Publication
Manual
of the American Psychological Association

Sixth Edition

Publication Manual of the American Psychological Association

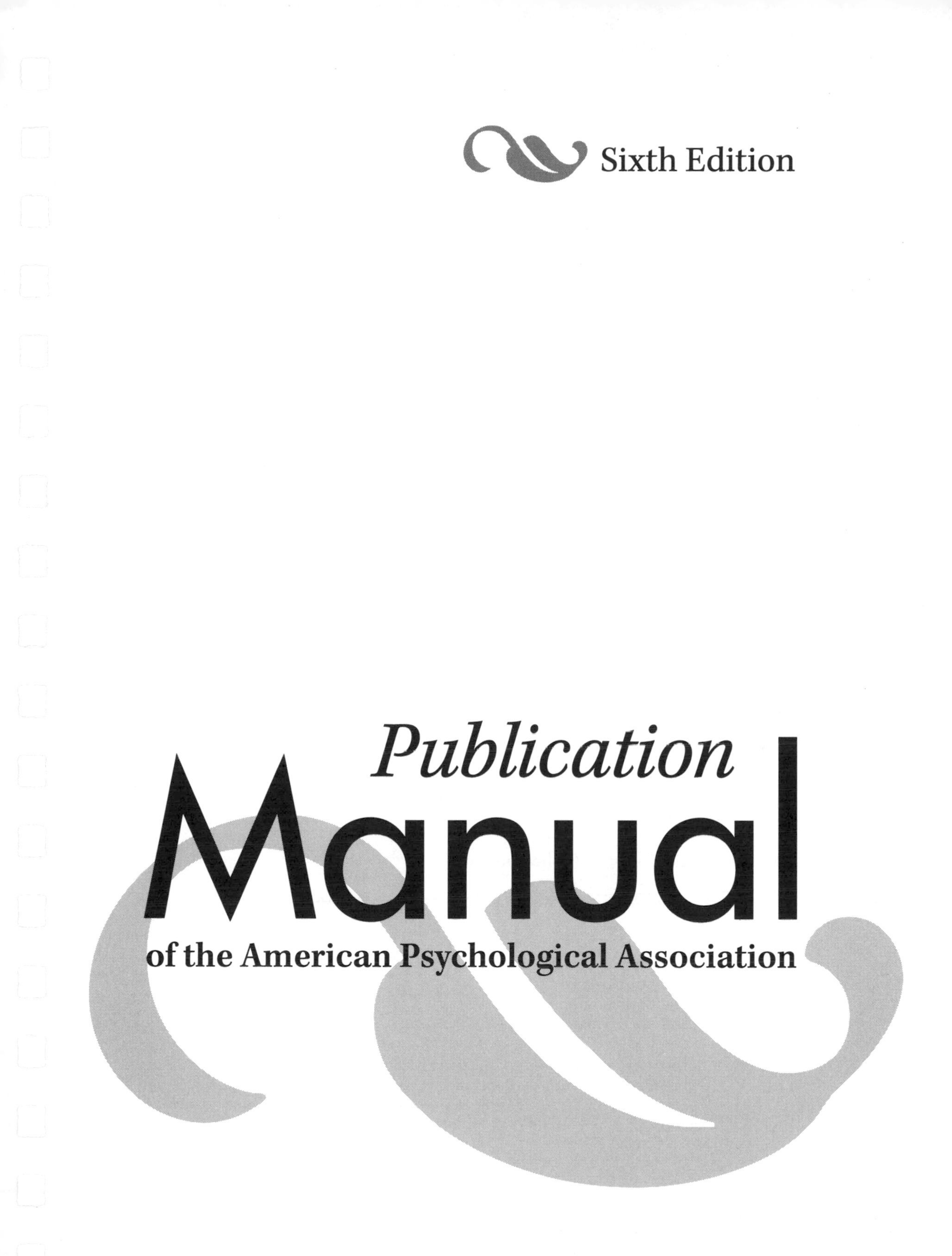

American Psychological Association • *Washington, DC*

Second printing: August 2009

Published by
American Psychological Association
750 First Street, NE
Washington, DC 20002
www.apa.org

To order
APA Order Department
P.O. Box 92984
Washington, DC 20090-2984
Tel: (800) 374-2721; Direct: (202) 336-5510
Fax: (202) 336-5502; TDD/TTY: (202) 336-6123
Online: www.apa.org/books/
E-mail: order@apa.org

In the U.K., Europe, Africa, and the Middle East, copies may be ordered from
American Psychological Association
3 Henrietta Street
Covent Garden, London
WC2E 8LU England

Typeset in Sabon, Futura, and Universe by Circle Graphics, Columbia, MD
Printer: Automated Graphic Systems, White Plains, MD
Cover Designer: Naylor Design, Washington, DC
Production Manager: Jennifer L. Macomber

Library of Congress Cataloging-in-Publication Data

Publication manual of the American Psychological Association. — 6th ed.
p. cm.
Includes bibliographical references and index.
ISBN-10: 1-4338-0561-8 (softcover)
ISBN-10: 1-4338-0559-6 (hardcover)
ISBN-10: 1-4338-0562-6 (spiral bound)
ISBN-13: 978-1-4338-0561-5 (softcover)
[etc.]
1. Psychology—Authorship—Style manuals. 2. Social sciences—Authorship—Style manuals. 3. Psychological literature—Publishing—Handbooks, manuals, etc. 4. Social science literature—Publishing—Handbooks, manuals, etc. I. American Psychological Association.
BF76.7.P83 2010
808'.06615—dc22

2009010391

British Library Cataloguing-in-Publication Data
A CIP record is available from the British Library.

Printed in the United States of America
Sixth Edition

Contents

List of Tables and Figures

Tables

Figures

Foreword

From its inception as a brief journal article in 1929, the *Publication Manual of the American Psychological Association* has been designed to advance scholarship by setting sound and rigorous standards for scientific communication. The creators of the 1929 manuscript included psychologists, anthropologists, and business managers who convened under the sponsorship of the National Research Council. They sought to establish a simple set of procedures, or *style rules*, that would codify the many components of scientific writing to increase the ease of reading comprehension. This goal was subsequently embraced not only by psychologists but also by scholars in other social and behavioral sciences who wished to enhance the dissemination of knowledge in their respective fields.

Uniform style helps us to cull articles quickly for key points and findings. Rules of style in scientific writing encourage full disclosure of essential information and allow us to dispense with minor distractions. Style helps us express the key elements of quantitative results, choose the graphic form that will best suit our analyses, report critical details of our research protocol, and describe individuals with accuracy and respect. It removes the distraction of puzzling over the correct punctuation for a reference or the proper form for numbers in text. Those elements are codified in the rules we follow for clear communication, allowing us to focus our intellectual energy on the substance of our research.

Today, APA Style sets a standard that is realized in APA journals, books, and electronic databases. In my tenure as APA publisher, the APA Journals program has grown from one that publishes 17,700 pages a year to one that publishes 37,000 pages a year. The APA Books program has grown from 12 books to over 1,214 books as well as 160 psychotherapy training videos. APA electronic products have grown from one database to five databases that offer users immediate connection to abstracts, books, journals, reviews, and quality gray literature. This profusion of scholarship has been supported and defined by the guidance provided in the *Publication Manual*. Together with the *APA Dictionary of*

Psychology and *Encyclopedia of Psychology*, it establishes a sound foundation for the advancement of the field.

The *Publication Manual* is consulted not only by psychologists but also by students and researchers in education, social work, nursing, business, and many other behavioral and social sciences. Its standards are available in English as well as Spanish, Portuguese, Korean, Chinese, and many other languages. A central focus of deliberation for this edition has been the way in which web-based technological innovations have altered the way we conceptualize, conduct, and consume scientific research. The sixth edition of the *Publication Manual* is devoted in large part to interpreting these advances and incorporating them into the style lexicon. It is my hope that, in concert with our other reference products, it will serve as a solid base for all of your scientific communications.

Gary R. VandenBos, PhD
Publisher, American Psychological Association

Preface

To better understand the complex changes in scientific publishing and address them in this edition, many experts and professional groups were consulted. We began the revision process in 2006 by looking closely at the fifth edition, analyzing more than five years of accumulated user feedback; evaluating published criticism; and commissioning reviews from senior editors in psychology, education, nursing, history, and business. After deliberation of and debate about these comments, the APA Publications and Communications Board set broad parameters for the revision and appointed a panel of experienced editors and scientists from diverse specialty areas to collaborate with dedicated staff on the revision.

The six-member *Publication Manual* Revision Task Force met for the first time in February 2007. They determined that revisions were needed in seven key areas: ethics, journal article reporting standards, reducing bias in language, graphics, writing style, references, and statistics. Working groups of experts were established to support the work of the task force in each area.

As the revision progressed, APA staff continued to solicit recommendations for revision from the APA Council of Editors, from *Publication Manual* users at the www.apastyle.org website, from APA members at professional meetings, and from APA boards and committees. Those recommendations were passed along to working group and task force members for consideration.

Thus, this edition of the *Publication Manual* is the result of creative collaboration with many groups and individuals. We must first thank the members of the *Publication Manual* Revision Task Force. They devoted many hours to analyzing reviews, considering the scholarly publishing climate, identifying topics in need of greater coverage, meeting with working group members to generate and revise text, critiquing and discussing new drafts, and poring over the final draft with a persistent commitment to getting it right. We are fortunate to have benefited so thoroughly from their enthusiastic and generous support of this project.

We are also grateful for the contributions that came from the working groups of experts who helped shape this edition. They dialed in faithfully to join Webex conference calls, collaborating to ensure accurate and comprehensive coverage for their respective areas. We benefited from the welcome blend of tact, humor, and insight that they brought to this project.

Early in the revision process, we solicited critiques from selected core users, that is, from senior editors and writers in the areas of psychology, nursing, education, and business. The overall recommendations gained from those individuals greatly influenced the approach taken in planning this edition of the *Publication Manual*. For sharing their insights and suggestions, we thank Barney Beins, Geoff Cumming, Janet Shibley Hyde, Judy Nemes, Kathryn Riley, Henry Roediger III, Peter W. Schroth, Martha Storandt, and Sandra P. Thomas. On a related note, we are indebted to Linda Beebe and the PsycINFO staff for their invaluable guidance on how evolving technologies continue to affect the reading, storage, and retrieval of scholarly work.

To guide us in our commitment to provide sound and timely instruction on scientific reporting, we solicited comments from several APA boards and committees. We are grateful for recommendations received from the APA Committee on Ethnic Minority Affairs; the APA Board of Scientific Affairs; the APA History Oversight Committee; the APA Committee on Disability Issues in Psychology; the American Psychological Association of Graduate Students; the APA Task Force on Gender Identity, Gender Variance, and Intersex Conditions; and the APA Committee on Socioeconomic Status.

Several writing instructors and coaches contacted us with suggestions for making APA Style more accessible for students. For taking the time to share their recommendations, we are most grateful to Dee Seligman, Wendy Packman, Scott Hines, Geeta Patangay, Mylea Charvat, and Jeff Zuckerman.

Last, we thank the APA Office of Publications and Databases staff for their many contributions to this edition, including Paige Jackson, Susan Herman, Annie Hill, Harriet Kaplan, Edward Porter, Shenyun Wu, Amy Pearson, Ron Teeter, Hal Warren, Beverly Jamison, Susan Harris, and Julia Frank-McNeil. Nora Kisch, Julianne Rovesti, Peter Gaviorno, and the entire sales and marketing team have worked tirelessly to inform the broad social science community about the new edition. We are particularly grateful to Jennifer Macomber for her skilled and meticulous care in shepherding the manuscript through production. Finally, we thank Anne Woodworth Gasque, who managed the process with ingenuity and grace, for her superb stewardship of this project.

Mary Lynn Skutley
Editorial Director, APA Books

Gary R. VandenBos, PhD
Publisher, American Psychological Association

Publication Manual of the American Psychological Association, Sixth Edition Editorial Staff

Publication Manual Revision Task Force

Mark Appelbaum, Chair
Lillian Comas-Diaz
Harris Cooper
Leah Light
Peter Ornstein
Lois Tetrick

Editor in Chief

Gary R. VandenBos

Project Director

Mary Lynn Skutley

Senior Editors

Anne Woodworth Gasque
Paige Jackson

Publication Manual Revision Working Groups

Bias-Free Language

Lillian Comas-Diaz, Co-Chair
Peter Ornstein, Co-Chair
Norman Abeles
Kevin Cokley
Sari H. Dworkin
Alba A. Ortiz
Denise Sekaquaptewa
Nathan Grant Smith
Glen W. White

Ethics

Leah L. Light, Co-Chair
Lois Tetrick, Co-Chair
Celia B. Fisher
Lenore W. Harmon
Mieke Verfaellie

Graphics

Mark Appelbaum, Co-Chair
Lois Tetrick, Co-Chair
John Jonides
Penny Pexman
David Thissen
Howard Wainer

Journal Article Reporting Standards (JARS)

Mark Appelbaum, Co-Chair
Harris Cooper, Co-Chair
Scott E. Maxwell
Valerie F. Reyna
Kenneth J. Sher
Arthur Stone

References

Mark Appelbaum, Co-Chair
Peter Ornstein, Co-Chair
Susan Herman
Annie Hill

Statistics

Mark Appelbaum, Co-Chair
Harris Cooper, Co-Chair
Geoff Cumming
Michael Edwards
Joel Levin
Abigail Panter

Writing Style

Leah L. Light, Co-Chair
Peter Ornstein, Co-Chair
David F. Bjorklund
Catherine Haden
Annie Hill

Publication
Manual
of the American Psychological Association

Introduction

The *Publication Manual of the American Psychological Association* was first published in 1929 as a seven-page "standard of procedure, to which exceptions would doubtless be necessary, but to which reference might be made in cases of doubt" (Bentley et al., 1929, p. 57). Eighty years later, we launch the sixth edition of the *Publication Manual* in the same spirit. Over the years, the *Publication Manual* has grown by necessity from a simple set of style rules to an authoritative source on all aspects of scholarly writing, from the ethics of duplicate publication to the word choice that best reduces bias in language.

The rules of APA Style are drawn from an extensive body of psychological literature, from editors and authors experienced in scholarly writing, and from recognized authorities on publication practices. This edition of the *Publication Manual* has been extensively revised to reflect new standards in publishing and new practices in information dissemination. Since the last edition of the manual was published, we have gone from a population that reads articles to one that "consumes content." New technologies have made increasingly sophisticated analyses possible, just as they have accelerated the dissemination of those analyses in multiple forms, from blogs to personal web postings to articles published in online databases.

To provide readers with guidance on how these and other developments have affected scholarly publishing, we have reordered and condensed the manual significantly. Our first goal was to simplify the reader's job by compiling all information on a topic in a single place. We have ordered information in accordance with the publication process, beginning with the idea stage and ending with the publication stage. We have retained and strengthened the basic rules of APA writing style and the guidelines on avoiding bias in language that were first published by APA more than 30 years ago. Most important, we have significantly expanded guidance on ethics, statistics, journal article reporting standards, electronic reference formats, and the construction of tables and figures.

Key to this revision is an updated and expanded web presence, which exponentially increases the information we are able to provide. At www.apastyle.org, readers will find a full range of resources for learning APA Style as well as additional guidance on writing and publishing, which will evolve with changing standards and practices.

Organization of the Sixth Edition

In Chapter 1, we acquaint readers with the types of articles common in scholarly publications. We also describe the role of ethics in publishing and offer guidance in following best practices for compliance.

In Chapter 2, we define all parts of a scholarly manuscript, from title to appendix, emphasizing both function and form. We also summarize current reporting standards for journal articles. The chapter ends with sample papers that illustrate the rules of APA Style.

In Chapter 3, we offer basic guidance on planning and writing the article. We advise readers on how to organize their thoughts, choose effective words, and describe individuals with accuracy and sensitivity.

In Chapter 4, we instruct readers on the nuts and bolts of style: punctuation, spelling, capitalization, abbreviations, numbers, and statistics in text. Consistency in the use of these basic aspects of style is key to clear scientific communication.

In Chapter 5, we describe the effective use of graphic elements in text and provide readers with illustrations of graphic elements that are useful for the presentation of data in tables and figures.

In Chapter 6, we provide guidance on citing sources. We discuss ground rules for acknowledging contributions of others and for formatting quotations. We instruct readers on when and how to cite references in text and on how to construct a reference list that contains everything readers need to locate each source.

In Chapter 7, we provide a comprehensive selection of reference examples in APA Style. The examples cover a range of categories, from periodicals to podcasts, with an emphasis on references to electronic formats.

In Chapter 8, we provide an overview of the journal publishing process. We emphasize the author's responsibilities in manuscript preparation and at each subsequent stage of publication.

Specific Changes in the Sixth Edition

General Approach

We considered two broad issues in planning this revision. First, given the wide use of the *Publication Manual* by readers outside the field of psychology, to what extent should this edition focus specifically on the APA journals program? Detailed information on APA journals is available on the web (see http://www.apa.org/journals/); each journal has its own web page, which includes specific instructions to authors. We decided to remove from the *Publication Manual* much of the APA-specific information that is readily accessible on the web, where guidelines are kept current. In this edition of the *Publication Manual,* we emphasize general principles that researchers need to know as well as principles of clear textual and visual communication.

Second, to what extent should the *Publication Manual* be prescriptive rather than descriptive of current practices in the field? A section in the foreword to the fourth edition is relevant:

> The *Publication Manual* presents explicit style requirements but acknowledges that alternatives are sometimes necessary; authors should balance the rules of the *Publication Manual* with good judgment. Because the written language of psychology changes more slowly than psychology itself, the *Publication Manual* does not offer solutions for all stylistic problems. In that sense, it is a transitional document: Its style requirements are based on the existing scientific literature rather than imposed on the literature. (American Psychological Association, 1994, p. xxiii)

Because of the diversity of practices in the social and behavioral sciences, we anticipated that the *Publication Manual* would likely prescribe new direction for some subdisciplines and merely describe the current state of scientific reporting for other subdisciplines.

New and Expanded Content

Chapter 1. Because of the importance of ethical issues that affect the conduct of scientific inquiry, we have placed ethics discussions in this opening chapter and have significantly expanded coverage of several topics. New guidance is included on determining authorship and terms of collaboration, duplicate publication, plagiarism and self-plagiarism, disguising of participants, validity of instrumentation, and making data available to others for verification.

Chapter 2. In Chapter 2, we provide comprehensive information on specific manuscript parts, which were located in several chapters in the last edition. For each manuscript part, we describe purpose and core content as well as how it should appear in text. This chapter has been significantly expanded with the addition of journal article reporting standards to help readers report empirical research with clarity and precision. We also provide an expanded discussion of statistical methods, including guidance on reporting effect sizes. In addition, we provide a new section on the use and preparation of supplemental materials for the web. We close the chapter with a new selection of sample papers that instantiate elements of APA Style.

Chapter 3. In this chapter, we offer two areas with significantly changed content. First, we have simplified APA heading style to make it more conducive to electronic publication. Second, we have updated guidelines for reducing bias in language to reflect current practices and preferences. A new section on presenting historical language that is inappropriate by present standards has been added, and examples of good and bad language choices have been expanded and moved to the web, where they are more accessible to all and can be easily updated.

Chapter 4. New content in Chapter 4 includes guidelines for reporting inferential statistics and a significantly revised table of statistical abbreviations. A new discussion of using supplemental files containing lengthy data sets and other media is also included.

Chapter 5. Procedures for developing graphic material have changed dramatically since the last edition of the *Publication Manual* was published. This chapter contains significantly expanded content on the electronic presentation of data. It will help readers understand the purpose of each kind of display and choose the best match for communicating the results of the investigation. We provide new examples for a variety of displays, including electrophysiological, imaging, and other biological data.

Chapter 6. In this chapter, we have consolidated information on all aspects of citations, beginning with guidance on how much to cite, how to format quotations, and how to navigate the permission process. Basic in-text citation styles and reference components are covered in detail. The discussion of electronic sources has been greatly expanded, emphasizing the role of the digital object identifier as a reliable way to locate information.

Chapter 7. Chapter 7 contains a significantly expanded set of reference examples, with an emphasis on electronic formats, for readers to use in mastering the changes described in Chapter 6. New examples have been added for a number of online sources, from data sets and measurement instruments to software and online discussion forums.

Chapter 8. Chapter 8 has been revised to focus more on the publication process and less on specific APA policies and procedures. It includes an expanded discussion of the function and process of peer review; a discussion of ethical, legal, and policy requirements in publication; and guidelines on working with the publisher while the article is in press.

How to Use the *Publication Manual*

The *Publication Manual* describes requirements for the preparation and submission of manuscripts for publication. Chapters in the *Publication Manual* provide substantively different kinds of information and are arranged in the sequence in which one considers the elements of manuscript preparation, from initial concept through publication. Although each chapter is autonomous, individuals new to the publication process may benefit from reading the book from beginning to end to get a comprehensive overview.

Organizational Aids

We have included checklists throughout the book to help you organize tasks and review your progress. These are listed below.

Checklist name	Page
Ethical Compliance Checklist	20
Table Checklist	150
Figure Checklist	167
Checklist for Manuscript Submission	240

We have also provided sample papers to illustrate applications of APA Style. These include a one-experiment paper (Figure 2.1, pp. 41–53), a two-experiment paper (Figure 2.2, pp. 54–56), and a sample paper reporting a meta-analysis (Figure 2.3, pp. 57–59).

Format Aids

Examples of points of style or format that appear throughout the book are in a contrasting typeface. This typeface is intended to help you locate examples quickly.

This is an example of the typeface used to illustrate style points.

The following are other formatting aids that are designed to help the reader locate specific information quickly:

- A detailed table of contents lists the sections for each chapter and will help you locate categories of information quickly.
- An abbreviated table of contents appears inside the front cover for ease in locating broad categories of information.
- A list of tables and figures follows the table of contents and will help you locate specific tables and figures.
- An abbreviated index of commonly used references appears inside the back cover.

We hope that these format aids will assist you in finding the instruction you need in the pages that follow.[1]

[1]You may find that the appearance of these pages occasionally deviates from APA Style rules. For example, sections may not be double-spaced and may not be in 12-point Times Roman typeface. APA Style rules are designed for ease of reading in manuscript form. Published work often takes a different form in accordance with professional design standards.

1

Writing for the Behavioral and Social Sciences

Research is complete only when the results are shared with the scientific community. Although such sharing is accomplished in various ways, both formal and informal, the traditional medium for communicating research results is the scientific journal.

The scientific journal is the repository of the accumulated knowledge of a field. The findings and analyses, the successes and failures, and the perspectives of many investigators over many years are recorded in the literature. Familiarity with the literature allows an individual investigator to avoid needlessly repeating work that has been done before, to build on existing work, and in turn to contribute something new.

Just as each investigator benefits from the publication process, so the body of scientific literature depends for its vitality on the active participation of individual investigators. Authors of scientific articles contribute most to the literature when they communicate clearly and concisely.

In this chapter, we discuss several considerations that authors should weigh before writing for publication—considerations both about their own research and about the scientific publishing tradition. We begin by identifying the types of articles that appear in scientific journals. In the rest of the chapter, we focus on overarching ethical and legal standards in publishing that must be addressed as a first step in planning an investigation.

Types of Articles

Journal articles are usually reports of empirical studies, literature reviews, theoretical articles, methodological articles, or case studies. They are *primary* or original publications. Members of the scientific community generally agree that the characteristics of these publications are that (a) articles represent research not previously published (i.e., first disclosure; for a discussion of duplicate publication, see section 1.09.), (b) articles

are reviewed by peers before being accepted or rejected by a journal, and (c) articles are archival (i.e., retrievable for future reference).

1.01 Empirical Studies

Empirical studies are reports of original research. These include secondary analyses that test hypotheses by presenting novel analyses of data not considered or addressed in previous reports. They typically consist of distinct sections that reflect the stages in the research process and that appear in the following sequence:

- **introduction:** development of the problem under investigation, including its historical antecedents, and statement of the purpose of the investigation;
- **method:** description of the procedures used to conduct the investigation;
- **results:** report of the findings and analyses; and
- **discussion:** summary, interpretation, and implications of the results.

1.02 Literature Reviews

Literature reviews, including research syntheses and meta-analyses, are critical evaluations of material that has already been published. In *meta-analyses,* authors use quantitative procedures to statistically combine the results of studies. By organizing, integrating, and evaluating previously published material, authors of literature reviews consider the progress of research toward clarifying a problem. In a sense, literature reviews are tutorials, in that authors

- define and clarify the problem;
- summarize previous investigations to inform the reader of the state of research;
- identify relations, contradictions, gaps, and inconsistencies in the literature; and
- suggest the next step or steps in solving the problem.

The components of literature reviews can be arranged in various ways (e.g., by grouping research based on similarity in the concepts or theories of interest, methodological similarities among the studies reviewed, or the historical development of the field).

1.03 Theoretical Articles

In *theoretical articles,* authors draw on existing research literature to advance theory. Literature reviews and theoretical articles are often similar in structure, but theoretical articles present empirical information only when it advances a theoretical issue. Authors of theoretical articles trace the development of theory to expand and refine theoretical constructs or present a new theory or analyze existing theory, pointing out flaws or demonstrating the advantage of one theory over another. In this type of article, authors customarily examine a theory's internal consistency and external validity. The sections of a theoretical article, like those of a literature review, can vary in order of their content.

1.04 Methodological Articles

Methodological articles present new methodological approaches, modifications of existing methods, or discussions of quantitative and data analytic approaches to the community of researchers. These articles focus on methodological or data analytic approaches and introduce empirical data only as illustrations of the approach. Methodological articles are presented at a level that makes them accessible to the well-read researcher and provide sufficient detail for researchers to assess the applicability of the methodology to their research problem. Further, the article allows the reader to compare the proposed methods with those in current use and to implement the proposed methods. In methodological articles, highly technical materials (e.g., derivations, proofs, details of simulations) should be presented in appendices or as supplemental materials to improve the overall readability of the article.

1.05 Case Studies

Case studies are reports of case materials obtained while working with an individual, a group, a community, or an organization. Case studies illustrate a problem; indicate a means for solving a problem; and/or shed light on needed research, clinical applications, or theoretical matters. In writing case studies, authors carefully consider the balance between providing important illustrative material and using confidential case material responsibly. (See section 1.11 for a discussion on confidentiality.)

1.06 Other Types of Articles

Other, less frequently published types of articles include brief reports, comments and replies on previously published articles, book reviews, obituaries, letters to the editor, and monographs. Consult with the editor of the journal to which you are considering submitting the manuscript for specific information regarding these kinds of articles.

Ethical and Legal Standards in Publishing

Much of the *Publication Manual* addresses scientific writing style. Style involves no inherent right or wrong. It is merely a conventional way of presenting information that is designed to ease communication. Different scholarly disciplines have different publication styles.

In contrast, basic ethical and legal principles underlie all scholarly research and writing. These long-standing principles are designed to achieve three goals:

- to ensure the accuracy of scientific knowledge,
- to protect the rights and welfare of research participants, and
- to protect intellectual property rights.

Writers in the social and behavioral sciences work to uphold these goals and follow the principles that have been established by their professional associations. The following guidance is drawn from the "Ethical Principles of Psychologists and Code of Conduct" (hereinafter referred to as the APA Ethics Code; APA, 2002; see also http://www.apa.org/ethics), which contains standards that address the reporting and publishing of scientific data. Note that the APA Ethics Code is not a static document—it may be revised and updated over time. Updates appear on the website as they become available.

Ensuring the Accuracy of Scientific Knowledge

1.07 Ethical Reporting of Research Results

The essence of the scientific method involves observations that can be repeated and verified by others. Thus, psychologists do not fabricate or falsify data (APA Ethics Code Standard 8.10a, Reporting Research Results). Modifying results, including visual images (for more discussion on visual images, see Chapter 5, section 5.29), to support a hypothesis or omitting troublesome observations from reports to present a more convincing story is also prohibited (APA Ethics Code Standard 5.01a, Avoidance of False or Deceptive Statements).

Careful preparation of manuscripts for publication is essential, but errors can still occur. Authors are responsible for making such errors public if the errors are discovered after publication. First, inform the editor and the publisher so that a correction notice can be published. The goal of such a notice is to correct the knowledge base so that the error is brought to the attention of future users of the information. Each correction notice is appended to the original article in an online database so that it will be retrieved whenever the original article is retrieved (for more details on correction notices, see section 8.06; APA Ethics Code Standard 8.10b, Reporting Research Results).

1.08 Data Retention and Sharing

Researchers must make their data available to the editor at any time during the review and publication process if questions arise with respect to the accuracy of the report. Refusal to do so can lead to rejection of the submitted manuscript without further consideration. In a similar vein, once an article is published, researchers must make their data available to permit other qualified professionals to confirm the analyses and results (APA Ethics Code Standard 8.14a, Sharing Research Data for Verification). Authors are expected to retain raw data for a minimum of five years after publication of the research. Other information related to the research (e.g., instructions, treatment manuals, software, details of procedures, code for mathematical models reported in journal articles) should be kept for the same period; such information is necessary if others are to attempt replication and should be provided to qualified researchers on request (APA Ethics Code Standard 6.01, Documentation of Professional and Scientific Work and Maintenance of Records).

APA encourages the open sharing of data among qualified investigators. Authors are expected to comply promptly and in a spirit of cooperation with requests for data sharing from other researchers. Before sharing data, delete any personally identifiable information or code that would make it possible to reestablish a link to an individual participant's identity. In addition to protecting the confidentiality of research participants, special proprietary or other concerns of the investigator or sponsor of the research sometimes must be addressed as well. Generally, the costs of complying with the request should be borne by the requester.

To avoid misunderstanding, it is important for the researcher requesting data and the researcher providing data to come to a written agreement about the conditions under which the data are to be shared. Such an agreement must specify the limits on how the shared data may be used (e.g., for verification of already published results, for inclusion in meta-analytic studies, for secondary analysis). The written agreement should also include a formal statement about limits on the distribution of the shared data (e.g., it may be used only by the person requesting the data, it may be used by the person requesting the data and individuals the requestor directly supervises, or there are no limits on the further distribution of the data). Furthermore, the agreement should specify limits on the dissemination (conference presentations, internal reports, journal articles, book chapters, etc.) of the results of analyses performed on the data and authorship expectations. Data-sharing arrangements must be entered into with proper consideration of copyright restrictions, consent provided by subjects, requirements of funding agencies, and rules promulgated by the employer of the holder of the data (APA Ethics Code Standard 8.14b, Sharing Research Data for Verification).

1.09 Duplicate and Piecemeal Publication of Data

The scientific literature is our institutional memory. Thus, reports in the literature must accurately reflect the independence of separate research efforts. Both duplicate and piecemeal publication of data constitute threats to these goals. *Duplicate publication* is the publication of the same data or ideas in two separate sources. *Piecemeal publication* is the unnecessary splitting of the findings from one research effort into multiple articles.

Duplicate publication. Misrepresentation of data as original when they have been published previously is specifically prohibited by APA Ethics Code Standard 8.13, Duplicate Publication of Data. Duplicate publication distorts the knowledge base by making it appear that there is more information available than really exists. It also wastes scarce resources (journal pages and the time and efforts of editors and reviewers). The prohibition against duplicate publication is especially critical for the cumulative knowledge of the field. Duplicate publication can give the erroneous impression that findings are more replicable than is the case or that particular conclusions are more strongly supported than is warranted by the cumulative evidence. Duplicate publication can also lead to copyright violations; authors cannot assign the copyright for the same material to more than one publisher.

Previously published research. Authors must not submit to an APA journal a manuscript describing work that has been published previously in whole or in substantial part elsewhere, whether in English or in another language. More important, authors should not submit manuscripts that have been published elsewhere in substantially similar form or with substantially similar content. Authors in doubt about what constitutes prior publication should consult with the editor of the journal in question.

This policy regarding duplicate publication does not necessarily exclude from consideration manuscripts previously published in abstracted form (e.g., in the proceedings of an annual meeting) or in a periodical with limited circulation or availability (e.g., in a report by a university department, by a government agency, or in a U.S. dissertation). This policy does exclude from consideration the same or overlapping material that has appeared in a publication that has been offered for public sale, such as conference proceedings or a book chapter; such a publication does not meet the criterion of "limited circulation." Publication of a brief report in an APA journal is with the understanding that an extended report will not be published elsewhere because APA brief reports include sufficient descriptions of methodology to allow for replication; the brief report is the archival record for the work. Similarly, the restraints against

duplicate publication do not preclude subsequent reanalysis of published data in light of new theories or methodologies, if the reanalysis is clearly labeled as such and provides new insights into the phenomena being studied.

Acknowledging and citing previous work. Authors sometimes want to publish what is essentially the same material in more than one venue to reach different audiences. However, such duplicate publication can rarely be justified, given the ready accessibility of computerized retrieval systems for published works. If it is deemed scientifically necessary to re-present previously published material—for instance, in reports of new analyses or to frame new research that follows up on previous work from the authors' laboratory—the following conditions must be met:

1. The amount of duplicated material must be small relative to the total length of the text.
2. The text must clearly acknowledge in the author note and other relevant sections of the article (i.e., Method and/or Result sections) that the information was reported previously, and the citation to the previous work must be given.
3. Any republished tables and figures must be clearly marked as reprinted or adapted, and the original source must be provided both in the text and in a footnote to the table or figure.
4. The original publication venue must be clearly and accurately cited in the reference list (see also the discussion on self-plagiarism in section 1.10).

When the original publication has multiple authors and the authorship is not identical on both publications, it is important that all authors receive agreed-upon credit (e.g., in an author note) for their contributions in the later publication.

Piecemeal publication. Authors are obligated to present work parsimoniously and as completely as possible within the space constraints of journal publications. Data that can be meaningfully combined within a single publication should be presented together to enhance effective communication. Piecemeal, or fragmented, publication of research findings can be misleading if multiple reports appear to represent independent instances of data collection or analyses; distortion of the scientific literature, especially in reviews or meta-analyses, may result. Piecemeal publication of several reports of the results from a single study is therefore undesirable unless there is a clear benefit to scientific communication. It may be quite difficult to determine whether such a benefit exists when multiple dependent variables that were observed in the same sample and at the same time are reported in separate manuscripts. Authors who wish to divide the report of a study into more than one article should inform the editor and provide such information as the editor requests. Whether the publication of two or more reports based on the same or on closely related research constitutes fragmented publication is a matter of editorial judgment.

Reanalysis of published data. There may be times, especially in instances of large-scale, longitudinal, or multidisciplinary projects, when it is both necessary and appropriate to publish multiple reports. Multidisciplinary projects often address diverse topics, and publishing in a single journal may be inappropriate. Repeated publication from a longitudinal study is often appropriate because the data at different ages make unique scientific contributions. Further, useful knowledge should be made available to others as soon as possible, which is precluded if publication is withheld until all the studies are completed.

As multiple reports from large-scale or longitudinal studies are created, authors are obligated to cite prior reports on the project to help the reader understand the work accurately. For example, in the early years of a longitudinal study, one might cite all previous publications from it. For a well-known or long-term longitudinal study, one might cite the original publication, a more recent summary, and earlier articles that focused on the same or related scientific questions addressed in the current report. Often it is not necessary to repeat the description of the design and methods of a longitudinal or large-scale project in its entirety. Authors may refer the reader to an earlier publication for this detailed information. It is important, however, to provide sufficient information so that the reader can evaluate the current report. It is also important to make clear the degree of sample overlap in multiple reports from large studies. Again, authors should inform and consult with the editor prior to the submission of a manuscript of this type.

Alerting the editor. Whether the publication of two or more reports based on the same or closely related research constitutes duplicate publication is a matter of editorial judgment, as is the determination of whether the manuscript meets other publication criteria. Any prior publication should be noted (see previous section on acknowledging and citing previous work) and referenced in the manuscript, and authors must inform the journal editor of the existence of any similar manuscripts that have already been published or accepted for publication or that may be submitted for concurrent consideration to the same journal or elsewhere. The editor can then make an informed judgment as to whether the submitted manuscript includes sufficient new information to warrant consideration. If, during the review or production process, a manuscript is discovered to be in violation of duplicate publication policies and authors have failed to inform the editor of the possible violation, then the manuscript can be rejected without further consideration. If such a violation is discovered after publication in an APA journal, appropriate action such as retraction by the publisher or notice of duplicate publication will be taken.

Journal articles sometimes are revised for publication as book chapters. Authors have a responsibility to reveal to the reader that portions of the new work were previously published and to cite and reference the source. If copyright is owned by a publisher or by another person, authors must acknowledge copyright and obtain permission to adapt or reproduce.

1.10 Plagiarism and Self-Plagiarism

Plagiarism. Researchers do not claim the words and ideas of another as their own; they give credit where credit is due (APA Ethics Code Standard 8.11, Plagiarism). Quotation marks should be used to indicate the exact words of another. *Each time* you paraphrase another author (i.e., summarize a passage or rearrange the order of a sentence and change some of the words), you need to credit the source in the text. The following paragraph is an example of how one might appropriately paraphrase some of the foregoing material in this section.

> As stated in the sixth edition of the *Publication Manual of the American Psychological Association* (APA, 2010), the ethical principles of scientific publication are designed to ensure the integrity of scientific knowledge and to protect the intellectual property rights of others. As the *Publication Manual* explains,

authors are expected to correct the record if they discover errors in their publications; they are also expected to give credit to others for their prior work when it is quoted or paraphrased.

The key element of this principle is that authors do not present the work of another as if it were their own work. This can extend to ideas as well as written words. If authors model a study after one done by someone else, the originating author should be given credit. If the rationale for a study was suggested in the Discussion section of someone else's article, that person should be given credit. Given the free exchange of ideas, which is very important to the health of intellectual discourse, authors may not know where an idea for a study originated. If authors do know, however, they should acknowledge the source; this includes personal communications. (For additional information on quotations and paraphrasing, see sections 6.03–6.08; for instructions on referencing publications and personal communications, see sections 6.11–6.20.)

Self-plagiarism. Just as researchers do not present the work of others as their own (plagiarism), they do not present their own previously published work as new scholarship (self-plagiarism). There are, however, limited circumstances (e.g., describing the details of an instrument or an analytic approach) under which authors may wish to duplicate without attribution (citation) their previously used words, feeling that extensive self-referencing is undesirable or awkward. When the duplicated words are limited in scope, this approach is permissible. When duplication of one's own words is more extensive, citation of the duplicated words should be the norm. What constitutes the maximum acceptable length of duplicated material is difficult to define but must conform to legal notions of fair use. The general view is that the core of the new document must constitute an original contribution to knowledge, and only the amount of previously published material necessary to understand that contribution should be included, primarily in the discussion of theory and methodology. When feasible, all of the author's own words that are cited should be located in a single paragraph or a few paragraphs, with a citation at the end of each. Opening such paragraphs with a phrase like "as I have previously discussed" will also alert readers to the status of the upcoming material.

Protecting the Rights and Welfare of Research Participants

1.11 Rights and Confidentiality of Research Participants

Certification of standards. Standards 8.01–8.09 of the APA Ethics Code specify the principles psychologists are to follow in conducting research with humans and animals. Authors, regardless of field, are required to certify that they have followed these standards as a precondition of publishing their articles in APA journals (see http://www.apa.org/journals; see also Figure 8.2, pp. 233–234). Authors are also encouraged to include such certifications in the description of participants in the text of the manuscript. Failure to follow these standards can be grounds for rejecting a manuscript for publication or for retraction of a published article.

Protecting confidentiality. When researchers use case studies to describe their research, they are prohibited from disclosing "confidential, personally identifiable information concerning their patients, individual or organizational clients, students, research participants, or other recipients of their services" (APA Ethics Code Standard 4.07, Use of Confidential Information for Didactic or Other Purposes). Confidentiality in case studies is generally handled by one of two means. One option is to prepare the descriptive case material, present it to the subject of the case report, and obtain written consent for its publication from the subject. In doing so, however, one must be careful not to exploit persons over whom one has supervisory, evaluative, or other authority such as clients, patients, supervisees, employees, or organizational clients (see APA Ethics Code Standard 3.08, Exploitative Relationships). The other option is to disguise some aspects of the case material so that neither the subject nor third parties (e.g., family members, employers) are identifiable. Four main strategies have emerged for achieving this: (a) altering specific characteristics, (b) limiting the description of specific characteristics, (c) obfuscating case detail by adding extraneous material, and (d) using composites.

Such disguising of cases is a delicate issue because it is essential not to change variables that would lead the reader to draw false conclusions related to the phenomena being described (Tuckett, 2000). For example, altering the subject's gender in a case illustrating a promising therapy for rape trauma might compromise its educative value if the client–patient's gender played a significant role in the treatment. Subject details should be omitted only if they are not essential to the phenomenon described. Subject privacy, however, should never be sacrificed for clinical or scientific accuracy. Cases that cannot adequately disguise identifiable subject information should not be submitted for publication. For additional information on the presentation of case material, see VandenBos (2001).

1.12 Conflict of Interest

In all scientific disciplines, professional communications are presumed to be based on objective interpretations of evidence and unbiased interpretation of fact. An author's economic and commercial interests in products or services used or discussed in a paper may color such objectivity. Although such relations do not necessarily constitute a conflict of interest, the integrity of the field requires disclosure of the possibilities of such potentially distorting influences where they may exist. In general, the safest and most open course of action is to disclose in an author note activities and relationships that if known to others might be viewed as a conflict of interest, even if you do not believe that any conflict or bias exists.

Whether an interest is significant will depend on individual circumstances and cannot be defined by a dollar amount. Holdings in a company through a mutual fund are not ordinarily sufficient to warrant disclosure, whereas salaries, research grants, consulting fees, and personal stock holdings would be. Being the copyright holder of and/or recipient of royalties from a psychological test might be another example. Participation on a board of directors or any other relationship with an entity or person that is in some way part of the paper should also be carefully considered for possible disclosure.

In addition to disclosure of possible sources of positive bias, authors should also carefully consider disclosure when circumstances could suggest bias against a product, service, facility, or person. For example, having a copyright or royalty interest in a competing psychological test or assessment protocol might be seen as a possible source of negative bias against another test instrument.

The previous examples refer to possible conflicts of interest of a researcher in the conduct of the research. It is important to recognize that reviewers of research reports also have potential conflicts of interest. In general, one should not review a manuscript from a colleague or collaborator, a close personal friend, or a recent student. Typically, the action editor will not select individuals to be reviewers in which this obvious conflict of interest may exist. However, if this might occur, a potential reviewer should consult with the action editor about whether recusal from the evaluation process would be appropriate.

Reviewers also have an ethical obligation to be open and fair in assessing a manuscript without bias. If for any reason a reviewer may find this difficult, it is appropriate to discuss the potential conflict of interest with the action editor as soon as this situation becomes apparent.

Last, reviewers have an obligation to maintain the confidentiality of a manuscript. This means, in general, that one does not discuss the manuscript with another individual. Moreover, as noted in section 1.14, "editors and reviewers may not use the material from an unpublished manuscript to advance their own or others' work without the author's consent."

Protecting Intellectual Property Rights

1.13 Publication Credit

Authorship is reserved for persons who make a substantial contribution to and who accept responsibility for a published work.

Definition of authorship. Individuals should only take authorship credit for work they have actually performed or to which they have substantially contributed (APA Ethics Code Standard 8.12a, Publication Credit). Authorship encompasses, therefore, not only those who do the actual writing but also those who have made substantial scientific contributions to a study. Substantial professional contributions may include formulating the problem or hypothesis, structuring the experimental design, organizing and conducting the statistical analysis, interpreting the results, or writing a major portion of the paper. Those who so contribute are listed in the byline. Lesser contributions, which do not constitute authorship, may be acknowledged in a note (see section 2.03). These contributions may include such supportive functions as designing or building the apparatus, suggesting or advising about the statistical analysis, collecting or entering the data, modifying or structuring a computer program, and recruiting participants or obtaining animals. Conducting routine observations or diagnoses for use in studies does not constitute authorship. Combinations of these (and other) tasks, however, may justify authorship.

Determining authorship. As early as practicable in a research project, the collaborators should decide on which tasks are necessary for the project's completion, how the work will be divided, which tasks or combination of tasks merits authorship credit, and on what level credit should be given (first author, second author, etc.). Collaborators may need to reassess authorship credit and order if changes in relative contribution are made in the course of the project (and its publication). This is especially true in faculty–student collaborations, when students may need more intensive supervision than originally anticipated, when additional analyses are required beyond the scope of a student's current level of training (Fisher, 2003), or when the level of the contribution of the student exceeds that originally anticipated.

When a paper is accepted by an editor, each person listed in the byline must verify in writing that he or she agrees to serve as an author and accepts the responsibilities of authorship (see the section on author responsibilities at the beginning of Chapter 8).

Order of authorship. Authors are responsible for determining authorship and for specifying the order in which two or more authors' names appear in the byline. The general rule is that the name of the principal contributor should appear first, with subsequent names in order of decreasing contribution, but this convention can vary from field to field. If authors played equal roles in the research and publication of their study, they may wish to note this in the author note (see section 2.03 for more information on author notes).

Principal authorship and the order of authorship credit should accurately reflect the relative contributions of persons involved (APA Ethics Code Standard 8.12b, Publication Credit). Relative status (i.e., department chair, junior faculty member, student) should not determine the order of authorship. Because doctoral work is expected to represent an independent and original contribution devised by students, except under rare circumstances, students should be listed as the principal author of any multiauthored papers substantially based on their dissertation (APA Ethics Code Standard 8.12c, Publication Credit). Unusual exceptions to doctoral student first authorship might occur when the doctoral dissertation is published as part of a collection of studies involving other researchers (Fisher, 2003). Whether students merit principal authorship on master's-level or other predoctoral research will depend on their specific contributions to the research. When master's-level students make the primary contributions to a study, they should be listed as the first author. When students are just beginning to acquire skills necessary to make a primary scientific contribution, they may conduct master's theses that involve the opportunity to learn these skills through collaboration on a faculty-originated project. In such cases, authorship should be determined by the relative contributions of student and faculty member to the project (Fisher, 2003).

1.14 Reviewers

Editorial review of a manuscript requires that the editors and reviewers circulate and discuss the manuscript. During the review process, the manuscript is a confidential and privileged document. Editors and reviewers may not, without authors' explicit permission, quote from a manuscript under review or circulate copies of it for any purpose other than editorial review (APA Ethics Code Standard 8.15, Reviewers; see section 8.01 for a detailed discussion of the peer review process). If reviewers for APA journals wish to consult with a colleague about some aspect of the manuscript, the reviewer must request permission from the editor prior to approaching the colleague. Publishers have different policies on this, and reviewers should consult with the editor about this matter. In addition, editors and reviewers may not use the material from an unpublished manuscript to advance their own or others' work without the author's consent.

1.15 Author's Copyright on an Unpublished Manuscript

Authors are protected by federal statute against unauthorized use of their unpublished manuscripts. Under the Copyright Act of 1976 (title 17 of the *United States Code*), an unpublished work is copyrighted from the moment it is fixed in tangible form—for example, typed on a page. Copyright protection is "an incident of the process of authorship" (U.S. Copyright Office, 1981, p. 3). Until authors formally transfer copyright (see section 8.05), they own the copyright on an unpublished manuscript, and all exclusive rights due the copyright owner of a published work are also due authors of an unpublished work. To ensure copyright protection, include the copyright notice on all published works (e.g., Copyright [year] by [name of copyright holder]). The notice need not appear on unpublished works; nonetheless, it is recommended that a copyright notice be included on all works, whether published or not. Registration of copyright provides a public record and is usually a prerequisite for any legal action.

1.16 Planning for Ethical Compliance

Regardless of the type of article involved, attention to ethical concerns begins long before a manuscript is submitted for publication. Authors submitting a manuscript to an APA journal are required to submit a form stating their compliance with ethical standards for publication as well as a form disclosing any conflicts of interest (see Chapter 8, Figures 8.2 and 8.3, pp. 233–235) once a manuscript is accepted. We encourage authors to consult these forms before beginning their research project and at regular intervals throughout the entire research process. Whether or not the work will be submitted to an APA journal, issues related to institutional approval, informed consent, deception in research, and participant protections should be carefully considered while the research is in the planning stages and may be the basis of questions for editors or reviewers (see Chapter 8). In particular, we urge researchers to review the following checklist.

Ethical Compliance Checklist

- ☐ Have you obtained permission for use of unpublished instruments, procedures, or data that other researchers might consider theirs (proprietary)?
- ☐ Have you properly cited other published work presented in portions of your manuscript?
- ☐ Are you prepared to answer questions about institutional review of your study or studies?
- ☐ Are you prepared to answer editorial questions about the informed consent and debriefing procedures you used?
- ☐ If your study involved animal subjects, are you prepared to answer editorial questions about humane care and use of animals in research?
- ☐ Have all authors reviewed the manuscript and agreed on responsibility for its content?
- ☐ Have you adequately protected the confidentiality of research participants, clients–patients, organizations, third parties, or others who were the source of information presented in this manuscript?
- ☐ Have all authors agreed to the order of authorship?
- ☐ Have you obtained permission for use of any copyrighted material you have included?

2

Manuscript Structure and Content

In this chapter, we describe the structure of the manuscript, with a focus on function and format. For each manuscript element, we detail current expectations for the content. In each section, the following kinds of information are included:

- a definition or description of the manuscript part,
- specific guidelines on content to be included, and
- guidelines on how the part should appear in text.[1]

In this edition of the *Publication Manual,* we present updated journal article reporting standards, and these are also discussed in this chapter. These reporting standards relate to material recommended to appear in the abstract, the introduction of the research problem, the method section, the results, and the discussion of the results. Also presented are three specific modules relating to studies with manipulated conditions or interventions. The chapter ends with sample papers that illustrate the function and format of the sections described.

Journal Article Reporting Standards

Reporting standards provide a degree of comprehensiveness in the information that is routinely included in reports of empirical investigations. The motivation for the development of reporting standards has come from within the disciplines of the behavioral, social, educational, and medical sciences. Uniform reporting standards make it easier to generalize across fields, to more fully understand the implications of individual studies, and to allow techniques of meta-analysis to proceed more efficiently. Also, decision makers in policy and practice have emphasized the importance of understanding how research was conducted and what was found. A set of comprehensive reporting standards facilitates this understanding.

[1]Note that guidelines for the formatting and preparation of the complete manuscript can be found in section 8.03.

Reporting standards are based on the research design and implementation of the study being reported, not on the topical focus of the study or the particular journal that might serve as the vehicle for its publication. Reporting standards are emergent and have not yet been developed for all types of studies.

In the next section, we describe a set of reporting standards relating to the material recommended to appear in (a) the abstract; (b) the introduction of the research problem; (c) subsections of the method section describing the characteristics of the participants; sampling procedures; sample size, power, and precision; measures and covariates; and the general descriptor of the research design; (d) the statistical results; and (e) the discussion of results. These standards relate to all types of research designs. Then we present three specific modules relating to studies with manipulated conditions or interventions. You can use (or a journal editor may ask you to use) these modules in addition to the general template if they are relevant to the research at hand. One module contains standards for describing the experimental manipulation or intervention itself, and the other two modules describe features of designs with experimental (i.e., random assignment) and quasi-experimental (i.e., nonrandom assignment) research designs. We also provide a flow chart to help you describe how subjects moved through the experimental or quasi-experimental study. In the same spirit, we include standards for reports of meta-analyses. Before you begin to write a manuscript, consult the particular journal to which you are considering submitting and see whether there are journal-specific guidelines regarding your research design.

We relied heavily on previous efforts to construct reporting standards in developing the standards presented here. For example, for the Journal Article Reporting Standards, Consolidated Standards of Reporting Trials (CONSORT; 2007; see http://www.consort-statement.org/) and Transparent Reporting of Evaluations With Nonexperimental Designs (TREND; see http://www.trend-statement.org/asp/trend.asp) were used. Four earlier efforts contributed to the meta-analysis reporting standards. A complete description of how the standards were developed can be found in "Reporting Standards for Research in Psychology: Why Do We Need Them? What Might They Be?" (APA Publications and Communications Board Working Group on Journal Article Reporting Standards, 2008).

Four sets of guidelines, which can be found in the Appendix, have been created to help you decide which elements are relevant to your study. These guidelines are from the *American Psychologist* article (see previous paragraph) and include entries beyond those discussed in this chapter. For information on content, refer to Table 1 of the Appendix, Journal Article Reporting Standards (JARS): Information Recommended for Inclusion in Manuscripts That Report New Data Collections Regardless of Research Design. The additional modules for designs involving experimental manipulations and interventions can be found in Table 2 of the Appendix, Module A: Reporting Standards for Studies With an Experimental Manipulation or Intervention (in Addition to Material Presented in Table 1) and Table 3 of the Appendix, Reporting Standards for Studies Using Random and Nonrandom Assignment of Participants to Experimental Groups. The fourth set of guidelines is titled Meta-Analysis Reporting Standards [MARS]: Information Recommended for Inclusion in Manuscripts Reporting Meta-Analyses, which can be found in Table 4 of the Appendix.

Not everything in these guidelines will be relevant to every article you prepare. Also, as descriptions of research expand, so does the space needed to report them. Technological changes now allow authors to supplement their articles with additional online-only material to facilitate complete reporting. Most scholarly publishers, including the APA, now make available to authors online supplemental archives that can be used to store supplemental materials associated with the articles that appear in print. So, some of the material in the appendices may not appear in the published article itself but rather in an online supplemental archive. We discuss supplemental material more fully in section 2.13.

Manuscript Elements

2.01 Title

A title should summarize the main idea of the manuscript simply and, if possible, with style. It should be a concise statement of the main topic and should identify the variables or theoretical issues under investigation and the relationship between them. An example of a good title is "Effect of Transformed Letters on Reading Speed."

A title should be fully explanatory when standing alone. Although its principal function is to inform readers about the study, a title is also used as a statement of article content for abstracting and reference purposes in databases such as APA's PsycINFO. A good title is easily shortened to the running head used within the published article.

Titles are commonly indexed and compiled in numerous reference works. Therefore, avoid words that serve no useful purpose; they increase length and can mislead indexers. For example, the words *method* and *results* do not normally appear in a title, nor should such terms as *A Study of* or *An Experimental Investigation of*. Occasionally a term such as *a research synthesis* or *a meta-analysis* or *fMRI study of* conveys important information for the potential reader and is included in the title. Avoid using abbreviations in a title; spelling out all terms helps ensure accurate, complete indexing of the article. The recommended length for a title is no more than 12 words.

The title should be typed in uppercase and lowercase letters, centered between the left and right margins, and positioned in the upper half of the page.

2.02 Author's Name (Byline) and Institutional Affiliation

Every manuscript includes the name of the author and the institutional affiliation of the author when the research was conducted.

Author's name (byline). The preferred form of an author's name is first name, middle initial(s), and last name; this form reduces the likelihood of mistaken identity. To assist researchers as well as librarians, use the same form for publication throughout your career; that is, do not use initials on one manuscript and the full name on a later one. Determining whether Juanita A. Smith is the same person as J. A. Smith, J. Smith, or A. Smith can be difficult, particularly when citations span several years and institutional affiliations change. Omit all titles (e.g., Dr., Professor) and degrees (e.g., PhD, PsyD, EdD).

Institutional affiliation. The affiliation identifies the location where the author or authors were when the research was conducted, which is usually an institution. Include a dual affiliation only if two institutions contributed substantial support to the study. Include no more than two affiliations per author. When an author has no institutional affiliation, list the city and state of residence below the author's name. If the institu-

Table 2.1. Author Bylines

Byline variation	Example
One author, no affiliation	Mary S. Haggerty Rochester, New York
Two authors (with suffixes), one affiliation	John Q. Foster II and Roy R. Davis Jr. Educational Testing Service, Princeton, New Jersey
Three authors, one affiliation	Juanita Fuentes, Paul Dykes, and Susan Watanabe University of Colorado at Boulder
Two authors, two affiliations	David Wolf University of California, Berkeley Amanda Blue Brandon University
Three authors, two affiliations	Mariah Meade and Sylvia Earleywine Georgetown University Jeffrey Coffee Dartmouth College

tional affiliation has changed since the work was completed, give the current affiliation in the author note (see Table 2.1).

The names of the authors should appear in the order of their contributions, centered between the side margins. For names with suffixes (e.g., Jr. and III), separate the suffix from the rest of the name with a space instead of a comma. The institutional affiliation should be centered under the author's name, on the next line.

John Q. Foster II and Roy R. Davis Jr.
Educational Testing Service, Princeton, New Jersey

2.03 Author Note

An author note appears with each printed article to identify each author's departmental affiliation, provide acknowledgments, state any disclaimers or perceived conflict of interest, and provide a point of contact for the interested reader. (Students should note that an author note is usually not a requirement for theses and dissertations.) Notes should be arranged as follows.

First paragraph: Complete departmental affiliation. Identify departmental affiliations at the time of the study for all authors. Format as follows: name of the author as it appears in the byline, comma, department name, comma, university name, semicolon, next author name, and so on, and end with a period. If an author is not affiliated with an institution, provide the city and state (provide city and country for authors whose affiliations are outside of the United States, and include province for authors in Canada or Australia). No degrees should be given, and state names should be spelled out.

Second paragraph: Changes of affiliation (if any). Identify any changes in author affiliation subsequent to the time of the study. Use the following wording: [author's name] is now at [affiliation]. The affiliation should include the department and institution.

Third paragraph.

Acknowledgments. Identify grants or other financial support (and the source, if appropriate) for your study; do not precede grant numbers by No. or #. Next, acknowledge colleagues who assisted in conducting the study or critiquing the manuscript. Do not acknowledge the persons routinely involved in the review and acceptance of manuscripts—peer reviewers or editors, associate editors, and consulting editors of the journal in which the article is to appear. (If you would like to acknowledge a specific idea raised by a reviewer, do so in the text where the idea is discussed.) In this paragraph, also explain any special agreements concerning authorship, such as if authors contributed equally to the study. End this paragraph with thanks for personal assistance, such as in manuscript preparation.

Special circumstances. If there are any special circumstances, disclose them before the acknowledgments in the third paragraph. For example, if the manuscript is based on data also used in a previously published report (e.g., a longitudinal study) or a doctoral dissertation, state that information in this paragraph. Also, acknowledge the publication of related reports (e.g., reports on the same database). If any relationships may be perceived as a conflict of interest (e.g., if you own stock in a company that manufactures a drug used in your study), explain them here. If your employer or granting organization requires a disclaimer stating, for example, that the research reported does not reflect the views of that organization, such a statement is included in this paragraph.

Fourth paragraph: Person to contact (mailing address, e-mail). Provide a complete mailing address for correspondence. End this paragraph with an e-mail address and no period.

> Jane Doe, Department of Psychology, University of Illinois at Urbana–Champaign; John Smith, Department of Educational Psychology, University of Chicago.
>
> John Smith is now at Department of Psychology, University of California, San Diego.
>
> This research was supported in part by grants from the National Institute on Aging and from the John D. and Catherine T. MacArthur Foundation.
>
> Correspondence concerning this article should be addressed to Jane Doe, Department of Psychology, University of Illinois, Champaign, IL 61820.
> E-mail: jdoe@uiuc.edu

Place the author note on the title page, below the title, byline, and affiliation. Center the label *Author Note.* Start each paragraph of the note with an indent, and type separate paragraphs for the authors' names and current affiliations, changes in affiliations, acknowledgments, and special circumstances, if any, along with the person to contact. The author note is not numbered or cited in the text.

2.04 Abstract

An abstract is a brief, comprehensive summary of the contents of the article; it allows readers to survey the contents of an article quickly and, like a title, it enables persons interested in the document to retrieve it from abstracting and indexing databases. Most scholarly journals require an abstract. Consult the instructions to authors or web page of the journal to which you plan to submit your article for any journal-specific instructions.

A well-prepared abstract can be the most important single paragraph in an article. Most people have their first contact with an article by seeing just the abstract, usually in comparison with several other abstracts, as they are doing a literature search. Readers frequently decide on the basis of the abstract whether to read the entire article. The abstract needs to be dense with information. By embedding key words in your abstract, you enhance the user's ability to find it. A good abstract is

- **accurate:** Ensure that the abstract correctly reflects the purpose and content of the manuscript. Do not include information that does not appear in the body of the manuscript. If the study extends or replicates previous research, note this in the abstract and cite the author's last name and the year of the relevant report. Comparing an abstract with an outline of the manuscript's headings is a useful way to verify its accuracy.
- **nonevaluative:** Report rather than evaluate; do not add to or comment on what is in the body of the manuscript.
- **coherent and readable:** Write in clear and concise language. Use verbs rather than their noun equivalents and the active rather than the passive voice (e.g., *investigated* rather than *an investigation of; The authors presented the results* instead of *Results were presented*). Use the present tense to describe conclusions drawn or results with continuing applicability; use the past tense to describe specific variables manipulated or outcomes measured.
- **concise:** Be brief, and make each sentence maximally informative, especially the lead sentence. Begin the abstract with the most important points. Do not waste space by repeating the title. Include in the abstract only the four or five most important concepts, findings, or implications. Use the specific words in your abstract that you think your audience will use in their electronic searches.

An abstract of a *report of an empirical study* should describe

- the problem under investigation, in one sentence if possible;
- the participants, specifying pertinent characteristics such as age, sex, and ethnic and/or racial group; in animal research, specifying genus and species;
- the essential features of study method—you have a limited number of words so restrict your description to essential and interesting features of the study methodology—particularly those likely to be used in electronic searches;
- the basic findings, including effect sizes and confidence intervals and/or statistical significance levels; and
- the conclusions and the implications or applications.

An abstract for a *literature review or meta-analysis* should describe

- the problem or relation(s) under investigation;
- study eligibility criteria;
- type(s) of participants included in primary studies;
- main results (including the most important effect sizes) and any important moderators of these effect sizes;

- conclusions (including limitations); and
- implications for theory, policy, and/or practice.

An abstract for a *theory-oriented* paper should describe

- how the theory or model works and/or the principles on which it is based and
- what phenomena the theory or model accounts for and linkages to empirical results.

An abstract for a *methodological* paper should describe

- the general class of methods being discussed;
- the essential features of the proposed method;
- the range of application of the proposed method; and
- in the case of statistical procedures, some of its essential features such as robustness or power efficiency.

An abstract for a *case study* should describe

- the subject and relevant characteristics of the individual, group, community, or organization presented;
- the nature of or solution to a problem illustrated by the case example; and
- the questions raised for additional research or theory.

Do not exceed the abstract word limit of the journal to which you are submitting your article. Word limits vary from journal to journal and typically range from 150 to 250 words. For information on how abstracts are used to retrieve articles, consult *Record Structure for APA Databases* (Sick, 2009).

When preparing your manuscript, begin the abstract on a new page and identify it with the running head or abbreviated title and the page number 2. The label *Abstract* should appear in uppercase and lowercase letters, centered, at the top of the page. Type the abstract itself as a single paragraph without paragraph indentation.

2.05 Introduction

Introduce the problem. The body of a manuscript opens with an introduction that presents the specific problem under study and describes the research strategy. Because the introduction is clearly identified by its position in the manuscript, it does not carry a heading labeling it the introduction.

Before writing the introduction, consider the following questions:

- Why is this problem important?
- How does the study relate to previous work in the area? If other aspects of this study have been reported previously, how does this report differ from, and build on, the earlier report?
- What are the primary and secondary hypotheses and objectives of the study, and what, if any, are the links to theory?
- How do the hypotheses and research design relate to one another?
- What are the theoretical and practical implications of the study?

A good introduction answers these questions in just a few pages and, by summarizing the relevant arguments and the past evidence, gives the reader a firm sense of what was done and why.

Explore importance of the problem. State why the problem deserves new research. For basic research, the statement about importance might involve the need to resolve any inconsistency in results of past work and/or extend the reach of a theoretical formulation. For applied research, this might involve the need to solve a social problem or treat a psychological disorder. When research is driven by the desire to resolve controversial issues, all sides in the debate should be represented in balanced measure in the introduction. Avoid animosity and ad hominem arguments in presenting the controversy. Conclude the statement of the problem in the introduction with a brief but formal statement of the purpose of the research that summarizes the material preceding it. For literature reviews as well as theoretical and methodological articles, also clearly state the reasons that the reported content is important and how the article fits into the cumulative understanding of the field.

Describe relevant scholarship. Discuss the relevant related literature, but do not feel compelled to include an exhaustive historical account. Assume that the reader is knowledgeable about the basic problem and does not require a complete accounting of its history. A scholarly description of earlier work in the introduction provides a summary of the most recent directly related work and recognizes the priority of the work of others. Citation of and specific credit to relevant earlier works are signs of scientific and scholarly responsibility and are essential for the growth of a cumulative science. In the description of relevant scholarship, also inform readers whether other aspects of this study have been reported on previously and how the current use of the evidence differs from earlier uses. At the same time, cite and reference only works pertinent to the specific issue and not those that are of only tangential or general significance. When summarizing earlier works, avoid nonessential details; instead, emphasize pertinent findings, relevant methodological issues, and major conclusions. Refer the reader to general surveys or research syntheses of the topic if they are available.

Demonstrate the logical continuity between previous and present work. Develop the problem with enough breadth and clarity to make it generally understood by as wide a professional audience as possible. Do not let the goal of brevity lead you to write a statement intelligible only to the specialist.

State hypotheses and their correspondence to research design. After you have introduced the problem and have developed the background material, explain your approach to solving the problem. In empirical studies, this usually involves stating your hypotheses or specific question and describing how these were derived from theory or are logically connected to previous data and argumentation. Clearly develop the rationale for each. Also, if you have some hypotheses or questions that are central to your purpose and others that are secondary or exploratory, state this prioritization. Explain how the research design permits the inferences needed to examine the hypothesis or provide estimates in answer to the question.

In preparing your manuscript, begin the introduction on a new page, identifying it with the running head and the page number 3. Type the title of the manuscript in uppercase and lowercase letters centered at the top of the page, and then type the text. The remaining sections of the article follow each other without a break; do not start a new page when a new heading occurs. Each remaining manuscript page should also carry the running head and a page number.

2.06 Method

The Method section describes in detail how the study was conducted, including conceptual and operational definitions of the variables used in the study. Different types of studies will rely on different methodologies; however, a complete description of the methods used enables the reader to evaluate the appropriateness of your methods and the reliability and the validity of your results. It also permits experienced investigators to replicate the study. If your manuscript is an update of an ongoing or earlier study and the method has been published in detail elsewhere, you may refer the reader to that source and simply give a brief synopsis of the method in this section (see also section 1.10, regarding self-plagiarism). The following is an example of such a synopsis:

> We present cross-sectional and 3-year longitudinal data from a study of adults aged 55 to 84. . . . The memory tasks were those used in our previous research (Zelinski et al., 1990; Zelinski, Gilewski, & Thompson, 1980).

If you are reporting on multiple experiments, see section 2.09.

Identify subsections. It is both conventional and expedient to divide the Method section into labeled subsections. These usually include a section with descriptions of the participants or subjects and a section describing the procedures used in the study. The latter section often includes description of (a) any experimental manipulations or interventions used and how they were delivered—for example, any mechanical apparatus used to deliver them; (b) sampling procedures and sample size and precision; (c) measurement approaches (including the psychometric properties of the instruments used); and (d) the research design. If the design of the study is complex or the stimuli require detailed description, additional subsections or subheadings to divide the subsections may be warranted to help readers find specific information.

Include in these subsections the information essential to comprehend and replicate the study. Insufficient detail leaves the reader with questions; too much detail burdens the reader with irrelevant information. Consider using appendices and/or a supplemental website for more detailed information (see section 2.13).

Participant (subject) characteristics. Appropriate identification of research participants is critical to the science and practice of psychology, particularly for generalizing the findings, making comparisons across replications, and using the evidence in research syntheses and secondary data analyses. If humans participated in the study, report the eligibility and exclusion criteria, including any restrictions based on demographic characteristics.

Describe the sample adequately. Detail the sample's major demographic characteristics, such as age; sex; ethnic and/or racial group; level of education; socioeconomic, generational, or immigrant status; disability status; sexual orientation; gender identity; and language preference as well as important topic-specific characteristics (e.g., achievement level in studies of educational interventions). As a rule, describe the groups as specifically as possible, with particular emphasis on characteristics that may have bearing on the interpretation of results. Often, participant characteristics can be important for understanding the nature of the sample and the degree to which results can be generalized. For example, the following is a useful characterization of a sample:

> The second group included 40 women between the ages of 20 and 30 years (*M* = 24.2, *SD* = 2.1), all of whom had emigrated from El Salvador; had at least 12 years of education; had been permanent residents of the United States for at least 10 years; and lived in Washington, DC.

To determine how far the data can be generalized, you may find it useful to identify subgroups:

> The Asian sample included 30 Chinese and 45 Vietnamese persons.

or

> Among the Latino and Hispanic American men, 20 were Mexican American and 20 were Puerto Rican.

Even when a characteristic is not used in analysis of the data, reporting it may give readers a more complete understanding of the sample and the generalizability of results and may prove useful in meta-analytic studies that incorporate the article's results.

When animals are used, report the genus, species, and strain number or other specific identification, such as the name and location of the supplier and the stock designation. Give the number of animals and the animals' sex, age, weight, and physiological condition.

Sampling procedures. Describe the procedures for selecting participants, including (a) the sampling method, if a systematic sampling plan was used; (b) the percentage of the sample approached that participated; and (c) the number of participants who selected themselves into the sample. Describe the settings and locations in which the data were collected as well as any agreements and payments made to participants, agreements with the institutional review board, ethical standards met, and safety monitoring procedures.

Sample size, power, and precision. Along with the description of subjects, give the intended size of the sample and number of individuals meant to be in each condition, if separate conditions were used. State whether the achieved sample differed in known ways from the target population. Conclusions and interpretations should not go beyond what the sample would warrant.

State how this intended sample size was determined (e.g., analysis of power or precision). If interim analysis and stopping rules were used to modify the desired sample size, describe the methodology and results.

When applying inferential statistics, take seriously the statistical power considerations associated with the tests of hypotheses. Such considerations relate to the likelihood of correctly rejecting the tested hypotheses, given a particular alpha level, effect size, and sample size. In that regard, routinely provide evidence that the study has sufficient power to detect effects of substantive interest. Be similarly careful in discussing the role played by sample size in cases in which not rejecting the null hypothesis is desirable (i.e., when one wishes to argue that there are no differences), when testing various assumptions underlying the statistical model adopted (e.g., normality, homogeneity of variance, homogeneity of regression), and in model fitting.

Alternatively, use calculations based on a chosen target precision (confidence interval width) to determine sample sizes. Use the resulting confidence intervals to justify conclusions concerning effect sizes (e.g., that some effect is negligibly small).

Measures and covariates. Include in the Method section information that provides definitions of all primary and secondary outcome measures and covariates, including measures collected but not included in this report. Describe the methods used to collect data (e.g., written questionnaires, interviews, observations) as well as methods used to enhance the quality of the measurements (e.g., the training and reliability of assessors or the use of multiple observations). Provide information on instruments used, including their psychometric and biometric properties and evidence of cultural validity.

Research design. Specify the research design in the Method section. Were subjects placed into conditions that were manipulated, or were they observed naturalistically? If multiple conditions were created, how were participants assigned to conditions, through random assignment or some other selection mechanism? Was the study conducted as a between-subjects or a within-subject design?

Different research designs have different reporting needs associated with them. Information that should be reported for all studies that involve experimental manipulations or interventions is summarized in Table 2 of the Appendix, Module A: Reporting Standards for Studies With an Experimental Manipulation or Intervention (in Addition to Material Presented in Table 1) and Table 3 of the Appendix, Reporting Standards for Studies Using Random and Nonrandom Assignment of Participants to Experimental Groups. When reporting studies that are not of the manipulation or intervention variety (e.g., observational, natural history studies), provide sufficient description of the study procedures to allow the reader to fully comprehend the complexity of the study and to be prepared to conduct a near replication of the study (see APA Publications and Communications Board Working Group on Journal Article Reporting Standards, 2008, for a discussion of the emergence of these standards).

Experimental manipulations or interventions. If interventions or experimental manipulations were used in the study, describe their specific content. Include the details of the interventions or manipulations intended for each study condition, including control groups (if any), and describe how and when interventions (experimental manipulations) were actually administered.

The description of manipulations or interventions should include several elements. Carefully describe the content of the intervention or specific experimental manipulations. Often, this will involve presenting a brief summary of instructions given to participants. If the instructions are unusual or compose the experimental manipulation, you may present them verbatim in an appendix or in an online supplemental archive. If the text is brief, you may present it in the body of the paper if it does not interfere with the readability of the report.

Describe the methods of manipulation and data acquisition. If a mechanical apparatus was used to present stimulus materials or collect data, include in the description of procedures the apparatus model number and manufacturer (when important, as in neuroimaging studies), its key settings or parameters (e.g., pulse settings), and its resolution (e.g., regarding stimulus delivery, recording precision). As with the description of the intervention or experimental manipulation, this material may be presented in the body of the paper, in an appendix, in an online supplemental archive, or as appropriate.

When relevant—such as, for example, in the delivery of clinical and educational interventions—the procedures should also contain a description of who delivered the intervention, including their level of professional training and their level of training in the specific intervention. Present the number of deliverers along with the mean, standard deviation, and range of number of individuals or units treated by each deliverer.

Provide information about (a) the setting where the intervention or manipulation was delivered, (b) the quantity and duration of exposure to the intervention or manipulation (i.e., how many sessions, episodes, or events were intended to be delivered and how long they were intended to last), (c) the time span taken for the delivery of the intervention or manipulation to each unit (e.g., would the manipulation delivery be complete in one session, or if participants returned for multiple sessions, how much time passed between the first and last session?), and (d) activities or incentives used to increase compliance.

When an instrument is translated into a language other than the language in which it was developed, describe the specific method of translation (e.g., back-translation, in which a text is translated into another language and then back into the first to ensure that it is equivalent enough that results can be compared).

Provide a description of how participants were grouped during data acquisition (i.e., was the manipulation or intervention administered individual by individual, in small groups, or in intact groupings such as classrooms?). Describe the smallest unit (e.g., individuals, work groups, classes) that was analyzed to assess effects. If the unit used for statistical analysis differed from the unit used to deliver the intervention or manipulation (i.e., was different from the unit of randomization), describe the analytic method used to account for this (e.g., adjusting the standard error estimates or using multilevel analysis).

2.07 Results

In the Results section, summarize the collected data and the analysis performed on those data relevant to the discourse that is to follow. Report the data in sufficient detail to justify your conclusions. Mention all relevant results, including those that run counter to expectation; be sure to include small effect sizes (or statistically nonsignificant findings) when theory predicts large (or statistically significant) ones. Do not hide uncomfortable results by omission. Do not include individual scores or raw data, with the exception, for example, of single-case designs or illustrative examples. In the spirit of data sharing (encouraged by APA and other professional associations and sometimes required by funding agencies), raw data, including study characteristics and individual effect sizes used in a meta-analysis, can be made available on supplemental online archives. See section 2.13 for a detailed discussion of the use of supplemental online archives. Discussing the implications of the results should be reserved for presentation in the Discussion section.

Recruitment. Provide dates defining the periods of recruitment and follow-up and the primary sources of the potential subjects, where appropriate. If these dates differ by group, provide the values for each group.

Statistics and data analysis. Analysis of data and the reporting of the results of those analyses are fundamental aspects of the conduct of research. Accurate, unbiased, complete, and insightful reporting of the analytic treatment of data (be it quantitative or qualitative) must be a component of all research reports. Researchers in the field of psychology use numerous approaches to the analysis of data, and no one approach is uniformly preferred as long as the method is appropriate to the research questions being asked and the nature of the data collected. The methods used must support their analytic burdens, including robustness to violations of the assumptions that underlie them, and they must provide clear, unequivocal insights into the data.

Historically, researchers in psychology have relied heavily on null hypothesis statistical significance testing (NHST) as a starting point for many (but not all) of its analytic approaches. APA stresses that NHST is but a starting point and that additional reporting elements such as effect sizes, confidence intervals, and extensive description are needed to convey the most complete meaning of the results. The degree to which any journal emphasizes (or de-emphasizes) NHST is a decision of the individual editor. However, complete reporting of all tested hypotheses and estimates of appropriate effect sizes and confidence intervals are the minimum expectations for all APA journals.[2] The research scientist is always responsible for the accurate and responsible reporting of the results of research studies.

Assume that your reader has a professional knowledge of statistical methods. Do not review basic concepts and procedures or provide citations for the most commonly used statistical procedures. If, however, there is any question about the appropriateness of a particular statistical procedure, justify its use by clearly stating the evidence that exists for the robustness of the procedure as applied.

Similarly, missing data can have a detrimental effect on the legitimacy of the inferences drawn by statistical tests. For this reason, it is critical that the frequency or percentages of missing data be reported along with any empirical evidence and/or theoretical arguments for the causes of data that are missing. For example, data might be described as missing completely at random (as when values of the missing variable are not related to the probability that they are missing or to the value of any other variable in the data set); missing at random (as when the probability of missing a value on a variable is not related to the missing value itself but may be related to other completely observed variables in the data set); or not missing at random (as when the probability of observing a given value for a variable is related to the missing value itself). It is also important to describe the methods for addressing missing data, if any were used (e.g., multiple imputation).

When reporting the results of inferential statistical tests or when providing estimates of parameters or effect sizes, include sufficient information to help the reader fully understand the analyses conducted and possible alternative explanations for the outcomes of those analyses. Because each analytic technique depends on different aspects of the data and assumptions, it is impossible to specify what constitutes a "sufficient set of statistics" for every analysis. However, such a set usually includes at least the following: the per-cell sample sizes; the observed cell means (or frequencies of cases in each category for a categorical variable); and the cell standard deviations, or the pooled within-cell variance. In the case of multivariable analytic systems, such as mul-

[2] Issues dealing with the controversy over the use of NHST and its alternatives are complex and outside the scope of a publication manual. For those interested in this controversy, a discussion of these and related issues can be found in the article by Wilkinson and the Task Force on Statistical Inference (1999); Harlow, Mulaik, and Steiger's (1997) *What If There Were No Significance Tests?* Kline's (2004) *Beyond Significance Testing: Reforming Data Analysis Methods in Behavioral Research*; and the article by Jones and Tukey (2000).

tivariate analyses of variance, regression analyses, structural equation modeling analyses, and hierarchical linear modeling, the associated means, sample sizes, and variance–covariance (or correlation) matrix or matrices often represent a sufficient set of statistics. At times, the amount of information that constitutes a sufficient set of statistics can be extensive; when this is the case, this information could be supplied in a supplementary data set or appendix (see section 2.13). For analyses based on very small samples (including single-case investigations), consider providing the complete set of raw data in a table or figure. Your work will more easily become a part of the cumulative knowledge of the field if you include enough statistical information to allow its inclusion in future meta-analyses.

For inferential statistical tests (e.g., t, F, and χ^2 tests), include the obtained magnitude or value of the test statistic, the degrees of freedom, the probability of obtaining a value as extreme as or more extreme than the one obtained (the exact p value), and the size and direction of the effect. When point estimates (e.g., sample means or regression coefficients) are provided, always include an associated measure of variability (precision), with an indication of the specific measure used (e.g., the standard error).

The inclusion of confidence intervals (for estimates of parameters, for functions of parameters such as differences in means, and for effect sizes) can be an extremely effective way of reporting results. Because confidence intervals combine information on location and precision and can often be directly used to infer significance levels, they are, in general, the best reporting strategy. The use of confidence intervals is therefore strongly recommended. As a rule, it is best to use a single confidence level, specified on an a priori basis (e.g., a 95% or 99% confidence interval), throughout the manuscript. Wherever possible, base discussion and interpretation of results on point and interval estimates.

For the reader to appreciate the magnitude or importance of a study's findings, it is almost always necessary to include some measure of effect size in the Results section.[3] Whenever possible, provide a confidence interval for each effect size reported to indicate the precision of estimation of the effect size. Effect sizes may be expressed in the original units (e.g., the mean number of questions answered correctly; kg/month for a regression slope) and are often most easily understood when reported in original units. It can often be valuable to report an effect size not only in original units but also in some standardized or units-free unit (e.g., as a Cohen's d value) or a standardized regression weight. Multiple degree-of-freedom effect-size indicators are often less useful than effect-size indicators that decompose multiple degree-of-freedom tests into meaningful one degree-of-freedom effects—particularly when the latter are the results that inform the discussion. The general principle to be followed, however, is to provide the reader with enough information to assess the magnitude of the observed effect.

Ancillary analyses. Report any other analyses performed, including subgroup analyses and adjusted analyses, indicating those that were prespecified and those that were exploratory (though not necessarily in the level of detail of primary analyses). Consider putting the detailed results of these analyses on the supplemental online archive. Discuss the implications, if any, of the ancillary analyses for statistical error rates.

Participant flow. For experimental and quasi-experimental designs, there must be a description of the flow of participants (human, animal, or units such as classrooms or

[3] Grissom and Kim (2005) provide a comprehensive discussion of effect sizes.

hospital wards) through the study. Present the total number of units recruited into the study and the number of participants assigned to each group. Provide the number of participants who did not complete the experiment or crossed over to other conditions and explain why. Note the number of participants used in the primary analyses. (This number might differ from the number who completed the study because participants might not show up for or complete the final measurement.) The flowchart in the Appendix (Figure 1) provides a useful device for displaying the flow of participants through each stage of a study (see also Figures 5.3 and 5.4, pp. 154–155).

Intervention or manipulation fidelity. If interventions or experimental manipulations were used, provide evidence on whether they were delivered as intended. In basic experimental research, this might be the results of checks on the manipulation. In applied research, this might be, for example, records and observations of intervention delivery sessions and attendance records.

Baseline data. Be sure that baseline demographic and/or clinical characteristics of each group are provided.

Statistics and data analysis. In studies reporting the results of experimental manipulations or interventions, clarify whether the analysis was by intent-to-treat. That is, were all participants assigned to conditions included in the data analysis regardless of whether they actually received the intervention, or were only participants who completed the intervention satisfactorily included? Give a rationale for the choice.

Adverse events. If interventions were studied, detail all important adverse events (events with serious consequences) and/or side effects in each intervention group.

2.08 Discussion

After presenting the results, you are in a position to evaluate and interpret their implications, especially with respect to your original hypotheses. Here you will examine, interpret, and qualify the results and draw inferences and conclusions from them. Emphasize any theoretical or practical consequences of the results. (When the discussion is relatively brief and straightforward, some authors prefer to combine it with the Results section, creating a section called Results and Discussion.)

Open the Discussion section with a clear statement of the support or nonsupport for your original hypotheses, distinguished by primary and secondary hypotheses. If hypotheses were not supported, offer post hoc explanations. Similarities and differences between your results and the work of others should be used to contextualize, confirm, and clarify your conclusions. Do not simply reformulate and repeat points already made; each new statement should contribute to your interpretation and to the reader's understanding of the problem.

Your interpretation of the results should take into account (a) sources of potential bias and other threats to internal validity, (b) the imprecision of measures, (c) the overall number of tests or overlap among tests, (d) the effect sizes observed, and (e) other limitations or weaknesses of the study. If an intervention is involved, discuss whether it was successful and the mechanism by which it was intended to work (causal pathways) and/or alternative mechanisms. Also, discuss barriers to implementing the intervention or manipulation as well as the fidelity with which the intervention or manipulation was implemented in the study, that is, any differences between the manipulation as planned and as implemented.

Acknowledge the limitations of your research, and address alternative explanations of the results. Discuss the generalizability, or external validity, of the findings. This critical analysis should take into account differences between the target population and the accessed sample. For interventions, discuss characteristics that make them more or less applicable to circumstances not included in the study, how and what outcomes were measured (relative to other measures that might have been used), the length of time to measurement (between the end of the intervention and the measurement of outcomes), incentives, compliance rates, and specific settings involved in the study as well as other contextual issues.

End the Discussion section with a reasoned and justifiable commentary on the importance of your findings. This concluding section may be brief or extensive provided that it is tightly reasoned, self-contained, and not overstated. In this section, you might briefly return to a discussion of why the problem is important (as stated in the introduction); what larger issues, those that transcend the particulars of the subfield, might hinge on the findings; and what propositions are confirmed or disconfirmed by the extrapolation of these findings to such overarching issues.

You may also consider the following issues:

- What is the theoretical, clinical, or practical significance of the outcomes, and what is the basis for these interpretations? If the findings are valid and replicable, what real-life psychological phenomena might be explained or modeled by the results? Are applications warranted on the basis of this research?
- What problems remain unresolved or arise anew because of these findings?

The responses to these questions are the core of the contribution of your study and justify why readers both inside and outside your own specialty should attend to the findings. Your readers should receive clear, unambiguous, and direct answers.

2.09 Multiple Experiments

If you are presenting several studies in one manuscript, make the rationale, logic, and method of each study clear to the reader. If appropriate, include for each study a short discussion of the results, or combine the discussion with the description of results (e.g., Results and Discussion). Always include a comprehensive general discussion of all the work after the last study. Report only conceptually linked studies in a single paper.

The arrangement of sections reflects the structure previously described. For example, label a series of experiments *Experiment 1, Experiment 2,* and so forth. They organize the subsections and make referring to a specific experiment convenient for the reader. The Method and Results sections (and the Discussion section, if a short discussion accompanies each study) appear under each study heading. (Refer to Figure 2.2, pp. 54–56, for the form of a two-experiment paper.)

2.10 Meta-Analyses

The same factors that have led to proposals for reporting standards for manuscripts that report new data collections have led to similar efforts to establish standards for reporting the methods and results of meta-analyses. Guidelines for reporting research syntheses and meta-analyses are in the Appendix (Table 4, Meta-Analysis Reporting Standards [MARS]: Information Recommended for Inclusion in Manuscripts Reporting Meta-Analyses). In the guidelines, it is assumed that the research synthesis being reported used quantitative procedures to combine the results of studies. However, many of the guidelines (e.g., regarding introductory material and literature searching procedures) could apply to a research synthesis even if meta-analytic procedures were not carried out. Because this type of research is more specialized, we do not detail each item. The terms and issues should be familiar to researchers undertaking a meta-analysis and are described in numerous texts.

Note that easy access to electronic storage of information means that all of the elements listed in the MARS guidelines need not appear in printed journal articles. The online supplemental archives of journals can be used to store supplemental materials associated with the articles that appear in print. This supplemental material might include, for example, the list of citations to the research included in a meta-analysis and the table giving descriptive information for each included study, especially when the number of included studies is large. If the number of articles contributing studies to the meta-analysis is relatively small (e.g., about 50 or fewer), they should appear in the reference list with an asterisk included to identify them. If the number of articles in the meta-analysis exceeds 50, then the references to the articles should be placed in a list and in a supplemental online archive. If an article is mentioned in the text of a meta-analytic article and the results reported in that article are included in the meta-analysis, the article should be cited both in the reference list and in the supplemental materials.

2.11 References

References acknowledge the work of previous scholars and provide a reliable way to locate it. References are used to document statements made about the literature, just as data in the manuscript support interpretations and conclusions. The references cited in the manuscript do not need to be exhaustive but should be sufficient to support the need for your research and to ensure that readers can place it in the context of previous research and theorizing.

The standard procedures for citation ensure that references are accurate, complete, and useful to investigators and readers. For detailed guidance on citing sources and preparing the reference list, consult Chapters 6 and 7.

Start the reference list on a new page. The word *References* should appear in uppercase and lowercase letters, centered. Double-space all reference entries. APA publishes references in a *hanging indent* format, meaning that the first line of each reference is set flush left and subsequent lines are indented.

2.12 Footnotes

Footnotes are used to provide additional content or to acknowledge copyright permission status.

Content footnotes. Content footnotes supplement or amplify substantive information in the text; they should not include complicated, irrelevant, or nonessential information. Because they can be distracting to readers, such footnotes should be included only if they strengthen the discussion. A content footnote should convey just one idea; if you find yourself creating paragraphs or displaying equations as you are writing a footnote, then the main text or an appendix probably would be a more suitable place to present your information. Another alternative is to indicate in a short footnote that the material is available online as supplemental material. In most cases, an author integrates an article best by presenting important information in the text, not in a footnote.

Copyright permission. Copyright permission footnotes acknowledge the source of lengthy quotations, scale and test items, and figures and tables that have been reprinted or adapted. Authors must obtain permission to reproduce or adapt material from a copyrighted source. (See Chapter 8 for a discussion of what authors should know about permissions and copyright.)

A numbered footnote is generally used to provide source material for long quotations. For tables, the source material is provided in a table note (see section 5.16), and for figures, the source is credited at the end of the caption (see section 5.23). Use the wording below for copyright permission footnotes.

Type of source	Copyright permission footnote
Journal	From [or The data in column 1 are from] "Title of Article," by A. N. Author and C. O. Author, year, *Title of Journal, Volume,* p. xx. Copyright [year] by the Name of Copyright Holder. Reprinted [or adapted] with permission.
Book	From [or The data in column 1 are from] *Title of Book* (p. xxx), by A. N. Author and C. O. Author, year, Place of Publication: Publisher. Copyright [year] by the Name of Copyright Holder. Reprinted [or adapted] with permission.

Number all footnotes consecutively in the order in which they appear in the manuscript with superscript Arabic numerals. Footnote numbers should be superscripted, like this,[1] following any punctuation mark except a dash. A footnote number that appears with a dash—like this[2]—always precedes the dash. (The number falls inside a closing parenthesis if it applies only to matter within the parentheses, like this.[3]) Do not place footnote numbers in text headings. Subsequent references to a footnote are by parenthetical note:

the same results (see Footnote 3)

When using the footnote function in your word-processing program, place each content or copyright permission footnote at the bottom of the page on which it is discussed. Footnotes may alternatively be placed in consecutive order on a separate page after the references. Be sure that the number of the footnote corresponds with the appropriate text discussion.

2.13 Appendices and Supplemental Materials

Sometimes, material that supplements article content would be distracting or inappropriate in the body of the manuscript. Material of this type can often be included in an appendix or in a supplemental materials section—the former being an element of the print version of the article, the latter being an online supplemental archive that the publisher of the archival source maintains.

Appendices. In general, an appendix is appropriate for materials that are relatively brief and that are easily presented in print format. Some examples of material suitable for an appendix are (a) a list of stimulus materials (e.g., those used in psycholinguistic research), (b) a detailed description of a complex piece of equipment, (c) a list of articles that provided the source data for a meta-analysis but are not directly referred to in any other way in an article, and (d) a detailed demographic description of subpopulations in the study and other detailed and/or complex reporting items suggested in the reporting standards section of this chapter.

If your manuscript has only one appendix, label it *Appendix;* if your manuscript has more than one appendix, label each one with a capital letter (*Appendix A, Appendix B,* etc.) in the order in which it is mentioned in the main text. Each appendix must have a title. In the text, refer to appendices by their labels:

> produced the same results for both studies (see Appendices A and B for complete proofs).

Like the main text, an appendix may include headings and subheadings as well as tables, figures, and displayed equations. Number each appendix table and figure, and number displayed equations if necessary for later reference; precede the number with the letter of the appendix in which it is included (e.g., Table A1). In a sole appendix, which is not labeled with a letter, precede all tables, figures, and equation numbers with the letter A to distinguish them from those of the main text. All appendix tables and figures must be cited within the appendix and numbered in order of citation.

If one table constitutes an entire appendix, the centered appendix label and title serve in lieu of a table number and title. Generally, treat multiple tables as separate appendices. If multiple tables (but no text) are combined into one appendix, number the tables.

Begin each appendix on a separate page. Center the word *Appendix* and the identifying capital letters (*A, B,* etc., in the order in which they are mentioned in text) at the top of the page. Center the title of the appendix, and use uppercase and lowercase letters. Begin the text of the appendix flush left, followed by indented paragraphs.

Supplemental materials. Web-based, online supplemental archives tend to be more appropriate for material that is more useful when available as a direct download as well as materials that are not easily presented in standard print format. Some examples of materials suitable for inclusion in online supplemental archives are (a) lengthy computer code, (b) details of mathematical or computational models, (c) audio or video clips, (d) oversized tables, (e) detailed intervention protocols, (f) primary or supplementary data sets, (g) expanded methodology sections, and (h) color figures. Because this content may be useful to the field, APA and many other publishers make it possible to provide them to a wide audience by posting them on the web, with a link to the published article. These files (like an appendix) then become part of the primary journal record and cannot be augmented, altered, or deleted.

Materials for inclusion in supplemental online archives should be submitted in formats that will be widely accessible. The following multimedia formats are generally widely available to most users and are preferred:

- Text—ASCII, Word, PDF, HTML
- Tables—Excel, Word, HTML, XHTML, XML
- Audio and Video—AVI, MPG, Quicktime, RM, MP3, WAV

- Animation—GIF, JPEG, Flash/Shockwave
- Images—GIF, JPEG, TIFF

Less widely used file formats, including TeX, LaTeX, any client- or server-side scripting (e.g., Java, CGI), executable files, and software applications, are acceptable but may be of less use to the reader who does not have access to specialized programs. Many users refuse to deal with executable files or operate from systems that refuse to access them.

For APA journals, the link to online supplemental archives that appears in the published article leads readers to a landing page that includes a bibliographic citation, a link to the published article, and a context statement and link for each supplemental material file (see an example of a sample landing page at www.apastyle.org). Supplemental materials should include enough information to make their contents interpretable when accompanied by the published text. For more information on supplemental materials, see Chapter 8.

Most journals make supplemental materials subject to peer review and require that they be submitted with the initial manuscript. Once accepted, the supplemental materials will be posted with no further editing or polishing.

Include an appendix or supplemental materials only if they help readers to understand, evaluate, or replicate the study or theoretical argument being made. Be sure that all relevant ethical standards have been followed for appendices and supplemental materials, including copyright protection, accurate representation of data, and protection of human subjects (e.g., content of video clips if human images).

Sample Papers

These sample papers illustrate three kinds of manuscripts: one-experiment (Figure 2.1), two-experiment (Figure 2.2), and meta-analysis (Figure 2.3). The three manuscripts have been adapted for the *Publication Manual* from articles published in APA journals. The numbers referred to in the shaded boxes refer to numbered sections in the *Publication Manual.*

Figure 2.1. Sample One-Experiment Paper (The numbers refer to numbered sections in the *Publication Manual.*)

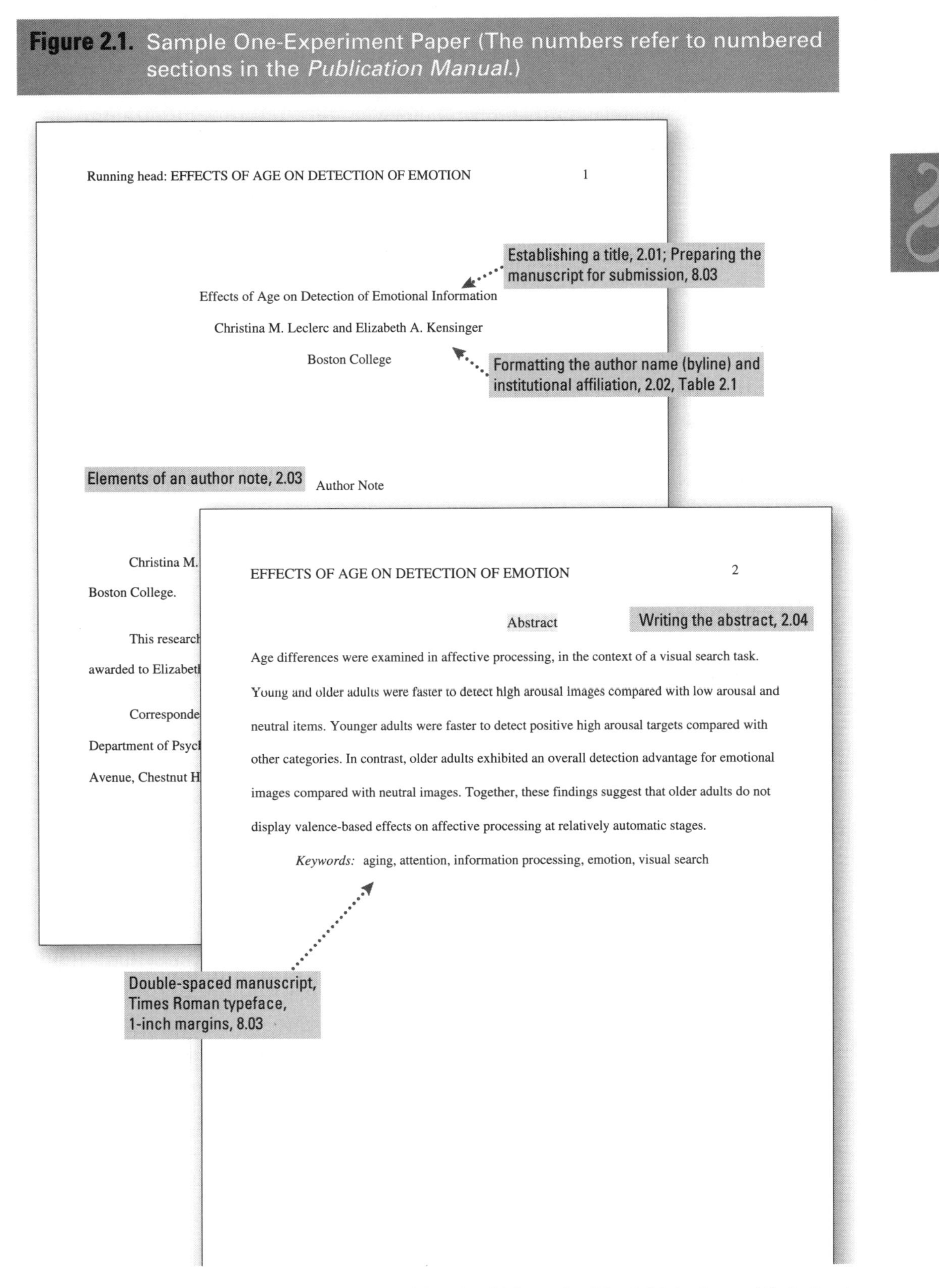

Paper adapted from "Effects of Age on Detection of Emotional Information," by C. M. Leclerc and E. A. Kensinger, 2008, *Psychology and Aging, 23,* pp. 209–215. Copyright 2008 by the American Psychological Association.

Figure 2.1. Sample One-Experiment Paper (continued)

Writing the introduction, 2.05

Effects of Age on Detection of Emotional Information

Frequently, people encounter situations in their environment in which it is impossible to attend to all available stimuli. It is therefore of great importance for one's attentional processes to select only the most salient information in the environment to which one should attend. Previous research has suggested that emotional information is privy to attentional selection in young adults (e.g., Anderson, 2005; Calvo & Lang, 2004; Carretie, Hinojosa, Marin-Loeches, Mecado, & Tapia, 2004; Nummenmaa, Hyona, & Calvo, 2006), an obvious service to evolutionary drives to approach rewarding situations and to avoid threat and danger (Davis & Whalen, 2001; Dolan & Vuilleumier, 2003; Lang, Bradley, & Cuthbert, 1997; LeDoux, 1995).

Ordering citations within the same parentheses, 6.16

Selecting the correct tense, 3.18

For example, Ohman, Flykt, and Esteves (2001) presented participants with 3 × 3 visual arrays with images representing four categories (snakes, spiders, flowers, mushrooms). In half the arrays, all nine images were from the same category, whereas in the remaining half of the arrays, eight images were from one category and one image was from a different category (e.g., eight flowers and one snake). Participants were asked to indicate whether the matrix included a discrepant stimulus. Results indicated that fear-relevant images were more quickly detected than fear-irrelev

Numbers that represent statistical or mathematical functions, 4.31

Numbers expressed in words, 4.32

Use of hyphenation for compound words, 4.13, Table 4.1

were fearfu

attention-g

not attende

Merikle, 2(

not limited

detected ra

Calvo & Lang, 2004; Carretie et al., 2004; Juth, Lundqvist, Karlsson, & Ohman, 2005; Nummenmaa et al., 2006).

From this research, it seems clear that younger adults show detection benefits for arousing information in the environment. It is less clear whether these effects are preserved across the adult life span. The focus of the current research is on determining the extent to which aging influences the early, relatively automatic detection of emotional information.

Continuity in presentation of ideas, 3.05

Regions of the brain thought to be important for emotional detection remain relatively intact with aging (reviewed by Chow & Cummings, 2000). Thus, it is plausible that the detection of emotional information remains relatively stable as adults age. However, despite the preservation of emotion-processing regions with age (or perhaps because of the contrast between the preservation of these regions and age-related declines in cognitive-processing regions; Good et al., 2001; Hedden & Gabrieli, 2004; Ohnishi, Matsuda, Tabira, Asada, & Uno, 2001; Raz, 2000; West, 1996), recent behavioral research has revealed changes that occur with aging in the regulation and processing of emotion. According to the socioemotional selectivity theory (Carstensen, 1992), with aging, time is perceived as increasingly limited, and as a result, emotion regulation becomes a primary goal (Carstensen, Isaacowitz, & Charles, 1999). According to socioemotional selectivity theory, age is associated with an increased motivation to derive emotional meaning from life and a simultaneous decreasing motivation to expand one's knowledge base. As a consequence of these motivational shifts, emotional aspects of the

Citing one work by six or more authors, 6.12

No capitalization in naming theories, 4.16

Figure 2.1. Sample One-Experiment Paper (continued)

EFFECTS OF AGE ON DETECTION OF EMOTION 5

To maintain positive affect in the face of negative age-related change (e.g., limited time remaining, physical and cognitive decline), older adults may adopt new cognitive strategies. One such strategy, discussed recently, is the positivity effect (Carstensen & Mikels, 2005), in which older adults spend proportionately more time processing positive emotional material and less time processing negative emotional material. Studies examining the influence of emotion on memory (Charles, Mather, & Carstensen, 2003; Kennedy, Mather, & Carstensen, 2004) have found that compared with younger adults, older adults recall proportionally more positive information and proportionally less negative information. Similar results have been found when examining eye-tracking patterns: Older adults looked at positive images longer than younger adults did, even when no age differences were observed in looking time for negative stimuli (Isaacowitz, Wadlinger, Goren, & Wilson, 2006). However, this positivity effect has not gone uncontested; some researchers have found evidence inconsistent with the positivity effect (e.g., Grühn, Smith, & Baltes, 2005; Kensinger, Brierley, Medford, Growdon, & Corkin, 2002).

Based on this previously discussed research, three competing hypotheses exist to explain age differences in emotional processing associated with the normal aging process. First, emotional information m

facilitated detection of er

emotional information m

detection of emotional in

principally on positive er

not negative, emotional i

The primary goal

To do so, we employed a

Using the colon between two grammatically complete clauses, 4.05

Capitalization of words beginning a sentence after a colon, 4.14

Hypotheses and their correspondence to research design, Introduction, 2.05

EFFECTS OF AGE ON DETECTION OF EMOTION

rapidly detect emotional information. We hypothesized that on the whole, older adults would be slower to detect information than young adults would be (consistent with Hahn, Carlson, Singer, & Gronlund, 2006; Mather & Knight, 2006); the critical question was whether the two age groups would show similar or divergent facilitation effects with regard to the effects of emotion on item detection. On the basis of the existing literature, the first two previously discussed hypotheses seemed to be more plausible than the third alternative. This is because there is reason to think that the positivity effect may be operating only at later stages of processing (e.g., strategic, elaborative, and emotion regulation processes) rather than at the earlier stages of processing involved in the rapid detection of information (see Mather & Knight, 2005, for discussion). Thus, the first two hypotheses, that emotional information maintains its importance across the life span or that emotional information in general takes on greater importance with age, seemed particularly applicable to early stages of emotional processing.

Indeed, a couple of prior studies have provided evidence for intact early processing of emotional facial expressions with aging. Mather and Knight (2006) examined young and older adults' abilities to detect happy, sad, angry, or neutral faces presented in a complex visual array. Mather and Knight found that like younger adults, older adults detected threatening faces more quickly than they detected other types of emotional stimuli. Similarly, Hahn et al. (2006) also found no age differences in efficiency of search time when angry faces were presented in an array of neutral faces, compared with happy faces in neutral face displays. When angry faces, compared with positive and neutral faces, served as nontarget distractors in the visual search arrays, however, older adults were more efficient in searching, compared with younger adults,

Using the semicolon to separate two independent clauses not joined by a conjunction, 4.04

Using the comma between elements in a series, 4.03

Punctuation with citations in parenthetical material, 6.21

Citing references in text, inclusion of year within paragraph, 6.11, 6.12

Prefixes and suffixes that do not require hyphens, Table 4.2

Figure 2.1. Sample One-Experiment Paper (continued)

negative stimuli were not of equivalent arousal levels (fearful faces typically are more arousing than happy faces; Hansen & Hansen, 1988). Given that arousal is thought to be a key factor in modulating the attentional focus effect (Hansen & Hansen, 1988; Pratto & John, 1991; Reimann & McNally, 1995), to more clearly understand emotional processing in the context of aging, it is necessary to include both positive and negative emotional items with equal levels of arousal.

In the current research, therefore, we compared young and older adults' detection of four categories of emotional information (positive high arousal, positive low arousal, negative high arousal, and negative low arousal) with their detection of neutral information. The positive and negative stimuli were carefully matched on arousal level, and the categories of high and low arousal were closely matched on valence to assure that the factors of valence (positive, negative) and arousal (high, low) could be investigated independently of one another. Participants were presented with a visual search task including images from these different categories (e.g., snakes, cars, teapots). For half of the multi-image arrays, all of the images were of the same item, and for the remaining half of the arrays, a sin

items was included. Participants were

the array, and their reaction times we

differences in response times (RTs) b

categories. We reasoned that if young

information, then we would expect si

stimuli for the two age groups. By co

were younger adults, older adults sho

emotional items (relative to the neutra

Prefixed words that require hyphens, Table 4.3

Using abbreviations, 4.22; Explanation of abbreviations, 4.23; Abbreviations used often in APA journals, 4.25; Plurals of abbreviations, 4.29

Identifying subsections within the Method section, 2.06

Using numerals to express numbers representing age, 4.31

for the arousing items than shown by the young adults (resulting in an interaction between age and arousal).

Method

Elements of the Method section, 2.06; Organizing a manuscript with levels of heading, 3.03

Participants

Younger adults (14 women, 10 men, M_{age} = 19.5 years, age range: 18–22 years) were recruited with flyers posted on the Boston College campus. Older adults (15 women, nine men, M_{age} = 76.1 years, age range: 68–84 years) were recruited through the Harvard Cooperative on Aging (see Table 1, for demographics and test scores).[1] Participants were compensated $10 per hour for their participation. There were 30 additional participants, recruited in the same way as described above, who provided pilot rating values: five young and five old participants for the assignment of items within individual categories (i.e., images depicting cats), and 10 young and 10 old participants for the assignment of images within valence and arousal categories. All participants were asked to bring corrective eyewear if needed, resulting in normal or corrected to normal vision for all participants.

Participant (subject) characteristics, Method, 2.06

Materials and Procedure

The visual search task was adapted from Ohman et al. (2001). There were 10 different types of items (two each of five Valence × Arousal categories: positive high arousal, positive low arousal, neutral, negative low arousal, negative high arousal), each containing nine individual exemplars that were used to construct 3 × 3 stimulus matrices. A total of 90 images were used, each appearing as a target and as a member of a distracting array. A total of 360 matrices were presented to each participant; half contained a target item (i.e., eight items of one type and one target item of another type) and half did not (i.e., all nine images of the same type). Within the

Figure 2.1. Sample One-Experiment Paper (continued)

EFFECTS OF AGE ON DETECTION OF EMOTION 9

matrix. Within the 180 target trials, each of the five emotion categories (e.g., positive high arousal, neutral, etc.) was represented in 36 trials. Further, within each of the 36 trials for each emotion category, nine trials were created for each of the combinations with the remaining four other emotion categories (e.g., nine trials with eight positive high arousal items and one neutral item). Location of the target was randomly varied such that no target within an emotion category was presented in the same location in arrays of more than one other emotion category (i.e., a negative high arousal target appeared in a different location when presented with positive high arousal array images than when presented with neutral array images).

The items within each category of grayscale images shared the same verbal label (e.g., mushroom, snake), and the items were selected from online databases and photo clipart packages. Each image depicted a photo of the actual object. Ten pilot participants were asked to write down the name corresponding to each object; any object that did not consistently generate the intended response was eliminated from the set. For the remaining images, an additional 20 pilot participants rated the emotional valence and arousal of the objects and assessed the degree of visual similarity among objects within a set (i.e., how similar the mushrooms were to one another) and between objects across sets (i.e., how similar the mushrooms were to the snakes).

Valence and arousal ratings. Valence and arousal were judged on 7-point scales (1 = *negative valence* or *low arousal* and 7 = *positive valence* or *high arousal*). Negative objects received mean valence ratings of 2.5 or lower, neutral objects received mean valence ratings of 3.5 to 4.5, and positive objects received mean valence ratings of 5.5 or higher. High arousal objects received mean arousal ratings greater than 5, and low arousal objects (including all neutral stimuli) received mean arousal ratings of less than 4. We selected categories for which both young and older adults agreed on the valence and arousal classifications, and stimuli were

Latin abbreviations, 4.26

Numbers expressed in words at beginning of sentence, 4.32

Italicization of anchors of a scale, 4.21

10

positive high arousal
h arousal.
etween-categories
exemplars (e.g., a set
the rest of the
ipants made these
ual dimensions in
ated how similar
lar the mushrooms
equated on within-
s well as for the

overall similarity of the object categories (*p*s > .20). For example, we selected particular mushrooms and particular cats so that the mushrooms were as similar to one another as were the cats (i.e., within-group similarity was held constant across the categories). Our object selection also assured that the categories differed from one another to a similar degree (e.g., that the mushrooms were as similar to the snakes as the cats were similar to the snakes).

Procedure

Each trial began with a white fixation cross presented on a black screen for 1,000 ms; the matrix was then presented, and it remained on the screen until a participant response was recorded. Participants were instructed to respond as quickly as possible with a button marked *yes* if there was a target present, or a button marked *no* if no target was present. Response latencies and accuracy for each trial were automatically recorded with E-Prime (Version 1.2) experimental

Figure 2.1. Sample One-Experiment Paper (continued)

software. Before beginning the actual task, participants performed 20 practice trials to assure compliance with the task instructions.

Results

Elements of the Results section, 2.07

Analyses focus on participants' RTs to the 120 trials in which a target was present and was from a different emotional category from the distractor (e.g., RTs were not included for arrays containing eight images of a cat and one image of a butterfly because cats and butterflies are both positive low arousal items). RTs were analyzed for 24 trials of each target emotion category. RTs for error trials were excluded (less than 5% of all responses) as were RTs that were ±3 *SD* from each participant's mean (approximately 1.5% of responses). Median RTs were then calculated for each of the five emotional target categories, collapsing across array type (see Table 2 for raw RT values for each of the two age groups). This allowed us to examine, for example, whether participants were faster to detect images of snakes than images of mushrooms, regardless of the type of array in which they were presented. Because our main interest was in examining the effects of valence and arousal on participants' target detection times, we created scores for each emotional target category that controlled for the participant's RTs to detect neutral targets (e.g., subtracting the RT to detect neutral targets from the RT to detect positive high arousal targets). These difference scores were then examined with a 2 × 2 × 2 (Age [young, older] × Valence [positive, negative] × Arousal [high, low]) analysis of variance (ANOVA). This ANOVA revealed only a significant main effect of arousal, $F(1, 46) = 8.41$, $p = .006$, $\eta_p^2 = .16$, with larger differences between neutral and high arousal images ($M = 137$) than between neutral and low arousal images ($M = 93$; i.e., high arousal items processed more quickly across both age groups compared with low arousal items; see Figure 1). There was no significant main effect for valence, nor was there an interaction between valence and arousal. It is critical that the analysis

Abbreviations accepted as words, 4.24

Symbols, 4.45; Numbers, 4.31

Nouns followed by numerals or letters, 4.17

Reporting *p* values, decimal fractions, 4.35

Statistical symbols, 4.46, Table 4.5

Numbering and discussing figures in text, 5.05

Figure 2.1. Sample One-Experiment Paper (continued)

revealed only a main effect of age but no interactions with age. Thus, the arousal-mediated effects on detection time appeared stable in young and older adults.

The results described above suggested that there was no influence of age on the influences of emotion. To further test the validity of this hypothesis, we submitted the RTs to the five categories of targets to a 2 × 5 (Age [young, old] × Target Category [positive high arousal, positive low arousal, neutral, negative low arousal, negative high arousal]) repeated measures ANOVA.[2] Both the age group, $F(1, 46) = 540.32, p < .001, \eta_p^2 = .92$, and the target category, $F(4, 184) = 8.98, p < .001, \eta_p^2 = .16$, main effects were significant, as well as the Age Group × Target Category interaction, $F(4, 184) = 3.59, p = .008, \eta_p^2 = .07$. This interaction appeared to reflect the fact that for the younger adults, positive high arousal targets were detected faster than targets from all other categories, $ts(23) < -1.90, p < .001$, with no other target categories differing significantly from one another (although there were trends for negative high arousal and negative low arousal targets to be detected more rapidly than neutral targets ($p < .12$). For older adults, all emotional categories of targets were detected more rapidly than were neutral targets, $ts(23) > 2.56, p < .017$, and RTs to the different emotion categories of targets did not differ significantly from one another. Thus, these results provided some evidence that older adults may show a broader advantage for detection of any type of emotional information, whereas young adults' benefit may be more narrowly restricted to only certain categories of emotional information.

Discussion

As outlined previously, there were three plausible alternatives for young and older adults' performance on the visual search task: The two age groups could show a similar pattern of enhanced detection of emotional information, older adults could show a greater advantage for

Statistics in text, 4.44

Spacing, alignment, and punctuation of mathematical copy, 4.46

Capitalize effects or variables when they appear with multiplication signs, 4.20

Elements of the Discussion section, 2.08

Figure 2.1. Sample One-Experiment Paper (continued)

EFFECTS OF AGE ON DETECTION OF EMOTION 13

emotional detection than young adults, or older adults could show a greater facilitation than young adults only for the detection of positive information. The results lent some support to the first two alternatives, but no evidence was found to support the third alternative.

In line with the first alternative, no effects of age were found when the influence of valence and arousal on target detection times was examined; both age groups showed only an arousal effect. This result is consistent with prior studies that indicated that arousing information can be detected rapidly and automatically by young adults (Anderson, Christoff, Panitz, De Rosa, & Gabrieli, 2003; Ohman & Mineka, 2001) and that older adults, like younger adults, continue to display a threat detection advantage when searching for negative facial targets in arrays of positive and neutral distractors (Hahn et al., 2006; Mather & Knight, 2006). Given the relative preservation of

& Bennett, 2004; Jenni

to take advantage of the

However, despi

age groups, the present

age-related enhanceme

the five categories of e

high arousal images (as

advantage for detecting

suggests a broader infl

for the hypothesis that

It is interesting

that the positivity effec

Clear statement of support or nonsupport of hypotheses, Discussion, 2.08

EFFECTS OF AGE ON DETECTION OF EMOTION 14

processing, given that no effects of valence were observed in older adults' detection speed. In the present study, older adults were equally fast to detect positive and negative information, consistent with prior research that indicated that older adults often attend equally to positive and negative stimuli (Rosler et al., 2005). Although the pattern of results for the young adults has differed across studies—in the present study and in some past research, young adults have shown facilitated detection of positive information (e.g., Anderson, 2005; Calvo & Lang, 2004; Carretie et al., 2004; Juth et al., 2005; Nummenmaa et al., 2006), whereas in other studies, young adults have shown an advantage for negative information (e.g., Armony & Dolan, 2002; Hansen & Hansen, 1988; Mogg, Bradley, de Bono, & Painter, 1997; Pratto & John, 1991; Reimann & McNally, 1995; Williams, Mathews, & MacLeod, 1996)—what is important to note is that the older adults detected both positive and negative stimuli at equal rates. This equivalent detection of positive and negative information provides evidence that older adults display an advantage for the detection of emotional information that is not valence-specific.

Thus, although younger and older adults exhibited somewhat divergent patterns of emotional detection on a task reliant on early, relatively automatic stages of processing, we found no evidence of an age-related positivity effect. The lack of a positivity focus in the older adults is in keeping with the proposal (e.g., Mather & Knight, 2006) that the positivity effect does not arise through automatic attentional influences. Rather, when this effect is observed in older adults, it is likely due to age-related changes in emotion regulation goals that operate at later stages of processing (i.e., during consciously controlled processing), once information has been attended to and once the emotional nature of the stimulus has been discerned.

Although we cannot conclusively say that the current task relies strictly on automatic processes, there are two lines of evidence suggesting that the construct examined in the current

Use of an em dash to indicate an interruption in the continuity of a sentence, 4.06; Description of an em dash, 4.13

Figure 2.1. Sample One-Experiment Paper (continued)

EFFECTS OF AGE ON DETECTION OF EMOTION 15

research examines relatively automatic processing. First, in their previous work, Ohman et al. (2001) compared RTs with both 2 × 2 and 3 × 3 arrays. No significant RT differences based on the number of images presented in the arrays were found. Second, in both Ohman et al.'s (2001) study and the present study, analyses were performed to examine the influence of target location on RT. Across both studies, and across both age groups in the current work, emotional targets were detected more quickly than were neutral targets, regardless of their location. Together, these findings suggest that task performance is dependent on relatively automatic detection processes rather than on controlled search processes.

Although further work is required to gain a more complete understanding of the age-related changes in the early processing of emotional information, our findings indicate that young and older adults

study provides further

of emotional images ar

(Fleischman et al., 200

although there is evide

information (e.g., Cars

present results suggest

tasks require relatively

Use of parallel construction with coordinating conjunctions used in pairs, 3.23

Discussion section ending with comments on importance of findings, 2.08

EFFECTS OF AGE ON DETECTION OF EMOTION 16

References

Construction of an accurate and complete reference list, 6.22; General desciption of references, 2.11

Anderson, A. K. (2005). Affective influences on the attentional dynamics supporting awareness. *Journal of Experimental Psychology: General*, *154*, 258–281. doi:10.1037/0096-3445.134.2.258

Anderson, A. K., Christoff, K., Panitz, D., De Rosa, E., & Gabrieli, J. D. E. (2003). Neural correlates of the automatic processing of threat facial signals. *Journal of Neuroscience*, *23*, 5627–5633.

Armony, J. L., & Dolan, R. J. (2002). Modulation of spatial attention by fear-conditioned stimuli: An event-related fMRI study. *Neuropsychologia*, *40*, 817–826. doi:10.1016/S0028-3932%2801%2900178-6

Beck, A. T., Epstein, N., Brown, G., & Steer, R. A. (1988). An inventory for measuring clinical anxiety: Psychometric properties. *Journal of Consulting and Clinical Psychology*, *56*, 893–897. doi:10.1037/0022-006X.56.6.893

Calvo, M. G., & Lang, P. J. (2004). Gaze patterns when looking at emotional pictures: Motivationally biased attention. *Motivation and Emotion*, *28*, 221–243. doi: 10.1023/B%3AMOEM.0000040153.26156.ed

Carretie, L., Hinojosa, J. A., Martin-Loeches, M., Mecado, F., & Tapia, M. (2004). Automatic attention to emotional stimuli: Neural correlates. *Human Brain Mapping*, *22*, 290–299. doi:10.1002/hbm.20037

Carstensen, L. L. (1992). Social and emotional patterns in adulthood: Support for socioemotional selectivity theory. *Psychology and Aging*, *7*, 331–338. doi:10.1037/0882-7974.7.3.331

Carstensen, L. L., Fung, H., & Charles, S. (2003). Socioemotional selectivity theory and the regulation of emotion in the second half of life. *Motivation and Emotion*, *27*, 103–123.

Figure 2.1. Sample One-Experiment Paper (continued)

EFFECTS OF AGE ON DETECTION OF EMOTION 17

Carstensen, L. L., & Mikels, J. A. (2005). At the intersection of emotion and cognition: Aging and the positivity effect. *Current Directions in Psychological Science, 14*, 117–121. doi: 10.1111/j.0963-7214.2005.00348.x

Charles, S. T., Mather, M., & Carstensen, L. L. (2003). Aging and emotional memory: The forgettable na

Psychology: C

Chow, T. W., & Cum

Aggleton (Ed.

Oxford Unive

Davis, M., & Whalen

EFFECTS OF AGE ON DETECTION OF EMOTION 18

Grühn, D., Smith, J., & Baltes, P. B. (2005). No aging bias favoring memory for positive material: Evidence from a heterogeneity-homogeneity list paradigm using emotionally toned words. *Psychology and Aging, 20*, 579–588. doi:10.1037/0882-7974.20.4.579

Hahn, S., Carlson, C., Singer, S., & Gronlund, S. D. (2006). Aging and visual search: Automatic

doi:

rity

nitive

Aging,

:

379–395.

-related

EFFECTS OF AGE ON DETECTION OF EMOTION 19

Kensinger, E. A., Brierley, B., Medford, N., Growdon, J. H., & Corkin, S. (2002). Effects of normal aging and Alzheimer's disease on emotional memory. *Emotion, 2*, 118–134. doi: 10.1037/1528-3542.2.2.118

Lang, P. J., Bradley, M. M., & Cuthbert, B. N. (1997). Motivated attention: Affect, activation, and action. In P. J. Lang, R. F. Simons, & M. Balaban (Eds.), *Attention and orienting: Sensory and motivational processes* (pp. 97–135). Mahwah, NJ: Erlbaum.

Leclerc, C. M., & Hess, T. M. (2005, August). *Age differences in processing of affectively primed information*. Poster session presented at the 113th Annual Convention of the American Psychological Association, Washington, DC.

LeDoux, J. E. (1995). Emotion: Clues from the brain. *Annual Review of Psychology, 46*, 209–235. doi:10.1146/annurev.ps.46.020195.001233

Mather, M., & Knight, M. (2005). Goal-directed memory: The role of cognitive control in older adults' emotional memory. *Psychology and Aging, 20*, 554–570. doi:10.1037/0882-7974.20.4.554

Mather, M., & Knight, M. R. (2006). Angry faces get noticed quickly: Threat detection is not impaired among older adults. *Journals of Gerontology, Series B: Psychological Sciences, 61B*, P54–P57.

Mogg, K., Bradley, B. P., de Bono, J., & Painter, M. (1997). Time course of attentional bias for threat information in non-clinical anxiety. *Behavioral Research Therapy, 35*, 297–303.

Nelson, H. E. (1976). A modified Wisconsin card sorting test sensitive to frontal lobe defects. *Cortex, 12*, 313–324.

Digital object identifier as article identifier, 6.31; Example of reference to a periodical, 7.01

Example of reference to a book chapter, print verison, no DOI, 7.02, Example 25

Figure 2.1. Sample One-Experiment Paper (continued)

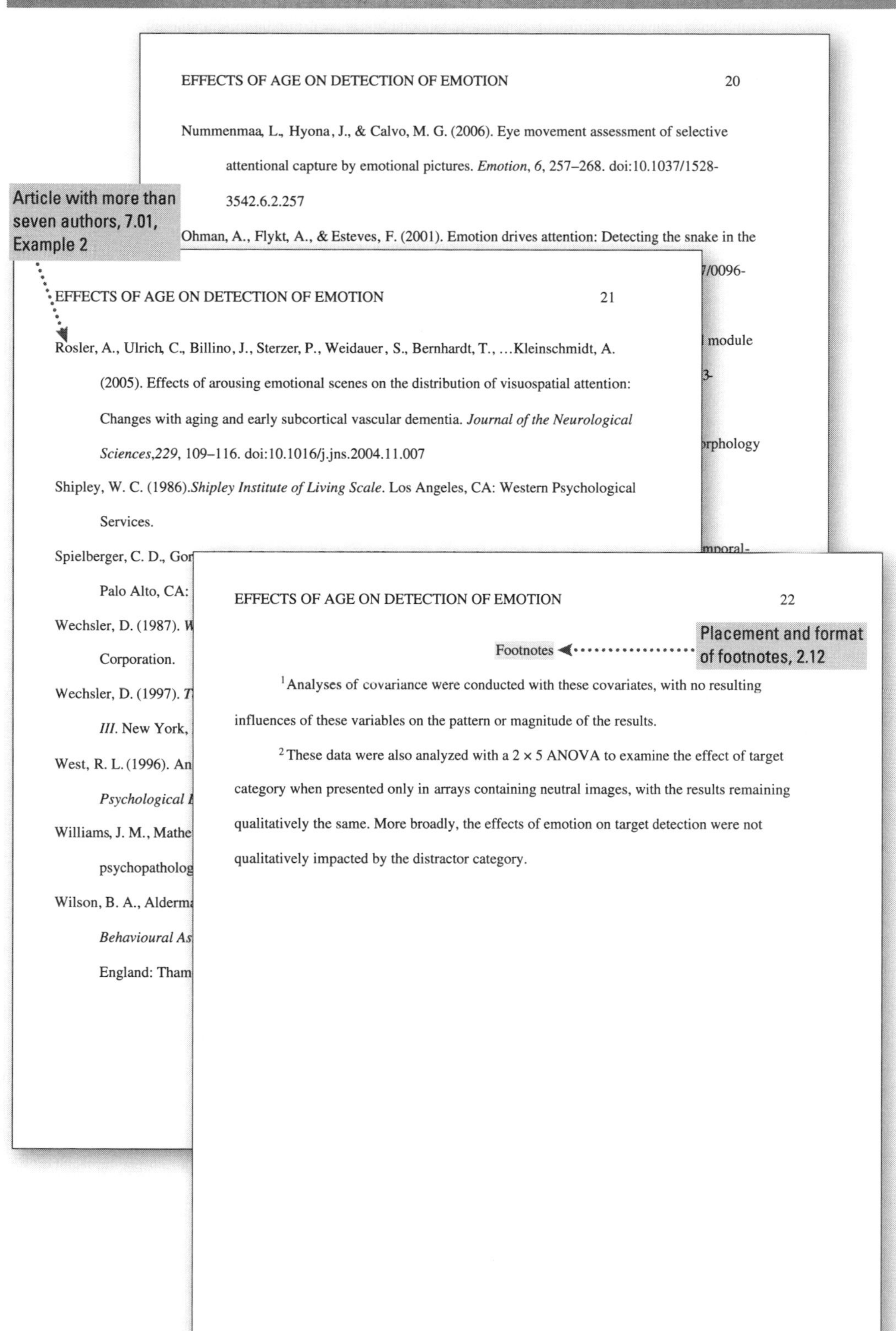
EFFECTS OF AGE ON DETECTION OF EMOTION 20

Nummenmaa, L., Hyona, J., & Calvo, M. G. (2006). Eye movement assessment of selective attentional capture by emotional pictures. *Emotion, 6,* 257–268. doi:10.1037/1528-3542.6.2.257

Ohman, A., Flykt, A., & Esteves, F. (2001). Emotion drives attention: Detecting the snake in the

EFFECTS OF AGE ON DETECTION OF EMOTION 21

Rosler, A., Ulrich, C., Billino, J., Sterzer, P., Weidauer, S., Bernhardt, T., ... Kleinschmidt, A. (2005). Effects of arousing emotional scenes on the distribution of visuospatial attention: Changes with aging and early subcortical vascular dementia. *Journal of the Neurological Sciences,229,* 109–116. doi:10.1016/j.jns.2004.11.007

Shipley, W. C. (1986).*Shipley Institute of Living Scale.* Los Angeles, CA: Western Psychological Services.

Spielberger, C. D., Gor

Palo Alto, CA:

Wechsler, D. (1987). W

Corporation.

Wechsler, D. (1997). T

III. New York,

West, R. L. (1996). An

Psychological I

Williams, J. M., Mathe

psychopatholog

Wilson, B. A., Alderma

Behavioural As

England: Tham

EFFECTS OF AGE ON DETECTION OF EMOTION 22

Footnotes

[1] Analyses of covariance were conducted with these covariates, with no resulting influences of these variables on the pattern or magnitude of the results.

[2] These data were also analyzed with a 2 × 5 ANOVA to examine the effect of target category when presented only in arrays containing neutral images, with the results remaining qualitatively the same. More broadly, the effects of emotion on target detection were not qualitatively impacted by the distractor category.

Figure 2.1. Sample One-Experiment Paper (continued)

EFFECTS OF AGE ON DETECTION OF EMOTION 23

Table 1

Participant Characteristics

Measure	Younger group *M*	Younger group *SD*	Older group *M*	Older group *SD*	*F* (1, 46)	*p*
Years of education	13.92	1.28	16.33	2.43	18.62	<.001
Beck Anxiety Inventory	9.39	5.34	6.25	6.06	3.54	.066
BADS–DEX	20.79	7.58	13.38	8.29	10.46	.002
STAI–State	45.79	4.44	47.08	3.48	1.07	.306
STAI–Trait	45.64	4.50	45.58	3.15	0.02	.963
Digit Symbol Substitution	49.62	7.18	31.58	6.56	77.52	<.001
Generative naming	46.95	9.70	47.17	12.98	.004	.951
Vocabulary	33.00	3.52	35.25	3.70	4.33	.043
Digit Span–Backward	8.81	2.09	8.25	2.15	0.78	.383
Arithmetic	16.14	2.75	14.96	3.11	1.84	.182
Mental Control	32.32	3.82	23.75	5.13	40.60	<.001
Self-Ordered Pointing	1.73	2.53	9.25	9.40	13.18	.001
WCST perseverative errors	0.36	0.66	1.83	3.23	4.39	.042

Note. The Beck Anxiety Inventory is from Beck et al. (1988); the Behavioral Assessment of the Dysexecutive Syndrome—Dysexecutive Questionnaire (BADS-DEX) is from Wilson et al. (1996); the State–Trait Inventory (STAI) measures are from Spielberger et al. (1970); and the Digit Symbol Substitution, Digit Span Backward, and Arithmetic Wechsler Adult Intelligence and Memory Scale–III measures are from Wechsler (1997). Generative naming scores represent the total number of words produced in 60 s each for letter *F*, *A*, and *S*. The Vocabulary measure is from Shipley (1986); the Mental Control measure is from Wechsler (1987); the Self-Ordered Pointing measure was adapted from Petrides and Milner (1982); and the Wisconsin Card Sorting Task (WCST) measure is from Nelson (1976). All values represent raw, nonstandardized scores.

Selecting effective presentation, 4.41; Logical and effective table layout, 5.08

Elements of table notes, 5.16

EFFECTS

Table 2

Raw Resp

Category
Positive h
Positive l
Neutral
Negative
Negative

Note. Valu
of the sam
positive hi
arousal, an
recorded i

Figure 2.1. Sample One-Experiment Paper (continued)

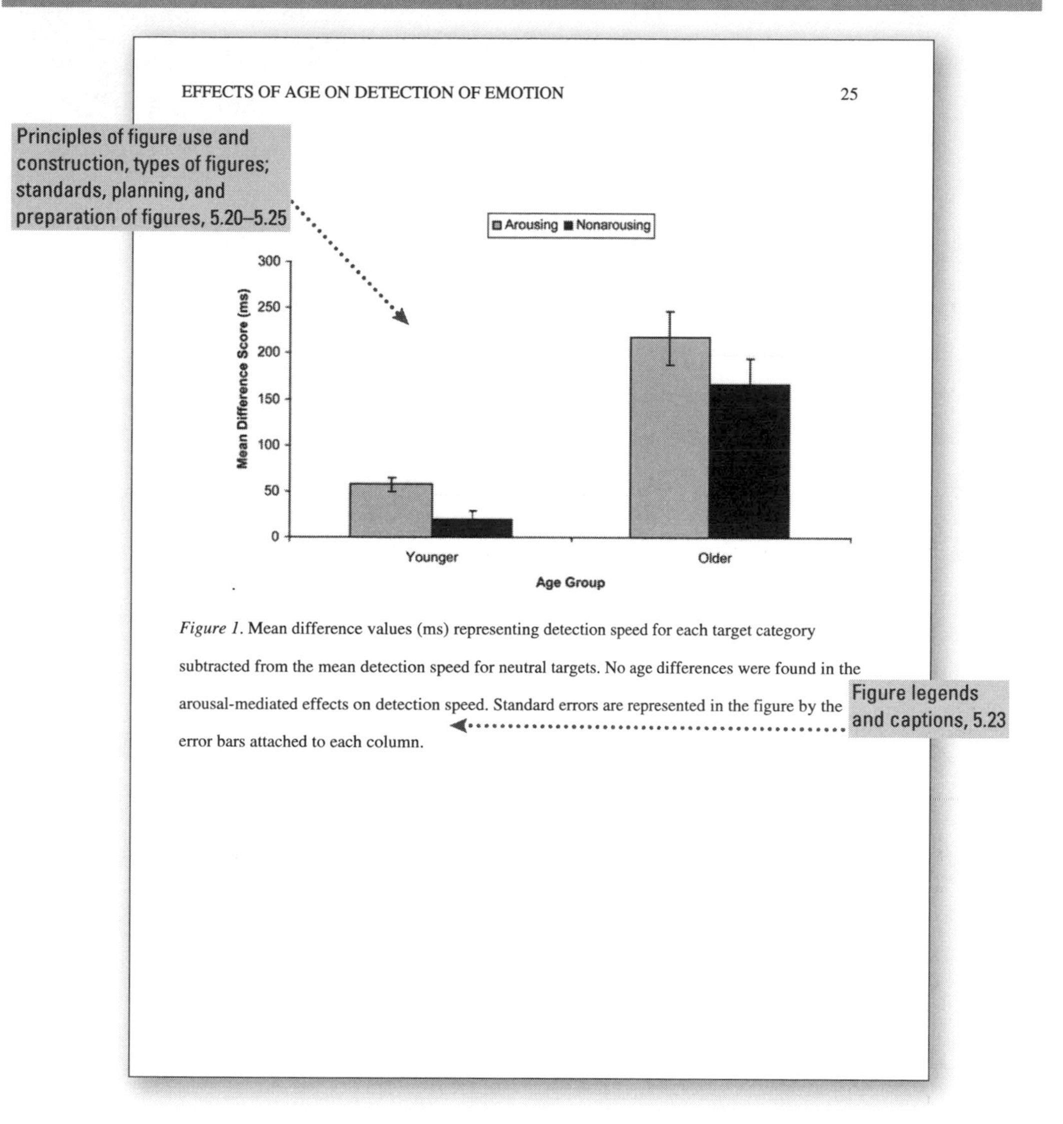
EFFECTS OF AGE ON DETECTION OF EMOTION 25

Figure 1. Mean difference values (ms) representing detection speed for each target category subtracted from the mean detection speed for neutral targets. No age differences were found in the arousal-mediated effects on detection speed. Standard errors are represented in the figure by the error bars attached to each column.

Figure 2.2. Sample Two-Experiment Paper (The numbers refer to numbered sections in the *Publication Manual*. This abridged manuscript illustrates the organizational structure characteristic of multiple-experiment papers. Of course, a complete multiple-experiment paper would include a title page, an abstract page, and so forth.)

INHIBITORY INFLUENCES ON ASYCHRONY 1

Inhibitory Influences on Asychrony as a Cue for Auditory Segregation

Auditory grouping involves the formation of auditory objects from the sound mixture reaching the ears. The cues used to integrate or segregate these sounds and so form auditory objects have been defined by several authors (e.g., Bregman, 1990; Darwin, 1997; Darwin & Carlyon, 1995). The key acoustic cues for segregating concurrent acoustic elements are differences in onset time (e.g., Dannenbring & Bregman, 1978; Rasch, 1978) and harmonic relations (e.g., Brunstrom & Roberts, 1998; Moore, Glasberg, & Peters, 1986). In an example of the importance of onset time, Darwin (1984a, 1984b) showed that increasing the level of a harmonic near the first formant (F1) frequency by adding a synchronous pure tone changes the phonetic quality of a vowel. However, when the added tone began a few hundred milliseconds before the vowel, it was essentially removed from the vowel percept.... [section continues].

General Method ◄······ Elements of empirical studies, 1.01

Overview

In the experiments reported here, we used a paradigm developed by Darwin to assess the perceptual integration of additional energy in the F1 region of a vowel through its effect on phonetic quality (Darwin, 1984a, 1984b; Darwin & Sutherland, 1984)....[section continues].

Stimuli

Amplitude and phase values for the vowel harmonics were obtained from the vocal-tract transfer function using cascaded formant resonators (Klatt, 1980). F1 values varied in 10-Hz steps from 360–550 Hz—except in Experiment 3, which used values from 350–540 Hz—to produce a continuum of 20 tokens....[section continues].

Listeners

Paper adapted from "Inhibitory Influences on Asychrony as a Cue for Auditory Segregation," by S. D. Holmes and B. Roberts, 2006, *Journal of Experimental Psychology: Human Perception and Performance, 32,* pp. 1231–1242.

Figure 2.2. Sample Two-Experiment Paper (continued)

INHIBITORY INFLUENCES ON ASYCHRONY 2

Listeners were volunteers recruited from the student population of the University of Birmingham and were paid for their participation. All listeners were native speakers of British English who reported normal hearing and had successfully completed a screening procedure (described below). For each experiment, the data for 12 listeners are presented....[section continues].

Plural forms of nouns of foreign origin, 3.19

Procedure

At the start of each session, listeners took part in a warm-up block. Depending on the number of conditions in a particular experiment, the warm-up block consisted of one block of all the experimental stimuli or every second or fourth F1 step in that block. This gave between 85 and 100 randomized trials.... [section continues].

Data Analysis

The data for each listener consisted of the number of /I/ responses out of 10 repetitions for each nominal F1 value in each condition. An estimate of the F1 frequency at the phoneme boundary was obtained by fitting a probit function (Finney, 1971) to a listener's identification data for each condition. The phoneme boundary was defined as the mean of the probit function (the 50% point)....[section continues].

Multiple Experiments, 2.09

Experiment 1

In this experim[...] pure-tone captor. Each [...] tone captor and a cente[...] continues].

Method

INHIBITORY INFLUENCES ON ASYCHRONY 3

There were nine conditions: the three standard ones (vowel alone, incremented fourth, and leading fourth) plus three captor conditions and their controls. A lead time of 240 ms was used for the added 500-Hz tone.... [section continues].

Abbreviating units of measurement, 4.27, Table 4.4

Results and Discussion

Figure 4 shows the mean phoneme boundaries for all conditions and the restoration effect for each captor type. The restoration effects are shown above the histogram bars both as a boundary shift in hertz and as a percentage of the difference in boundary position between the incremented-fourth and leading-fourth conditions.... [section continues].

Experiment 2

This experiment considers the case where the added 500-Hz tone begins at the same time as the vowel but continues after the vowel ends.... [section continues].

Method

There were five conditions: two of the standard ones (vowel alone and incremented fourth), a lagging-fourth condition (analogous to the leading-fourth condition used elsewhere), and a captor condition and its control. A lag time of 240 ms was used for the added 500-Hz tone.... [section continues]

Policy on metrication, 4.39; Style for metric units, 4.40

Results and Discussion

Figure 2.2. Sample Two-Experiment Paper (continued)

1984; Roberts & Holmes, 2006). This experiment used a gap between captor offset and vowel onset to measure the decay time of the captor effect ...[section continues].

Method

There were 17 conditions: the three standard ones (vowel alone, incremented fourth, and leading fourth), five captor conditions and their controls, and four additional conditions (described separately below). A lead time of 320 ms was used for the added 500-Hz tone. The captor conditions were created by adding a 1.1-kHz pure-tone captor, of various durations, to each member of the leading-fourth continuum....[section continues].

Results

Use of statistical term rather than symbol in text, 4.45

Figure 6 shows the mean phoneme boundaries for all conditions. There was a highly significant effect of condition on the phoneme boundary values, $F(16, 176) = 39.10, p < .001$. Incrementing the level of the fourth harmonic lowered the phoneme boundary relative to the vowel-alone condition (by 58 Hz, $p < .001$), which indicates that the extra energy was integrated into the vowel percept....[section continues].

Discussion

The results of this experiment show that the effect of the captor disappears somewhere between 80 and 160 ms after captor offset. This indicates that the captor effect takes quite a long time to decay away relative to the time constants typically found for cells in the CN using physiological measures (e.g., Needham & Paolini, 2003)....[section continues].

Summary and Concluding Discussion

Darwin and Sutherland (1984) first demonstrated that accompanying the leading portion of additional energy in the F1 region of a vowel with a captor tone partly reversed the effect of the onset asynchrony on perceived vowel quality. This finding was attributed to the formation of

a perceptual group between the leading portion and the captor tone, on the basis of their common onset time and harmonic relationship, leaving the remainder of the extra energy to integrate into the vowel percept... .[section continues].

[Follow the form of the one-experiment sample paper to type references, the author note, footnotes, tables, and figure captions.]

Figure 2.3. Sample Meta-Analysis (The numbers refer to numbered sections in the *Publication Manual*. This abridged manuscript illustrates the organizational structure characteristic of reports of meta-analyses. Of course, a complete meta-analysis would include a title page, an abstract page, and so forth.)

THE SLEEPER EFFECT IN PERSUASION 1

The Sleeper Effect in Persuasion:

A Meta-Analytic Review

Persuasive messages are often accompanied by information that induces suspicions of invalidity. For instance, recipients of communications about a political candidate may discount a message coming from a representative of the opponent party because they do not perceive the source of the message as credible (e.g., Lariscy & Tinkham, 1999). Because the source of the political message serves as a discounting cue and temporarily decreases the impact of the message, recipients may not be persuaded by the advocacy immediately after they receive the communication. Over time, however, recipients of an otherwise influential message may recall the message but not the noncredible source and thus become more persuaded by the message at that time than they were immediately following the communication. The term *sleeper effect* was used to denote such a d

noncredible source) be

memory of the messag

Italicize key terms, 4.21

Sample of Studies

We retrieved re

means of multiple proc

(1887–2003), Dissertati

Social-Science-Citation

credibility, *source cred*

persistence, *attitude m*

THE SLEEPER EFFECT IN PERSUASION 2

retention, *attitude and decay*, and *persuasion and decay*. Because researchers often use the terms *opinion* and *belief*, instead of *attitude*, we conducted searches using these substitute terms as well.

Second, … [section continues].

Description of meta-analysis, 1.02; Guidelines for reporting meta-analysis, 2.10; see also Appendix

Selection Criteria

We used the following criteria to select studies for inclusion in the meta-analysis.

1. We only included studies that involved the presentation of a communication containing persuasive arguments. Thus, we excluded studies in which the participants played a role or were asked to make a speech that contradicted their opinions. We also excluded developmental studies involving delayed effects of an early event (e.g., child abuse), which sometimes are also referred to as sleeper effects….[section continues].

Moderators

Identification of elements in a series within a sentence, 3.04

For descriptive purposes, we recorded (a) the year and (b) source (i.e., journal article, unpublished dissertations and theses, or other unpublished document) of each report as well as (c) the sample composition (i.e., high-school students, university students, or other) and (d) the country in which the study was conducted.

We also coded each experiment in terms of ….[section continues].

Studies were coded independently by the first author and another graduate student.

Paper adapted from "The Sleeper Effect in Persuasion: A Meta-Analytic Review," by G. Kumkale and D. Albarracin, 2004, *Psychological Bulletin, 130*, pp. 143–172. Copyright 2004 by the American Psychological Association.

Figure 2.3. Sample Meta-Analysis (continued)

THE SLEEPER EFFECT IN PERSUASION 3

was satisfactory (Orwin, 1994). We resolved disagreements by discussion and consultation with colleagues. Characteristics of the individual studies included in this review are presented in Table 1. The studies often contained several independent datasets such as different messages and different experiments. The characteristics that distinguish different datasets within a report appear on the second column of the table.

Dependent Measures and Computation of Effect Sizes

We calculated effect sizes for (a) persuasion and (b) recall–recognition of the message content. Calculations were based on the data described in the primary reports as well as available responses of the authors to requests of further information....[section continues].

Analyses of Effect Sizes

There are two n

effects....[section conti

To benefit from the str

conduct analyses using

The data analys

estimation of overall ef

Sample of Studies and

Descriptive cha

Table 2....[section con

Overview of the Aver

A thorough und

condition differences a

THE SLEEPER EFFECT IN PERSUASION 4

place over time....[section continues].

In light of these requirements, we first examined whether discounting cues led to a decrease in agreement with the communication (boomerang effect). Next,...[section continues].

Ruling out a nonpersisting boomerang effect. To determine whether or not a delayed increase in persuasion represents an absolute sleeper effect, one needs to rule out a nonpersisting boomerang effect, which takes place when a message initially backfires but later loses this reverse effect (see panel A of Figure 1)....[section continues].

Average sleeper effect. Relevant statistics corresponding to average changes in persuasion from the immediate to the delayed posttest appear in Table 4, organized by the different conditions we considered (i.e., acceptance-cue, discounting-cue, no-message control, and message-only control). In Table 4, positive effect sizes indicate increases in persuasion over time, negative effect sizes indicate decay in persuasion, and zero effects denote stability in persuasion. Confidence intervals that do not include zero indicate significant changes over time. The first row of Table 4 shows that recipients of acceptance cues agreed with the message less as time went by (fixed-effects, $d_+ = -0.21$; random-effects, $d_+ = -0.23$). In contrast to the decay in persuasion for recipients of acceptance cues, there was a slight increase in persuasion for recipients of discounting cues over time ($d_+ = 0.08$). It is important to note that change in discounting-cue conditions significantly differed from change in acceptance-cue conditions, (fixed-effects; $B = -0.29$, $SE = 0.04$), $Q_B(1) = 58.15$, $p < .0001$; $Q_E(123) = 193.82$, $p < .0001$....[section continues].

Summary and variability of the overall effect. The overall analyses identified a relative sleeper effect in persuasion, but no absolute sleeper effect. The latter was not surprising, because the sleeper effect was expected to emerge under specific conditions....[section continues].

Use at least two subheadings in a section, 3.02

Figure 2.3. Sample Meta-Analysis (continued)

THE SLEEPER EFFECT IN PERSUASION 5

Moderator Analyses

Although overall effects have descriptive value, the variability in the change observed in discounting-cue conditions makes it unlikely that the same effect was present under all conditions. Therefore, we tested the hypotheses that the sleeper effect would be more likely (e.g., more consistent with the absolute pattern in Panel B1 of Figure 1) when...[section continues].

Format for references included in a meta-analysis with less than 50 references, 6.26

THE SLEEPER EFFECT IN PERSUASION 6

References

References marked with an asterisk indicate studies included in the meta-analysis.

Albarracín, D. (2002). Cognition in persuasion: An analysis of information processing in response to persuasive communications. In M. P. Zanna (Ed.), *Advances in experimental social psychology* (Vol. 34, pp. 61–130). doi:10.1016/S0065-2601(02)80004-1

... [references continue]

Johnson, B. T., & Eagly, A. H. (1989). Effects of involvement in persuasion: A meta-analysis. *Psychological Bulletin, 106,* 290–314. doi:10.1037/0033-2909.106.2.290

*Johnson, H. H., Torcivia, J. M., & Poprick, M. A. (1968). Effects of source credibility on the relationship between authoritarianism and attitude change. *Journal of Personality and Social Psychology, 9,* 179–183. doi:10.1037/h0021250

*Johnson, H. H., & Watkins, T. A. (1971). The effects of message repetitions on immediate and delayed attitude change. *Psychonomic Science, 22,* 101–103.

Jonas, K., Diehl, M., & Bromer, P. (1997). Effects of attitudinal ambivalence on information processing and attitude-intention consistency. *Journal of Experimental Social Psychology, 33,* 190–210. doi:10.1006/jesp.1996.1317

... [references continue]

[Follow the form of the one-experiment sample paper to type the author note, footnotes, tables, and figure captions.]

3

Writing Clearly and Concisely

This chapter provides some general principles of expository writing and suggests ways to improve writing style. We focus first on the benefits of planning and choosing the best organizational structure to develop your argument. We next describe some basic principles for writing with clarity and precision and for avoiding bias in language. Last, we demonstrate how correct grammar is the foundation of clear, effective, and persuasive communication.

Organization

Before beginning to write, consider the best length and structure for the findings you wish to share. Ordering your thoughts logically, both at the paragraph and at the sentence levels, will strengthen the impact of your writing.

3.01 Length

The optimal length of a manuscript is the number of pages needed to effectively communicate the primary ideas of the study, review, or theoretical analysis. As a rule "less is more." Discursive writing often obscures an author's main points, and condensing long manuscripts often improves them. If a paper is too long, shorten it by stating points clearly and directly, confining the discussion to the specific problem under investigation, deleting or combining data displays, eliminating repetition across sections, and writing in the active voice. At times, a paper may need to be divided into two or more papers, each with a more specific focus (however, see section 1.09 on piecemeal publication). Journals differ in average length of articles published. It is generally wise to be consistent with the usual practices of the journal to which you are submitting your paper.

3.02 Organizing a Manuscript With Headings

In scientific writing, sound organizational structure is the key to clear, precise, and logical communication. This includes the use of headings to effectively organize ideas within a study as well as seriation to highlight important items within sections. Concise headings help the reader anticipate key points and track the development of your argument.

Readers familiar with earlier editions of the *Publication Manual* will note that we have changed and simplified the heading styles in this edition. This change was motivated by the desire to make planning a less complicated process for the writer and to make articles more accessible for those reading them in electronic formats.

Levels of heading establish the hierarchy of sections via format or appearance. All topics of equal importance have the same level of heading throughout a manuscript. For example, in a multiexperiment paper, the headings for the Method and Results sections in Experiment 1 should be the same level as the headings for the Method and Results sections in Experiment 2.

Avoid having only one subsection heading and subsection within a section, just as you would in an outline. Use at least two subsection headings within any given section, or use none (e.g., in an outline, you could divide a section numbered I into a minimum of A and B sections; just an A section could not stand alone).

3.03 Levels of Heading

The heading style recommended by APA consists of five possible formatting arrangements, according to the number of levels of subordination. Each heading level is numbered (see Table 3.1).

Regardless of the number of levels of subheading within a section, the heading structure for all sections follows the same top-down progression. Each section starts with the

Table 3.1. Format for Five Levels of Heading in APA Journals

Level of heading	Format
1	**Centered, Boldface, Uppercase and Lowercase Heading**[a]
2	**Flush Left, Boldface, Uppercase and Lowercase Heading**
3	**Indented, boldface, lowercase paragraph heading ending with a period.**[b]
4	***Indented, boldface, italicized, lowercase paragraph heading ending with a period.***
5	*Indented, italicized, lowercase paragraph heading ending with a period.*

[a]This type of capitalization is also referred to as *title case.* [b]In a *lowercase paragraph heading,* the first letter of the first word is uppercase and the remaining words are lowercase.

highest level of heading, even if one section may have fewer levels of subheading than another section. For example, the Method and Results sections of a paper may each have two levels of subheading, and the Discussion section may have only one level of subheading. There would then be three levels of heading for the paper overall: the section headings (**Method, Results,** and **Discussion**) and the two levels of subheading, as follows:

Method

Sample and Participant Selection

Assessments and Measures

  Q-sort measures of inhibition and aggressiveness.

  Life History Calendar.

Results

Outcome of Inhibited Children at 23 Years

  Personality and self-esteem.

  Social network.

  Life history and IQ.

Outcome of Aggressive Children at 23 Years

Discussion

Inhibited Children: Delayed Social Transitions During Emerging Adulthood

Inhibited Children: Weak Evidence for Internalizing Difficulties

Limitations of the Present Study

Conclusions and Future Prospects

The introduction to a manuscript does not carry a heading that labels it as the introduction. (The first part of a manuscript is assumed to be the introduction.)

Do not label headings with numbers or letters. (The sections and headings in the *Publication Manual* are numbered only to permit indexing and cross-referencing.) The number of levels of heading needed for your article will depend on its length and complexity. If only one level of heading is needed, use Level 1; for a paper with two levels of heading, use Levels 1 and 2; if three levels are needed, use Levels 1, 2, and 3; and so forth.

3.04 Seriation

Just as the heading structure alerts readers to the order of ideas within the paper, seriation helps the reader understand the organization of key points within sections, paragraphs, and sentences. In any series, all items should be syntactically and conceptually parallel (see section 3.23).

Separate paragraphs in a series, such as itemized conclusions or steps in a procedure, are identified by an Arabic numeral followed by a period but not enclosed in or followed by parentheses. Separate sentences in a series are also identified by an Arabic numeral followed by a period; the first word is capitalized, and the sentence ends with a period or correct punctuation.

> Using the learned helplessness theory, we predicted that the depressed and nondepressed participants would make the following judgments of control:

1. Individuals who . . . [paragraph continues].
2. Nondepressed persons exposed to . . . [paragraph continues].
3. Depressed persons exposed to . . . [paragraph continues].
4. Depressed and nondepressed participants in the no-noise groups . . . [paragraph continues].

The use of "numbered lists" may connote an unwanted or unwarranted ordinal position (e.g., chronology, importance, priority) among the items. If you wish to achieve the same effect without the implication of ordinality, items in the series should be identified by bullets. Symbols such as small squares, circles, and so forth, may be used in creating a bulleted list. At the time that an article accepted for publication is typeset, the bullet notation will be changed to the style used by that journal.

- Individuals who . . . [paragraph continues].
- Nondepressed persons exposed to . . . [paragraph continues].
- Depressed persons exposed to . . . [paragraph continues].
- Depressed and nondepressed participants in the no-noise groups . . . [paragraph continues].

Within a paragraph or sentence, identify elements in a series by lowercase letters in parentheses.

> The participant's three choices were (a) working with another participant, (b) working with a team, and (c) working alone.

Within a sentence, use commas to separate three or more elements that do not have internal commas; use semicolons to separate three or more elements that have internal commas.

> We tested three groups: (a) low scorers, who scored fewer than 20 points; (b) moderate scorers, who scored between 20 and 50 points; and (c) high scorers, who scored more than 50 points.

Alternatively, you may use bulleted lists within a sentence to separate three or more elements. In these instances, capitalize and punctuate the list as if it were a complete sentence.

> In accordance with this theory, these relations should be marked by

- equity, social justice, and equal opportunity;
- sensitivity to individual differences and promotion of a goodness-of-fit between individually different people and contexts;
- affirmative actions to correct ontogenetic or historical inequities in person–context fit;

- efforts to recognize and celebrate diversity; and
- promotion of universal participation in civic life, and hence democracy (Lerner, Balsano, Banik, & Naudeau, 2005, p. 45).

Writing Style

The prime objective of scientific reporting is clear communication. You can achieve this by presenting ideas in an orderly manner and by expressing yourself smoothly and precisely. Establishing a tone that conveys the essential points of your study in an interesting manner will engage readers and communicate your ideas more effectively.

3.05 Continuity in Presentation of Ideas

Readers will better understand your ideas if you aim for continuity in words, concepts, and thematic development from the opening statement to the conclusion. Continuity can be achieved in several ways. For instance, punctuation marks contribute to continuity by showing relationships between ideas. They cue the reader to the pauses, inflections, subordination, and pacing normally heard in speech. Use the full range of punctuation aids available: Neither overuse nor underuse one type of punctuation, such as commas or dashes. Overuse may annoy the reader; underuse may confuse. Instead, use punctuation to support meaning.

Another way to achieve continuity is through the use of transitional words. These words help maintain the flow of thought, especially when the material is complex or abstract. A pronoun that refers to a noun in the preceding sentence not only serves as a transition but also avoids repetition. Be sure the referent is obvious. Other transition devices are time links (*then, next, after, while, since*), cause–effect links (*therefore, consequently, as a result*), addition links (*in addition, moreover, furthermore, similarly*), and contrast links (*but, conversely, nevertheless, however, although*).

3.06 Smoothness of Expression

Scientific prose and creative writing serve different purposes. Devices that are often found in creative writing—for example, setting up ambiguity; inserting the unexpected; omitting the expected; and suddenly shifting the topic, tense, or person—can confuse or disturb readers of scientific prose. Therefore, try to avoid these devices and aim for clear and logical communication.

Because you have been so close to your material, you may not immediately see certain problems, especially contradictions the reader may infer. A reading by a colleague may uncover such problems. You can usually catch omissions, irrelevancies, and abruptness by putting the manuscript aside and rereading it later. Reading the paper aloud can make flaws more apparent. (See also section 3.11.)

If, on later reading, you find that your writing is abrupt, introducing more transition devices may be helpful. You may have abandoned an argument or theme prematurely; if so, you need to amplify the discussion.

Abruptness may result from sudden, unnecessary shifts in verb tense within the same paragraph or in adjacent paragraphs. By using verb tenses consistently, you can help ensure smooth expression. Past tense (e.g., "Smith *showed*") or present perfect tense (e.g., "researchers *have shown*") is appropriate for the literature review and the description of the procedure if the discussion is of past events. Stay within the chosen tense. Use past tense (e.g., "anxiety *decreased* significantly") to describe the results. Use the present tense (e.g., "the results of Experiment 2 *indicate*") to discuss implications of the results and to present the conclusions. By reporting conclusions in the present tense, you allow readers to join you in deliberating the matter at hand. (See section 3.19 for details on the use of verb tense.)

Noun strings, meaning several nouns used one after another to modify a final noun, create another form of abruptness. The reader is sometimes forced to stop to determine how the words relate to one another. Skillful hyphenation can clarify the relationships between words, but often the best approach is to untangle the string. For example, consider the following string:

commonly used investigative expanded issue control question technique

This is dense prose to the reader knowledgeable about studies on lie detection—and gibberish to a reader unfamiliar with such studies. Possible ways to untangle the string are as follows:

- a control-question technique that is commonly used to expand issues in investigations
- an expanded-issue control-question technique that is commonly used in investigations
- a common technique of using control questions to investigate expanded issues
- a common investigative technique of using expanded issues in control questions

One approach to untangling noun strings is to move the last word to the beginning of the string and fill in with verbs and prepositions. For example, *early childhood thought disorder misdiagnosis* might be rearranged to read *misdiagnosis of thought disorders in early childhood.*

Many writers strive to achieve smooth expression by using synonyms or near-synonyms to avoid repeating a term. The intention is commendable, but by using synonyms you may unintentionally suggest a subtle difference. Therefore, choose synonyms with care. The discreet use of pronouns can often relieve the monotonous repetition of a term without introducing ambiguity.

3.07 Tone

Although scientific writing differs in form from literary writing, it need not lack style or be dull. In describing your research, present the ideas and findings directly but aim for an interesting and compelling style and a tone that reflects your involvement with the problem.

Scientific writing often contrasts the positions of different researchers. Differences should be presented in a professional, noncombative manner. For example, "Fong and Nisbett did not address . . ." is acceptable, whereas "Fong and Nisbett completely overlooked . . ." is not.

One effective way to achieve the right tone is to imagine a specific reader you are intending to reach and to write in a way that will educate and persuade that individual. Envisioning a person familiar to you may make this technique more effective. You may wish to write, for example, to a researcher in a related field who is trying to keep abreast of the literature but is not familiar with jargon or insider perspectives. What would facilitate his or her understanding of and appreciation for the importance of your work?

3.08 Economy of Expression

Say only what needs to be said. The author who is frugal with words not only writes a more readable manuscript but also increases the chances that the manuscript will be accepted for publication. The number of printed pages a journal can publish is limited, and editors therefore often request that authors shorten submitted papers. You can tighten long papers by eliminating redundancy, wordiness, jargon, evasiveness, overuse of the passive voice, circumlocution, and clumsy prose. Weed out overly detailed descriptions of apparatus, participants, or procedures (beyond those called for in the reporting standards; see Chapter 2); elaborations of the obvious; and irrelevant observations or asides. Materials such as these may be placed, when appropriate, in an online supplemental archive (see sections 2.13 and 8.03 for further details).

Short words and short sentences are easier to comprehend than are long ones. A long technical term, however, may be more precise than several short words, and technical terms are inseparable from scientific reporting. Yet the technical terminology in a paper should be readily understood by individuals throughout each discipline. An article that depends on terminology familiar to only a few specialists does not sufficiently contribute to the literature.

Wordiness. Wordiness can also impede the ready grasp of ideas. Change *based on the fact that* to *because, at the present time* to *now,* and *for the purpose of* to simply *for* or *to.* Use *this study* instead of *the present study* when the context is clear. Change *there were several students who completed* to *several students completed.* Unconstrained wordiness lapses into embellishment and flowery writing, which are clearly inappropriate in scientific style.

Redundancy. Writers often use redundant language in an effort to be emphatic. Use no more words than are necessary to convey your meaning.

In the following examples, the italicized words are redundant and should be omitted:

they were *both* alike
a total of 68 participants
four *different* groups saw
instructions, which were *exactly* the same as those used
absolutely essential
has been *previously* found
small *in size*
one and the same
in *close* proximity
completely unanimous
just exactly
very close to significance
period of time
summarize *briefly*
the reason is *because*

Unit length. Although writing only in short, simple sentences produces choppy and boring prose, writing exclusively in long, involved sentences results in difficult, sometimes incomprehensible material. Varied sentence length helps readers maintain interest and comprehension. When involved concepts require long sentences, the components should proceed logically. Direct, declarative sentences with simple, common words are usually best.

Similar cautions apply to paragraph length. Single-sentence paragraphs are abrupt. Paragraphs that are too long are likely to lose the reader's attention. A new paragraph provides a pause for the reader—a chance to assimilate one step in the conceptual development before beginning another. If a paragraph runs longer than one double-spaced manuscript page, you may lose your readers. Look for a logical place to break a long paragraph, or reorganize the material.

3.09 Precision and Clarity

Word choice. Make certain that every word means exactly what you intend it to mean. In informal style, for example, *feel* broadly substitutes for *think* or *believe,* but in scientific style such latitude is not acceptable. A similar example is that *like* is often used when *such as* is meant:

Correct:

Articles by psychologists such as Skinner and Watson. . . .

Correct:

Like Watson, Skinner believed. . . .

Incorrect:

Articles by psychologists like Skinner and Watson. . . .

Colloquial expressions. Avoid colloquial expressions (e.g., *write up* for *report*), which diffuse meaning. Approximations of quantity (e.g., *quite a large part, practically all,* or *very few*) are interpreted differently by different readers or in different contexts. Approximations weaken statements, especially those describing empirical observations.

Jargon. *Jargon* is the continuous use of a technical vocabulary, even in places where that vocabulary is not relevant. Jargon is also the substitution of a euphemistic phrase for a familiar term (e.g., *monetarily felt scarcity* for *poverty*), and you should scrupulously avoid using such jargon. Federal bureaucratic jargon has had the greatest publicity, but scientific jargon also grates on the reader, encumbers the communication of information, and wastes space.

Pronouns. Pronouns confuse readers unless the referent for each pronoun is obvious; readers should not have to search previous text to determine the meaning of the term. Pronouns such as *this, that, these,* and *those* can be troublesome when they refer to something or someone in a previous sentence. Eliminate ambiguity by writing, for example, *this test, that trial, these participants,* and *those reports* (see also section 3.20).

Comparisons. Ambiguous or illogical comparisons result from omission of key verbs or from nonparallel structure. Consider, for example, "Ten-year-olds were more likely to play with age peers than 8-year-olds." Does this sentence mean that 10-year-olds were more likely than 8-year-olds to play with age peers? Or does it mean that 10-

year-olds were more likely to play with age peers and less likely to play with 8-year-olds? An illogical comparison occurs when parallelism is overlooked for the sake of brevity, as in "Her salary was lower than a convenience store clerk." Thoughtful attention to good sentence structure and word choice reduces the chance of this kind of ambiguity.

Attribution. Inappropriately or illogically attributing action in an effort to be objective can be misleading. Examples of undesirable attribution include use of the third person, anthropomorphism, and use of the editorial *we*.

Third person. To avoid ambiguity, use a personal pronoun rather than the third person when describing steps taken in your experiment.

Correct:

We reviewed the literature.

Incorrect:

The authors reviewed the literature.

Anthropomorphism. Do not attribute human characteristics to animals or to inanimate sources.

Correct:

Pairs of rats (cage mates) were allowed to forage together.

Incorrect:

Rat couples (cage mates) were allowed to forage together.

Correct:

The staff for the community program was persuaded to allow five of the observers to become tutors.

Incorrect:

The community program was persuaded to allow five of the observers to become tutors.

An experiment cannot *attempt to demonstrate, control unwanted variables,* or *interpret findings,* nor can tables or figures *compare* (all of these can, however, *show* or *indicate*). Use a pronoun or an appropriate noun as the subject of these verbs. *I* or *we* (meaning the author or authors) can replace *the experiment.*

***Editorial* we.** For clarity, restrict your use of *we* to refer only to yourself and your coauthors (use *I* if you are the sole author of the paper). Broader uses of *we* may leave your readers wondering to whom you are referring; instead, substitute an appropriate noun or clarify your usage:

Correct:

Researchers usually classify birdsong on the basis of frequency and temporal structure of the elements.

Incorrect:

We usually classify birdsong on the basis of frequency and temporal structure of the elements.

Some alternatives to *we* to consider are *people, humans, researchers, psychologists, nurses,* and so on. *We* is an appropriate and useful referent:

Correct:

As behaviorists, we tend to dispute . . .

Incorrect:

We tend to dispute . . .

3.10 Linguistic Devices

Devices that attract attention to words, sounds, or other embellishments instead of to ideas are inappropriate in scientific writing. Avoid heavy alliteration, rhyming, poetic expressions, and clichés. Use metaphors sparingly; although they can help simplify complicated ideas, metaphors can be distracting. Avoid mixed metaphors (e.g., *a theory representing one branch of a growing body of evidence*) and words with surplus or unintended meaning (e.g., *cop* for *police officer*), which may distract if not actually mislead the reader. Use figurative expressions with restraint and colorful expressions with care; these expressions can sound strained or forced.

3.11 Strategies to Improve Writing Style

Authors use various strategies in putting their thoughts on paper. The fit between author and strategy is more important than the particular strategy used. Three approaches to achieving professional and effective communication are (a) writing from an outline; (b) putting aside the first draft, then rereading it later; and (c) asking a colleague to review and critique the draft for you.

Writing from an outline helps preserve the logic of the research itself. An outline identifies main ideas, defines subordinate ideas, helps you discipline your writing and avoid tangential excursions, and helps you notice omissions. In an outline, you can also identify the subheadings that will be used in the article itself.

Rereading your own copy after setting it aside for a few days permits a fresh approach. Reading the paper aloud enables you not only to see faults that you overlooked on the previous reading but also to hear them. When these problems are corrected, give a polished copy to a colleague—preferably a person who has published in a related field but who is not familiar with your own work—for a critical review. Even better, get critiques from two colleagues, and you will have a trial run of a journal's review process.

These strategies, particularly the latter, may require you to invest more time in a manuscript than you had anticipated. The results of these strategies, however, may be greater accuracy and thoroughness and clearer communication.

Reducing Bias in Language

Scientific writing must be free of implied or irrelevant evaluation of the group or groups being studied. As an organization, APA is committed both to science and to the fair treatment of individuals and groups, and this policy requires that authors who write for APA publications avoid perpetuating demeaning attitudes and biased assumptions about people in their writing. Constructions that might imply bias against persons on the basis of gender, sexual orientation, racial or ethnic group, disability, or age are unacceptable.

Long-standing cultural practice can exert a powerful influence over even the most conscientious author. Just as you have learned to check what you write for spelling, grammar, and wordiness, practice rereading your work for bias. Another suggestion is to ask people from targeted groups to read and comment on your material.

What follows is a set of guidelines and discussions of specific issues that affect particular groups. These are not rigid rules. You may find that some attempts to follow the guidelines result in wordiness or clumsy prose. As always, good judgment is required. If your writing reflects respect for your participants and your readers and if you write with appropriate specificity and precision, you will be contributing to the goal of accurate, unbiased communication. Specific examples for each guideline are given in the Guidelines for Unbiased Language, which can be found on the APA Style website (www.apastyle.org).

General Guidelines for Reducing Bias

Guideline 1: Describe at the Appropriate Level of Specificity

Precision is essential in scientific writing; when you refer to a person or persons, choose words that are accurate, clear, and free from bias. The appropriate degree of specificity depends on the research question and the present state of knowledge in the field of study. When in doubt, be more specific rather than less, because it is easier to aggregate published data than to disaggregate them. For example, using *man* to refer to all human beings is simply not as accurate as the phrase *women and men.* To describe age groups, give a specific age range ("ages 65–83 years") instead of a broad category ("over 65 years"; see Schaie, 1993). When describing racial and ethnic groups, be appropriately specific and sensitive to issues of labeling. For example, instead of describing participants as Asian American or Hispanic American, it may be helpful to describe them by their nation or region of origin (e.g., Chinese Americans, Mexican Americans). If you are discussing sexual orientation, realize that some people interpret *gay* as referring to men and women, whereas others interpret the term as referring only to men (the terms *gay men* and *lesbians* currently are preferred).

Broad clinical terms such as *borderline* and *at risk* are loaded with innuendo unless properly explained. Specify the diagnosis that is borderline (e.g., "people with borderline personality disorder"). Identify the risk and the people it involves (e.g., "children at risk for early school dropout").

Gender is cultural and is the term to use when referring to women and men as social groups. *Sex* is biological; use it when the biological distinction is predominant. Note that the word *sex* can be confused with *sexual behavior. Gender* helps keep meaning unambiguous, as in the following example: "In accounting for attitudes toward the bill, sexual orientation rather than gender accounted for most of the variance. Most gay men and lesbians were for the proposal; most heterosexual men and women were against it."

Part of writing without bias is recognizing that differences should be mentioned only when relevant. Marital status, sexual orientation, racial and ethnic identity, or the fact that a person has a disability should not be mentioned gratuitously.

Guideline 2: Be Sensitive to Labels

Respect people's preferences; call people what they prefer to be called. Accept that preferences change with time and that individuals within groups often disagree about the designations they prefer. Make an effort to determine what is appropriate for your situation; you may need to ask your participants which designations they prefer, particularly when preferred designations are being debated within groups.

Avoid labeling people when possible. A common occurrence in scientific writing is that participants in a study tend to lose their individuality; they are broadly categorized as objects (noun forms such as *the gays* and *the elderly*) or, particularly in descriptions of people with disabilities, are equated with their conditions—*the amnesiacs, the depressives, the schizophrenics, the LDs,* for example. One solution is to use adjectival forms (e.g., "gay *men,*" "older *adults,*" "amnesic *patients*"). Another is to "put the person first," followed by a descriptive phrase (e.g., "people diagnosed with schizophrenia"). Note that the latter solution currently is preferred when describing people with disabilities.

When you need to mention several groups in a sentence or paragraph, such as when reporting results, do your best to balance sensitivity, clarity, and parsimony. For example, it may be cumbersome to repeat phrases such as "person with _______." If you provide operational definitions of groups early in your paper (e.g., "Participants scoring a minimum of X on the X scale constituted the high verbal group, and those scoring below X constituted the low verbal group"), it is scientifically informative and concise to describe participants thereafter in terms of the measures used to classify them (e.g., ". . . the contrast for the high verbal group was statistically significant, $p = .043$"), provided the terms are inoffensive. A label should not be used in any form that is perceived as pejorative; if such a perception is possible, you need to find more neutral terms. For example, *the demented* is not repaired by changing it to *demented group,* but *dementia group* would be acceptable. Abbreviations or series labels for groups usually sacrifice clarity and may offend: *LDs* or *LD group* to describe people with specific learning difficulties is offensive; *HVAs* for "high verbal ability group" is difficult to decipher. *Group A* is not offensive, but it is not descriptive either.

Recognize the difference between *case,* which is an occurrence of a disorder or illness, and *patient,* which is a person affected by the disorder or illness and receiving a doctor's care. "Manic–depressive cases were treated" is problematic; revise to "The patients with bipolar disorders were treated."

Bias may be promoted when the writer uses one group (often the writer's own group) as the standard against which others are judged, for example, citizens of the United States. In some contexts, the term *culturally deprived* may imply that one culture is the universally accepted standard. The unparallel nouns in the phrase *man and wife* may inappropriately prompt the reader to evaluate the roles of the individuals (i.e., the woman is defined only in terms of her relationship to the man) and the motives of the author. By contrast, the phrases *husband and wife* and *man and woman* are parallel. Usage of *normal* may prompt the reader to make the comparison with *abnormal,* thus stigmatizing individuals with differences. For example, contrasting lesbians with "the general public" or with "normal women" portrays lesbians as marginal to society. More appropriate comparison groups might be *heterosexual women, heterosexual women and men,* or *gay men.*

Also be aware of how order of presentation of social groups can imply that the first-mentioned group is the norm or standard and that later mentioned groups are deviant. Thus the phrases *men and women* and *White Americans and racial minorities* subtly reflect the perceived dominance of men and Whites over other groups. Similarly, when presenting group data, consider how placing socially dominant groups such as men and Whites on the left side of graphs and/or top of tables may also imply that these groups are the universal standard (Hegarty & Buechel, 2006). Avoid a consistent pattern of presenting information about socially dominant groups first.

Guideline 3: Acknowledge Participation

Write about the people in your study in a way that acknowledges their participation but is also consistent with the traditions of the field in which you are working. Thus, although descriptive terms such as *college students, children,* or *respondents* provide precise information about the individuals taking part in a research project, the more general terms *participants* and *subjects* are also in common usage. Indeed, for more than 100 years the term *subjects* has been used within experimental psychology as a general starting point for describing a sample, and its use is appropriate. *Subjects* and *sample* are customary when discussing certain established statistical terms (e.g., *within-subject* and *between-subjects* design). Further, the passive voice suggests individuals are *acted on* instead of being actors ("the students *completed* the survey" is preferable to "the students *were given* the survey" or "the survey was *administered* to the students"). "The subjects *completed* the trial" or "we *collected* data from the participants" is preferable to "the participants *were run.*" Consider avoiding terms such as *patient management* and *patient placement* when appropriate. In most cases, it is the treatment, not patients, that is managed; some alternatives are *coordination of care, supportive services,* and *assistance.* Also avoid the term *failed,* as in "eight participants failed to complete the Rorschach and the MMPI," because it can imply a personal shortcoming instead of a research result; *did not* is a more neutral choice (Knatterud, 1991).

As you read the rest of this chapter, consult www.apastyle.org for specific examples of problematic and preferred language in the Guidelines for Unbiased Language as well as further resources and information about nondiscriminatory language.

Reducing Bias by Topic

3.12 Gender

Remember that *gender* refers to role, not biological sex, and is cultural. Avoid ambiguity in sex identity or gender role by choosing nouns, pronouns, and adjectives that specifically describe your participants. Sexist bias can occur when pronouns are used carelessly, as when the masculine pronoun *he* is used to refer to both sexes or when the masculine or feminine pronoun is used exclusively to define roles by sex (e.g., "the nurse . . . *she*"). The use of *man* as a generic noun or as an ending for an occupational title (e.g., *policeman* instead of *police officer*) can be ambiguous and may imply incorrectly that all persons in the group are male. Be clear about whether you mean one sex or both sexes.

There are many alternatives to the generic *he* (see the Guidelines for Unbiased Language at www.apastyle.org), including rephrasing (e.g., from "When an individual conducts this kind of self-appraisal, *he* is a much stronger person" to "When an individual conducts this kind of self-appraisal, that person is much stronger" or "This kind of self-appraisal makes an individual much stronger"), using plural nouns or plural pronouns (e.g., from "A therapist who is too much like his client can lose *his* objectivity" to "Therapists who are too much like their clients can lose *their* objectivity"), replacing the pronoun with an article (e.g., from "A researcher must apply for *his* grant by September 1" to "A researcher must apply for *the* grant by September 1"), and dropping the pronoun (e.g., from "The researcher must avoid letting *his* own biases and expectations influence the interpretation of the results" to "The researcher must avoid letting biases and expectations influence the interpretation of the results"). Replacing *he* with *he or she* or *she or he* should be done sparingly because the repetition can become tiresome. Combination forms such as *he/she* or *(s)he* are awkward and distracting. Alternating between *he* and *she* also may be distracting and is not ideal; doing so implies that he or she can in fact be generic, which is not the case. Use of either pronoun unavoidably suggests that specific gender to the reader. Avoid referring to one sex as the *opposite sex:* an appropriate wording is the *other sex*. The term *opposite sex* implies strong differences between the two sexes; however, in fact, there are more similarities than differences between the two sexes (e.g., Hyde, 2005).

The adjective *transgender* refers to persons whose gender identity or gender expression differs from their sex at birth; *transgender* should not be used as a noun (National Lesbian & Gay Journalists Association, 2005). The word *transsexual* refers to transgender persons who live or desire to live full time as members of the sex other than their sex at birth, many of whom wish to make their bodies as congruent as possible with their preferred sex through surgery and hormonal treatment (American Psychiatric Association, 2000; Meyer et al., 2001). *Transsexual* can be used as a noun or as an adjective. The terms *female-to-male transgender person, male-to-female transgender person, female-to-male transsexual,* and *male-to-female transsexual* represent accepted usage (Gay & Lesbian Alliance Against Defamation, 2007). Transsexuals undergo *sex reassignment,* a term that is preferable to *sex change. Cross-dresser* is preferable to *transvestite.*

Refer to a transgender person using words (proper nouns, pronouns, etc.) appropriate to the person's gender identity or gender expression, regardless of birth sex. For example, use the pronouns *he, him,* or *his* in reference to a female-to-male transgender person. If gender identity or gender expression is ambiguous or variable, it may be best to avoid pronouns, as discussed earlier in this section (for more detailed information, see www.apastyle.org).

3.13 Sexual Orientation

Sexual orientation refers to an enduring pattern of attraction, behavior, emotion, identity, and social contacts. The term *sexual orientation* should be used rather than *sexual preference*. For a person having a bisexual orientation, the orientation is not chosen even though the sex of the partner may be a choice. For more information, see *Guidelines for Psychotherapy With Lesbian, Gay, and Bisexual Clients* (APA Committee on Lesbian, Gay, and Bisexual Concerns Joint Task Force on Guidelines for Psychotherapy With Lesbian, Gay, and Bisexual Clients, 2000; see also www.apastyle.org).

The terms *lesbians, gay men, bisexual men,* and *bisexual women* are preferable to *homosexual* when one is referring to people who identify this way. *Lesbian, gay,* and *bisexual* refer primarily to identities and to the culture and communities that have developed among people who share those identities. As such, the terms *lesbians, gay men,* and *bisexual individuals* are more accurate than *homosexual.* Furthermore, the term *homosexuality* has been and continues to be associated with negative stereotypes, pathology, and the reduction of people's identities to their sexual behavior. *Gay* can be interpreted broadly, to include men and women, or more narrowly, to include only men.

3.14 Racial and Ethnic Identity

Preferences for terms referring to racial and ethnic groups change often. One reason for this is simply personal preference; preferred designations are as varied as the people they name. Another reason is that over time, designations can become dated and sometimes negative. Authors are reminded of the two basic guidelines of specificity and sensitivity. In keeping with Guideline 2, use commonly accepted designations (e.g., Census categories) while being sensitive to participants' preferred designation. For example, some North American people of African ancestry prefer *Black* and others prefer *African American;* both terms currently are acceptable. On the other hand, *Negro* and *Afro-American* have become dated; therefore, usage of these terms generally is inappropriate. In keeping with Guideline 1, precision is important in the description of your sample (see section 2.06); in general, use the more specific rather than the less specific term.

Language that essentializes or reifies race is strongly discouraged and is generally considered inappropriate. For example, phrases such as *the Black race* and *the White race* are essentialist in nature, portray human groups monolithically, and often serve to perpetuate stereotypes. Authors sometimes use the word *minority* as a proxy for non-White racial and ethnic groups. This usage may be viewed pejoratively because *minority* is usually equated with being less than, oppressed, and deficient in comparison with the majority (i.e., Whites). Use a modifier (such as *ethnic* or *racial*) when using the word *minority.* When possible, use the actual name of the group or groups to which you are referring.

Racial and ethnic groups are designated by proper nouns and are capitalized. Therefore, use *Black* and *White* instead of *black* and *white* (the use of colors to refer to other human groups currently is considered pejorative and should not be used). Unparallel designations (e.g., *African Americans* and *Whites; Asian Americans* and *Black Americans*) should be avoided because one group is described by color while the other group is described by cultural heritage. For modifiers, do not use hyphens in multiword names, even if the names act as unit modifiers (e.g., *Asian American* participants).

Designations for some ethnic groups are described next. These groups frequently are included in studies published in APA journals. These examples are far from exhaustive but illustrate some of the complexities of naming (see the Guidelines for Unbiased Language at www.apastyle.org). Depending on where a person is from, individuals may prefer to be called *Hispanic, Latino, Chicano,* or some other designation; *Hispanic* is not necessarily an all-encompassing term, and authors should consult with their participants. In general, naming a nation or region of origin is helpful (e.g., *Cuban, Salvadoran,* or *Guatemalan* is more specific than *Central American* or *Hispanic*).

American Indian, Native American, and *Native North American* are all accepted terms for referring to indigenous peoples of North America. When referring to groups including Hawaiians and Samoans, you may use the broader designation *Native Americans.* The indigenous peoples of Canada may be referred to as *First Nations* or *Inuit* people. There are close to 450 Native North American groups, and authors are encouraged to name the participants' specific groups, recognizing that some groups prefer the name for their group in their native language (e.g., *Dine* instead of *Navajo, Tohono O'odham* instead of *Papago*).

The term *Asian* or *Asian American* is preferred to the older term *Oriental.* It is generally useful to specify the name of the Asian subgroup: Chinese, Vietnamese, Korean, Pakistani, and so on. People of Middle Eastern descent may also be identified by nation of origin: Iraqi, Lebanese, and so forth.

3.15 Disabilities

The overall principle for "nonhandicapping" language is to maintain the integrity (worth) of all individuals as human beings. Avoid language that objectifies a person by her or his condition (e.g., *autistic, neurotic*), that uses pictorial metaphors (e.g., *wheelchair bound* or *confined to a wheelchair*), that uses excessive and negative labels (e.g., *AIDS victim, brain damaged*), or that can be regarded as a slur (e.g., *cripple, invalid*). Use people-first language, and do not focus on the individual's disabling or chronic condition (e.g., *person with paraplegia, youth with autism*). Also use people-first language to describe groups of people with disabilities. For instance, say *people with intellectual disabilities* in contrast to *the retarded* (University of Kansas, Research and Training Center on Independent Living, 2008).

Avoid euphemisms that are condescending when describing individuals with disabilities (e.g., *special, physically challenged, handi-capable*). Some people with disabilities consider these terms patronizing and offensive. When writing about populations with disabilities or participants, emphasize both capabilities and concerns to avoid reducing them to a "bundle of deficiencies" (Rappaport, 1977). Do not refer to individuals with disabilities as *patients* or *cases* unless the context is within a hospital or clinical setting.

3.16 Age

Age should be reported as part of the description of participants in the Method section. Be specific in providing age ranges; avoid open-ended definitions such as "under 18 years" or "over 65 years." *Girl* and *boy* are correct terms for referring to individuals under the age of 12 years. *Young man* and *young woman* and *female adolescent* and *male adolescent* may be used for individuals aged 13 to 17 years. For persons 18 years and older, use *women* and *men.* The terms *elderly* and *senior* are not acceptable as nouns; some may consider their use as adjectives pejorative. Generational descriptors such as *boomer* or *baby boomer* should not be used unless they are related to a study on this topic. The term *older adults* is preferred. Age groups may also be described with adjectives. Gerontologists may prefer to use combination terms for older age groups (*young-old, old-old, very old, oldest old,* and *centenarians*); provide the specific ages of these groups and use them only as adjectives. Use *dementia* instead of *senility;* specify the type of dementia when known (e.g., *dementia of the Alzheimer's type*). For more references relating to age, see *Guidelines for the Evaluation of Dementia and Age-Related Cognitive Decline* (APA Presidential Task Force on the Assessment of Age-Consistent Memory Decline and Dementia, 1998) and "Guidelines for Psychological Practice With Older Adults" (APA, 2004; see also www.apastyle.org).

3.17 Historical and Interpretive Inaccuracies

Authors are encouraged to avoid perpetuating demeaning attitudes and biased assumptions about people in their writing. At the same time, authors need to avoid historical and interpretive inaccuracies. Historians and scholars writing literature reviews must be careful not to misrepresent ideas of the past in an effort to avoid language bias. Changes in nouns and pronouns may result in serious misrepresentation of the original author's ideas and give a false interpretation of that author's beliefs and intentions. In such writing, it is best to retain the original language and to comment on it in the discussion. Quotations should not be changed to accommodate current sensibilities (see sections 4.08 and 6.06).

Contemporary authors may indicate a historical author's original term by following it with an asterisk the first time it appears and by providing historical context directly following the quotation. Below is an example of historically appropriate use of a term that is considered biased by today's standards.

> In forming the elite scientific society called the Experimentalists, Titchener "wanted above all to have free, informal interchange between older and younger men* in the area of experimental psychology, with the goal of socializing the next generation into the profession" (Furumoto, 1988, p. 105).

*In this example, the term *men* seems to convey Titchener's intention to exclude women from the society. Substituting a more gender-neutral or inclusive term may be historically inaccurate.

Grammar and Usage

Incorrect grammar and careless construction of sentences distract the reader, introduce ambiguity, and generally obstruct communication. The examples in this section represent problems of grammar and usage that occur frequently in manuscripts received by journal editors.

3.18 Verbs

Verbs are vigorous, direct communicators. Use the active rather than the passive voice, and select tense or mood carefully.

Prefer the active voice.

Preferred:

We conducted the survey in a controlled setting.

Nonpreferred:

The survey was conducted in a controlled setting.

The passive voice is acceptable in expository writing and when you want to focus on the object or recipient of the action rather than on the actor. For example, "The speakers were attached to either side of the chair" emphasizes the placement of speakers, not who placed them—the more appropriate focus in the Method section. "The President was shot" emphasizes the importance of the person shot.

Select tense carefully. Use the past tense to express an action or a condition that occurred at a specific, definite time in the past, as when discussing another researcher's work and when reporting your results.

Correct:

Sanchez (2000) presented similar results.

Incorrect:

Sanchez (2000) presents similar results.

Use the present perfect tense to express a past action or condition that did not occur at a specific, definite time or to describe an action beginning in the past and continuing to the present.

Correct:

Since that time, several investigators have used this method.

Incorrect:

Since that time, several investigators used this method.

Select the appropriate mood. Use the subjunctive only to describe conditions that are contrary to fact or improbable; do not use the subjunctive to describe simple conditions or contingencies.

Correct:

If the experiment were not designed this way, the results could not be interpreted properly.

Incorrect:

If the experiment was not designed this way, the results could not be interpreted properly.

Use *would* with care. *Would* can correctly be used to mean *habitually,* as "The child would walk about the classroom," or to express a conditional action, as "We would sign the letter if we could." Do not use *would* to hedge; for example, change *it would appear that* to *it appears that.*

3.19 Agreement of Subject and Verb

A verb must agree in number (i.e., singular or plural) with its subject, regardless of intervening phrases that begin with such words as *together with, including, plus,* and *as well as.*

Correct:

The percentage of correct responses as well as the speed of the responses increases with practice.

Incorrect:

The percentage of correct responses as well as the speed of the responses increase with practice.

The plural form of some nouns of foreign origin, particularly those that end in the letter *a*, may appear to be singular and can cause authors to select a verb that does not agree in number with the noun.

Correct:

The data indicate that Terrence was correct.

Incorrect:

The data indicates that Terrence was correct.

Correct:

The phenomena occur every 100 years.

Incorrect:

The phenomena occurs every 100 years.

Consult a dictionary (APA prefers *Merriam-Webster's Collegiate Dictionary*, 2005) when in doubt about the plural form of nouns of foreign origin. For examples of agreement of subject and verb with collective nouns, see the APA Style website (www.apastyle.org).

3.20 Pronouns

Pronouns replace nouns. Each pronoun should refer clearly to its antecedent and should agree with the antecedent in number and gender.

A pronoun must agree in number (i.e., singular or plural) with the noun it replaces.

Correct:

Neither the highest scorer nor the lowest scorer in the group had any doubt about his or her competence.

Incorrect:

Neither the highest scorer nor the lowest scorer in the group had any doubt about their competence.

A pronoun must agree in gender (i.e., masculine, feminine, or neuter) with the noun it replaces. This rule extends to relative pronouns (pronouns that link subordinate clauses to nouns). Use *who* for human beings; use *that* or *which* for nonhuman animals and for things.

Correct:

The students who completed the task successfully were rewarded.

Correct:

The instructions that were included in the experiment were complex.

Incorrect:

The students that completed the task successfully were rewarded.

Use neuter pronouns to refer to animals (e.g., "the dog . . . it") unless the animals have been named:

The chimps were tested daily. . . . Sheba was tested unrestrained in an open testing area, which was her usual context for training and testing.

Pronouns can be subjects or objects of verbs or prepositions. Use *who* as the subject of a verb and *whom* as the object of a verb or a preposition. You can determine whether a relative pronoun is the subject or object of a verb by turning the subordinate clause around and substituting a personal pronoun. If you can substitute *he* or *she, who* is correct; if you can substitute *him* or *her, whom* is correct.

Correct:

Name the participant who you found achieved scores above the median. [You found *he* or *she* achieved scores above the median.]

Incorrect:

Name the participant whom you found achieved scores above the median. [You found *him* or *her* achieved scores above the median.]

Correct:

The participant whom I identified as the youngest dropped out. [I identified *him* or *her* as the youngest.]

Incorrect:

The participant who I identified as the youngest dropped out. [I identified *he* or *she* as the youngest.]

In a phrase consisting of a pronoun or noun plus a present participle (e.g., *running, flying*) that is used as an object of a preposition, the participle can be either a noun or a modifier of a noun, depending on the intended meaning. When you use a participle as a noun, make the other pronoun or noun possessive.

Correct:

We had nothing to do with their being the winners.

Incorrect:

We had nothing to do with them being the winners.

Correct:

The result is questionable because of one participant's performing at very high speed. [The result is questionable because of the performance, not because of the participant.]

Incorrect:

The result is questionable because of one participant performing at very high speed.

3.21 Misplaced and Dangling Modifiers and Use of Adverbs

An adjective or an adverb, whether a single word or a phrase, must clearly refer to the word it modifies.

Misplaced modifiers. Because of their placement in a sentence, misplaced modifiers ambiguously or illogically modify a word. You can eliminate misplaced modifiers by placing an adjective or an adverb as close as possible to the word it modifies.

Correct:

Using this procedure, the investigator tested the participants.

Correct:

The investigator tested the participants who were using the procedure.

Incorrect:

The investigator tested the participants using this procedure. [The sentence is unclear about whether the investigator or the participants used this procedure.]

Correct:

On the basis of this assumption, we developed a model. . . .

Correct:

Based on this assumption, the model. . . .

Incorrect:

Based on this assumption, we developed a model. . . . [This construction says, "we are based on an assumption."]

Many writers have trouble with the word *only.* Place *only* next to the word or phrase it modifies.

Correct:

These data provide only a partial answer.

Incorrect:

These data only provide a partial answer.

Dangling modifiers. Dangling modifiers have no referent in the sentence. Many of these result from the use of the passive voice. By writing in the active voice, you can avoid many dangling modifiers.

Correct:

Using this procedure, I tested the participants. [I, not the participants, used the procedure.]

Incorrect:

The participants were tested using this procedure.

Correct:

Mulholland and Williams (2000) found that this group performed better, a result that is congruent with those of other studies. [The result, not Mulholland and Williams, is congruent.]

Incorrect:

Congruent with other studies, Mulholland and Williams (2000) found that this group performed better.

Adverbs. Adverbs can be used as introductory or transitional words. Adverbs modify verbs, adjectives, and other adverbs and express manner or quality. Some adverbs, however—such as *fortunately, similarly, certainly, consequently, conversely,* and *regrettably*—can also be used as introductory or transitional words as long as the sense is confined to, for example, "it is fortunate that" or "in a similar manner." Use adverbs judiciously as introductory or transitional words. Ask yourself whether the introduction or transition is needed and whether the adverb is being used correctly.

Some of the more common introductory adverbial phrases are *importantly, more importantly, interestingly,* and *firstly.* Although *importantly* is used widely, whether its adverbial usage is proper is debatable. Both *importantly* and *interestingly* can often be recast to enhance the message of a sentence or simply be omitted without a loss of meaning.

Correct:

More important, the total amount of available long-term memory activation, and not the rate of spreading activation, drives the rate and probability of retrieval.

Correct:

Expressive behavior and autonomic nervous system activity also have figured importantly. . .

Incorrect:

More importantly, the total amount of available long-term memory activation, and not the rate of spreading activation, drives the rate and probability of retrieval.

Correct:

We were surprised to learn that the total. . . .

We find it interesting that the total. . . .

An interesting finding was that. . . .

Incorrect:

Interestingly, the total amount of available long-term memory activation, and not the rate of spreading activation, drives the rate and probability of retrieval.

Correct:

First, we hypothesized that the quality of the therapeutic alliance would be rated higher. . . .

Incorrect:

Firstly, we hypothesized that the quality of the therapeutic alliance would be rated higher. . . .

Another adverb often misused as an introductory or transitional word is *hopefully.* *Hopefully* means "in a hopeful manner" or "full of hope"; *hopefully* should not be used to mean "I hope" or "it is hoped."

Correct:

I hope this is not the case.

Incorrect:

Hopefully, this is not the case.

3.22 Relative Pronouns and Subordinate Conjunctions

Relative pronouns (*who, whom, that, which*) and subordinate conjunctions (e.g., *since, while, although*) introduce an element that is subordinate to the main clause of the sentence and reflect the relationship of the subordinate element to the main clause. Therefore, select these pronouns and conjunctions with care; interchanging them may reduce the precision of your meaning.

Relative pronouns.

That *versus* which. *That* clauses (called *restrictive*) are essential to the meaning of the sentence:

The materials that worked well in the first experiment were used in the second experiment.

Which clauses can merely add further information (nonrestrictive) or can be essential to the meaning (restrictive) of the sentence. APA prefers to reserve *which* for nonrestrictive clauses and use *that* in restrictive clauses.

Restrictive:

The cards that worked well in the first experiment were not useful in the second experiment. [Only those cards that worked well in the first experiment were not useful in the second; prefer *that.*]

Nonrestrictive:

The cards, which worked well in the first experiment, were not useful in the second experiment. [The second experiment was not appropriate for the cards.]

Consistent use of *that* for restrictive clauses and *which* for nonrestrictive clauses, which are set off with commas, will help make your writing clear and precise.

Subordinate conjunctions.

While *and* since. Some style authorities accept the use of *while* and *since* when they do not refer strictly to time; however, words like these, with more than one meaning, can cause confusion. Because precision and clarity are the standards in scientific writing, restricting your use of *while* and *since* to their temporal meanings is helpful. The following examples illustrate the temporal meanings of these terms:

> Bragg (1965) found that participants performed well while listening to music.
>
> Several versions of the test have been developed since the test was first introduced.

While *versus* although, and, or but. Use *while* to link events occurring simultaneously; otherwise, use *although, and,* or *but* in place of *while.*

Precise:

> Although these findings are unusual, they are not unique.

Imprecise:

> While these findings are unusual, they are not unique.

Precise:

> The argument is purely philosophical, but the conclusion can also yield an empirical hypothesis, amenable to empirical investigation.

Imprecise:

> While the argument is purely philosophical, the conclusion can also yield an empirical hypothesis, amenable to empirical investigation.

Since *versus* because. *Since* is more precise when it is used to refer only to time (to mean "after that"); otherwise, replace it with *because.*

Precise:

> Data for two participants were incomplete because these participants did not report for follow-up testing.

Imprecise:

> Data for two participants were incomplete since these participants did not report for follow-up testing.

3.23 Parallel Construction

To enhance the reader's understanding, present parallel ideas in parallel or coordinate form. Make certain that all elements of the parallelism are present before and after the coordinating conjunction (i.e., *and, but, or, nor*).

Correct:

> The results show that such changes could be made without affecting error rate and that latencies continued to decrease over time.

Incorrect:

> The results show that such changes could be made without affecting error rate and latencies continued to decrease over time.

With coordinating conjunctions used in pairs (*between . . . and, both . . . and, neither . . . nor, either . . . or, not only . . . but also*), place the first conjunction immediately before the first part of the parallelism.

Between* and *and.

Correct:

We recorded the difference between the performance of subjects who completed the first task and the performance of those who completed the second task. [The difference is between the subjects' performances, not between the performance and the task.]

Incorrect:

We recorded the difference between the performance of subjects who completed the first task and the second task.

Correct:

between 2.5 and 4.0 years of age

Incorrect:

between 2.5–4.0 years of age

Both* and *and.

Correct:

The names were difficult both to pronounce and to spell.

Incorrect:

The names were both difficult to pronounce and spell.

Never use *both* with *as well as*: The resulting construction is redundant.

Correct:

The names were difficult to pronounce as well as to spell.

Incorrect:

The names were difficult both to pronounce as well as to spell.

Neither* and *nor; either* and *or.

Correct:

Neither the responses to the auditory stimuli nor the responses to the tactile stimuli were repeated.

Incorrect:

Neither the responses to the auditory stimuli nor to the tactile stimuli were repeated.

Correct:

The respondents either gave the worst answer or gave the best answer.

or

The respondents gave either the worst answer or the best answer.

Incorrect:

The respondents either gave the worst answer or the best answer.

Not only* and *but also.

Correct:

It is surprising not only that pencil-and-paper scores predicted this result but also that all other predictors were less accurate.

Incorrect:

It is not only surprising that pencil-and-paper scores predicted this result but also that all other predictors were less accurate.

Elements in a series should also be parallel in form.

Correct:

The participants were told to make themselves comfortable, to read the instructions, and to ask about anything they did not understand.

Incorrect:

The participants were told to make themselves comfortable, to read the instructions, and that they should ask about anything they did not understand.

Take care to use parallel structure in lists and in table stubs (see sections 3.04 and 5.13).

4

The Mechanics of Style

When editors refer to *style,* they mean the rules or guidelines a publisher observes to ensure clear, consistent presentation in scholarly articles. Authors writing for a publication must follow the style rules established by the publisher to avoid inconsistencies among journal articles or book chapters. For example, without rules of style, three different manuscripts might use *sub-test, subtest,* and *Subtest* in one issue of a journal or in one book. Although the meaning of the word is the same and the choice of one style over the other may seem arbitrary (in this case, *subtest* is APA Style), such variations in style may distract or confuse the reader.

This chapter describes the style for APA journals regarding the most basic tools for conveying meaning—punctuation, spelling, capitalization, italics, abbreviations, numbers, metrication, and statistics. It omits general rules explained in widely available style manuals and examples of usage with little relevance to APA journals. Style manuals agree more often than they disagree; where they disagree, the *Publication Manual* takes precedence for APA publications.

Punctuation

Punctuation establishes the cadence of a sentence, telling the reader where to pause (comma, semicolon, and colon), stop (period and question mark), or take a detour (dash, parentheses, and brackets). Punctuation of a sentence usually denotes a pause in thought; different kinds of punctuation indicate different kinds and lengths of pauses.

4.01 Spacing After Punctuation Marks

Insert one space after

- commas, colons, and semicolons;
- periods that separate parts of a reference citation; and

- periods of the initials in personal names (e.g., J. R. Zhang).

Exception: Do not insert a space after internal periods in abbreviations (e.g., a.m., i.e., U.S.), including identity-concealing labels for study participants (F.I.M.), or around colons in ratios. Spacing twice after punctuation marks at the end of a sentence aids readers of draft manuscripts.

4.02 Period

Use a period to end a complete sentence. Periods are used with abbreviations as follows:

Use periods with

- initials of names (J. R. Smith).
- abbreviation for United States when it is used as an adjective (U.S. Navy).
- identity-concealing labels for study participants (F.I.M.). (See section 4.01 on spacing.)
- Latin abbreviations (a.m., cf., i.e., vs.).
- reference abbreviations (Vol. 1, 2nd ed., p. 6, F. Supp.).

Do not use periods with

- abbreviations of state names (NY; OH; Washington, DC) in reference list entries or in vendor locations (e.g., for drugs and apparatus described in the Method section).
- capital letter abbreviations and acronyms (APA, NDA, NIMH, IQ).
- abbreviations for routes of administration (icv, im, ip, iv, sc).
- web addresses in text or in the reference list (http://www.apa.org). In text, include these in parentheses when possible or revise the sentence to avoid ending a sentence with a URL and no punctuation.
- metric and nonmetric measurement abbreviations (cd, cm, ft, hr, kg, lb, min, ml, s).

Exception: The abbreviation for inch (in.) takes a period because without the period it could be misread.

4.03 Comma

Use a comma

- between elements (including before *and* and *or*) in a series of three or more items.

  Correct:

  the height, width, or depth
  in a study by Stacy, Newcomb, and Bentler (1991)

  Incorrect:

  in a study by Stacy, Newcomb and Bentler (1991)

- to set off a nonessential or nonrestrictive clause, that is, a clause that embellishes a sentence but if removed would leave the grammatical structure and meaning of the sentence intact.

  Switch A, which was on a panel, controlled the recording device.

Statistically significant differences were found for both ratings of controllability by self, $F(3, 132) = 19.58$, $p < .001$, est $\eta^2 = .31$, 95% CI [.17, .43], and ratings of controllability by others, $F(3, 96) = 3.21$, $p = .026$, est $\eta^2 = .09$, [.00, .20].

- to separate two independent clauses joined by a conjunction.

Cedar shavings covered the floor, and paper was available for shredding and nest building.

- to set off the year in exact dates.

April 18, 1992, was the correct date.

but

April 1992 was the correct month.

- to set off the year in parenthetical reference citations.

(Patrick, 1993)
(Kelsey, 1993, discovered . . .)

- to separate groups of three digits in most numbers of 1,000 or more (see section 4.37 for exceptions).

Do not use a comma

- before an essential or restrictive clause, that is, a clause that limits or defines the material it modifies. Removal of such a clause from the sentence would alter the intended meaning.

The switch that stops the recording device also controls the light.

- between the two parts of a compound predicate.

Correct:

All subjects completed the first phase of the experiment and returned the following week for Phase 2.

Incorrect:

All subjects completed the first phase of the experiment, and returned the following week for Phase 2.

- to separate parts of measurement.

8 years 2 months   3 min 40 s

4.04 Semicolon

Use a semicolon

- to separate two independent clauses that are not joined by a conjunction.

The participants in the first study were paid; those in the second were unpaid.

- to separate elements in a series that already contain commas. (See section 3.04 for the use of semicolons in numbered or lettered series.)

  The color order was red, yellow, blue; blue, yellow, red; or yellow, red, blue.

  (Davis & Hueter, 1994; Pettigrew, 1993)

  age, $M = 34.5$ years, 95% CI [29.4, 39.6]; years of education, $M = 10.4$ [8.7, 12.1]; and weekly income, $M = 612$ [522, 702];

4.05 Colon

Use a colon

- between a grammatically complete introductory clause (one that could stand as a sentence) and a final phrase or clause that illustrates, extends, or amplifies the preceding thought. If the clause following the colon is a complete sentence, it begins with a capital letter.

  For example, Freud (1930/1961) wrote of two urges: an urge toward union with others and an egoistic urge toward happiness.

  They have agreed on the outcome: Informed participants perform better than do uninformed participants.

- in ratios and proportions.

  The proportion (saltwater) was 1:8.

- in references between place of publication and publisher.

  New York: Wiley. St. Louis, MO: Mosby.

Do not use a colon

- after an introduction that is not an independent clause or complete sentence.

  The formula is $r_i = a_i + e$.

  The instructions for the task were

  > Your group's task is to rank the 15 items in terms of their importance for the crew's survival.

4.06 Dash

Use a dash to indicate only a sudden interruption in the continuity of a sentence. Overuse weakens the flow of material. (See also section 4.15 for capitalization following dashes in titles.)

These two participants—one from the first group and one from the second—were tested separately.

4.07 Quotation Marks

Observe the following guidelines for uses of double quotation marks other than in material quoted directly from a source.

Use double quotation marks

- to introduce a word or phrase used as an ironic comment, as slang, or as an invented or coined expression. Use quotation marks the first time the word or phrase is used; thereafter, do not use quotation marks.

  Correct:

  considered "normal" behavior

  the "good-outcome" variable . . . the good-outcome variable [no quotation marks after the initial usage]

  Incorrect:

  considered 'normal' behavior

  the "good-outcome" variable . . . the "good-outcome" variable

- to set off the title of an article or chapter in a periodical or book when the title is mentioned in text.

  Riger's (1992) article, "Epistemological Debates, Feminist Voices: Science, Social Values, and the Study of Women"

- to reproduce material from a test item or verbatim instructions to participants.

  The first fill-in item was "could be expected to _______."

If instructions are long, set them off from text in a block format without quotation marks. (See sections 4.08 and 6.03 for discussion of block format.)

Do not use double quotation marks

- to identify the anchors of a scale. Instead, italicize them.

  We ranked the items on a scale ranging from 1 (*all of the time*) to 5 (*never*).

- to cite a letter, word, phrase, or sentence as a linguistic example. Instead, italicize the term.

  He clarified the distinction between *farther* and *further.*

- to introduce a technical or key term. Instead, italicize the term.

  The term *zero-base budgeting* appeared frequently in the speech.

  She compared it with *meta-analysis,* which is described in the next section.

■ to hedge. Do not use any punctuation with such expressions.

Correct:

The teacher rewarded the class with tokens.

Incorrect:

The teacher "rewarded" the class with tokens.

4.08 Double or Single Quotation Marks

In text. Use double quotation marks to enclose quotations in text. Use single quotation marks within double quotation marks to set off material that in the original source was enclosed in double quotation marks.

Correct:

Miele (1993) found that "the 'placebo effect,' which had been verified in previous studies, disappeared when [only the first group's] behaviors were studied in this manner" (p. 276).

Incorrect:

Miele (1993) found that "the "placebo effect," which had been verified in previous studies, disappeared when [only the first group's] behaviors were studied in this manner" (p. 276).

In block quotations (any quotations of 40 or more words). Do not use quotation marks to enclose block quotations. Do use double quotation marks to enclose any quoted material within a block quotation.

Correct:

Miele (1993) found the following:

> The "placebo effect," which had been verified in previous studies, disappeared when behaviors were studied in this manner. Furthermore, the behaviors *were never exhibited again* [emphasis added], even when reel [*sic*] drugs were administered. Earlier studies (e.g., Abdullah, 1984; Fox, 1979) were clearly premature in attributing the results to a placebo effect. (p. 276)

Incorrect:

Miele (1993) found the following:

> "The 'placebo effect,' which had been verified in previous studies, disappeared when behaviors were studied in this manner. Furthermore, the behaviors *were never exhibited again* [emphasis added], even when reel [*sic*] drugs were administered. Earlier studies (e.g., Abdullah, 1984; Fox, 1979) were clearly premature in attributing the results to a placebo effect (p. 276)."

With other punctuation. Place periods and commas within closing single or double quotation marks. Place other punctuation marks inside quotation marks only when they are part of the quoted material.

4.09 Parentheses

Use parentheses

- to set off structurally independent elements.

  The patterns were statistically significant (see Figure 5).

  (When a complete sentence is enclosed in parentheses, place punctuation in the sentence inside the parentheses, like this.) If only part of a sentence is enclosed in parentheses (like this), place punctuation outside the parentheses (like this).

- to set off reference citations in text (see sections 6.09–6.19 and Appendix 7.1 for further discussion of reference citations in text).

  Dumas and Dore (1991) reported

  is fully described elsewhere (Hong & O'Neil, 1992) in the *Diagnostic and Statistical Manual of Mental Disorders* (4th ed., text rev.; *DSM–IV–TR;* American Psychiatric Association, 2000)

- to introduce an abbreviation.

  effect on the galvanic skin response (GSR)

- to set off letters that identify items in a series within a sentence or paragraph (see also section 3.04 on seriation).

  The subject areas included (a) synonyms associated with cultural interactions, (b) descriptors for ethnic group membership, and (c) psychological symptoms and outcomes associated with bicultural adaptation.

- to group mathematical expressions (see also sections 4.10 and 4.47).

  (k – 1)/(g – 2)

- to enclose the citation or page number of a direct quotation (see also section 6.03).

  The author stated, "The effect disappeared within minutes" (Lopez, 1993, p. 311), but she did not say which effect.

  Lopez (1993) found that "the effect disappeared within minutes" (p. 311), but she did not say which effect.

- to enclose numbers that identify displayed formulas and equations.

  $$M_j = \alpha M_{j-1} + f_j + g_j * g_{j'} \quad (1)$$

- to enclose statistical values.

  was statistically significant ($p = .031$)

- to enclose degrees of freedom.

  $t(75) = 2.19$
  $F(2, 116) = 3.71$

Do not use parentheses

- to enclose material within other parentheses.

  (the Beck Depression Inventory [BDI]) [Use brackets to avoid nested parentheses.]
  were statistically different, $F(4, 132) = 13.62$, $p < .001$. [Use a comma before the statistics to avoid nested parentheses.]

- back to back.

  Correct:
  (e.g., defensive pessimism; Norem & Cantor, 1986)
  Incorrect:
  (e.g., defensive pessimism) (Norem & Cantor, 1986)

4.10 Brackets

Use brackets

- to enclose the values that are the limits of a confidence interval.

  95% CIs [−7.2, 4.3], [9.2, 12.4], and [−1.2, −0.5]

- to enclose material inserted in a quotation by some person other than the original writer.

  "when [his own and others'] behaviors were studied" (Hanisch, 1992, p. 24)

- to enclose parenthetical material that is already within parentheses.

  (The results for the control group [$n = 8$] are also presented in Figure 2.)

Exception 1: Do not use brackets if the material can be set off easily with commas without confounding meaning.

  (as Imai, 1990, later concluded)
  not
  (as Imai [1990] later concluded)

Exception 2: In mathematical material, the placement of brackets and parentheses is reversed; that is, parentheses appear within brackets. (See section 4.47 for further discussion of brackets in equations.)

Do not use brackets

- to set off statistics that already include parentheses.

Correct:

was statistically significant, $F(1, 32) = 4.37$, $p = .045$.

Incorrect:

was statistically significant ($F[1, 32] = 4.37$, $p = .045$).

Incorrect:

was statistically significant [$F(1, 32) = 4.37$, $p = .045$].

4.11 Slash

Use a slash (also called a *virgule, solidus,* or *shill*)

- to clarify a relationship in which a hyphenated compound is used.

the classification/similarity-judgment condition
hits/false-alarms comparison

- to separate numerator from denominator.

X/Y

- to indicate *per* to separate units of measurement accompanied by a numerical value (see section 4.27).

0.5 deg/s 7.4 mg/kg

but

luminance is measured in candelas per square meter

- to set off English phonemes.

/o/

- to cite a republished work in text.

Freud (1923/1961)

Do not use a slash

- when a phrase would be clearer.

Each child handed the ball to her mother or guardian.

not

Each child handed the ball to her mother/guardian.

- for simple comparisons. Use a hyphen or short dash (en dash) instead.

  test–retest reliability

  not

  test/retest reliability

- more than once to express compound units. Use centered dots and parentheses as needed to prevent ambiguity.

  nmol • hr^{-1} • mg^{-1}

  not

  nmol/hr/mg

Spelling

4.12 Preferred Spelling

Spelling should conform to standard American English as exemplified in *Merriam-Webster's Collegiate Dictionary* (2005), the standard spelling reference for APA journals and books; spelling of psychological terms should conform to the *APA Dictionary of Psychology* (VandenBos, 2007). If a word is not in *Webster's Collegiate,* consult the more comprehensive *Webster's Third New International Dictionary* (2002). If the dictionary gives a choice, use the first spelling listed; for example, use *aging* and *canceled* rather than *ageing* and *cancelled.*

Plural forms of some words of Latin or Greek origin can be troublesome; a list of preferred spellings of some of the more common ones follows. Authors are reminded that plural nouns take plural verbs.

Singular	Plural
appendix	appendices
cannula	cannulas
datum	data
phenomenon	phenomena

In general, the possessive of a singular name is formed by adding an apostrophe and an *s,* even when a name ends in *s;* the possessive of a plural name is formed by adding an apostrophe. A list of examples follows as well as some exceptions.

Singular	Plural
Freud's	the Freuds'
James's	the Jameses'
Watson's	the Watsons'
Skinner's	the Skinners'

Exceptions: Use an apostrophe only with the singular form of names ending in unpronounced *s* (e.g., Descartes'). It is preferable to include *of* when referring to the plural form of names ending in unpronounced *s* (e.g., the home of the Descartes).

4.13 Hyphenation

Compound words take many forms; that is, two words may be written as (a) two separate words; (b) a hyphenated word; or (c) one unbroken, "solid" word. Choosing the proper form is sometimes frustrating. For example, is *follow up, follow-up,* or *followup* the form to be used? The dictionary is an excellent guide for such decisions, especially for nonscientific words (the term is *follow-up* when functioning as a noun or adjective but *follow up* when functioning as a verb). When a compound can be found in the dictionary, its usage is established and it is known as a *permanent compound* (e.g., *high school, caregiver,* and *self-esteem*). Dictionaries do not always agree on the way a compound should be written (open, solid, or hyphenated); APA follows *Webster's Collegiate* in most cases. Compound terms are often introduced into the language as separate or hyphenated words, and as they become more commonplace, they tend to fuse into a solid word. For example, the hyphen was dropped from *life-style* in the 11th edition of *Webster's Collegiate,* and *data base* is now *database.*

There is another kind of compound—the *temporary compound*—which is made up of two or more words that occur together, perhaps only in a particular paper, to express a thought. Because language is constantly expanding, especially in science, temporary compounds develop that are not yet listed in the dictionary. If a temporary compound modifies another word, it may or may not be hyphenated, depending on (a) its position in the sentence and (b) whether the pairing of a compound with another word can cause the reader to misinterpret meaning. The main rule to remember is that if a temporary compound precedes what it modifies, it may need to be hyphenated, and if it follows what it modifies, it usually does not. If a compound is not in the dictionary, follow the general principles of hyphenation given here and in Table 4.1. If you are still in doubt, use hyphens for clarity rather than omitting them. (See also Tables 4.2 and 4.3 for treatment of prefixes and suffixes.)

Hyphens, dashes, and minus signs are each typed differently.

- **hyphen:** Use no space before or after (e.g., trial-by-trial analysis).
- **em dash:** An em dash is longer than a hyphen or an en dash and is used to set off an element added to amplify or to digress from the main clause (e.g., Studies—published and unpublished—are included). Use no space before or after an em dash. If an em dash is not available on your keyboard, use two hyphens with no space before or after.
- **en dash:** An en dash is longer and thinner than a hyphen yet shorter than an em dash and is used between words of equal weight in a compound adjective (e.g., Chicago–London flight). Type as an en dash or, if the en dash is not available on your keyboard, as a single hyphen. In either case, use no space before or after.
- **minus sign:** A typeset minus sign is the same length as an en dash, but it is slightly thicker and slightly higher. If a minus sign is not available in your word-processing program, use a hyphen with a space on both sides (e.g., a - b). For a negative value, use a hyphen rather than a minus sign, with a space before but no space after (e.g., -5.25).

Table 4.1. Guide to Hyphenating Terms

Rule	Example
Hyphenate	
1. A compound with a participle when it precedes the term it modifies	■ role-playing technique ■ anxiety-arousing condition ■ water-deprived animals
2. A phrase used as an adjective when it precedes the term it modifies	■ trial-by-trial analysis ■ to-be-recalled items ■ all-or-none questionnaire
3. An adjective-and-noun compound when it precedes the term it modifies	■ high-anxiety group ■ middle-class families ■ low-frequency words
4. A compound with a number as the first element when the compound precedes the term it modifies	■ two-way analysis of variance ■ six-trial problem ■ 12th-grade students ■ 16-s interval
5. A fraction used as an adjective	■ two-thirds majority
Do not hyphenate	
1. A compound including an adverb ending in *ly*	■ widely used text ■ relatively homogeneous sample ■ randomly assigned participants
2. A compound including a comparative or superlative adjective	■ better written paper ■ less informed interviewers ■ higher scoring students ■ higher order learning
3. Chemical terms	■ sodium chloride solution ■ amino acid compound
4. Foreign phrases used as adjectives or adverbs	■ a posteriori test ■ post hoc comparisons ■ fed ad lib [but hyphenate the adjectival form: ad-lib feeding; see *Webster's Collegiate*]
5. A modifier including a letter or numeral as the second element	■ Group B participants ■ Type II error ■ Trial 1 performance
6. Common fractions used as nouns	■ one third of the participants

General Principle 1

If a compound adjective can be misread, use a hyphen.

General Principle 2

In a temporary compound that is used as an adjective before a noun, use a hyphen if the term can be misread or if the term expresses a single thought (i.e., all words together

Table 4.2. Prefixes and Suffixes That Do Not Require Hyphens

Prefix or suffix	Example	Prefix or suffix	Example
able	retrievable	**mini**	minisession
after	aftereffect	**multi**	multiphase
anti	antisocial	**non**	nonsignificant
bi	bilingual	**over**	overaggressive
cede	intercede	**phobia**	agoraphobia
co	coworker	**post**	posttest
counter	counterbalance	**pre**	preexperimental
equi	equimax	**pro**	prowar
extra	extracurricular	**pseudo**	pseudoscience
gram	cardiogram	**quasi**	quasiperiodic
infra	infrared	**re**	reevaluate
inter	interstimulus	**semi**	semidarkness
intra	intraspecific	**socio**	socioeconomic
like	wavelike	**sub**	subtest
macro	macrocosm	**super**	superordinate
mega	megawatt	**supra**	supraliminal
meta	metacognitive	**ultra**	ultrahigh
meter	micrometer	**un**	unbiased
micro	microcosm	**under**	underdeveloped
mid	midterm		

Exceptions: Use a hyphen in *meta-analysis* and *quasi-experimental.*

modify the noun). For example, are *different word lists* (a) word lists that are different from other word lists (if so, *different* modifies *word lists;* thus, write *different word lists*) or (b) lists that present different words (if so, the first word modifies the second, and together they modify *lists,* thus, *different-word lists*). Likewise, "the adolescents resided in two parent homes" means that two homes served as residences, whereas if the adolescents resided in "two-parent homes," they each would live in a household headed by two parents. A properly placed hyphen helps the reader understand the intended meaning.

General Principle 3

Most compound adjective rules are applicable only when the compound adjective precedes the term it modifies. If a compound adjective follows the term, do not use a hyphen, because relationships are sufficiently clear without one. The following examples are all correctly hyphenated:

client-centered counseling

Table 4.3. Prefixed Words That Require Hyphens

Occurrence	Example
1. Compounds in which the base word is capitalized	■ pro-Freudian
a number	■ post-1970
an abbreviation	■ pre-UCS trial
more than one word	■ non-achievement-oriented students
2. All *self-* compounds, whether they are adjectives or nouns[a]	■ self-report technique ■ the test was self-paced ■ self-esteem
3. Words that could be misunderstood	■ re-pair [pair again] ■ re-form [form again] ■ un-ionized
4. Words in which the prefix ends and the base word begins with the same vowel[b]	■ meta-analysis ■ anti-intellectual ■ co-occur

[a]But *self psychology.* [b]*Pre* and *re* compounds are usually set solid to base words beginning with *e.*

but

the counseling was client centered

t-test results

but

results from *t* tests

same-sex children

but

children of the same sex

General Principle 4

Write most words formed with prefixes as one word (see Table 4.2). Table 4.3 contains some exceptions.

General Principle 5

When two or more compound modifiers have a common base, that base is sometimes omitted in all except the last modifier, but the hyphens are retained.

long- and short-term memory

2-, 3-, and 10-min trials

Capitalization

Use an uppercase letter for the first letter of a word according to the guidelines in the following sections.

4.14 Words Beginning a Sentence

Capitalize

- the first word in a complete sentence.

Note: If a name that begins with a lowercase letter begins a sentence, then it should be capitalized. Do not begin a sentence with a statistical term (e.g., t test or p value; see section 4.30 for abbreviations beginning a sentence).

Correct:

De Waal (1994) concluded the following

Incorrect:

de Waal (1994) concluded the following

- the first word after a colon that begins a complete sentence.

The author made one main point: No explanation that has been suggested so far answers all questions.

4.15 Major Words in Titles and Headings

Capitalize

- major words in titles of books and articles within the body of the paper. Conjunctions, articles, and short prepositions are not considered major words; however, capitalize all words of four letters or more. Capitalize all verbs (including linking verbs), nouns, adjectives, adverbs, and pronouns. When a capitalized word is a hyphenated compound, capitalize both words. Also, capitalize the first word after a colon or a dash in a title.

In her book, *History of Pathology*

The criticism of the article, "Attitudes Toward Mental Health Workers"

"Ultrasonic Vocalizations Are Elicited From Rat Pups"

"Memory in Hearing-Impaired Children: Implications for Vocabulary Development"

Exception: In titles of books and articles in reference lists, capitalize only the first word, the first word after a colon or em dash, and proper nouns. Do not capitalize the second word of a hyphenated compound. (See Chapter 6 for further discussion of reference style.)

Liu, D., Wellman, H. M., Tardif, T., & Sabbagh, M. A. (2008). Theory of mind development in Chinese children: A meta-analysis of false-belief understanding across cultures and languages. *Developmental Psychology, 44,* 523–531. doi:10.1037/0012-1649.44.2.523

Cantor, A. B. (1996). Sample-size calculations for Cohen's kappa. *Psychological Methods, 1,* 150–153. doi:10.1037/1082-989X.1.2.150

- major words in article headings and subheadings.

Exception: In indented paragraph (Levels 3, 4, and 5) headings, capitalize only the first word and proper nouns (see section 3.03).

- major words in table titles and figure legends. In table headings and figure captions, capitalize only the first word and proper nouns (see sections 5.13 for table headings and 5.23 for figure captions).
- references to titles of sections within the same article.

  as explained in the Method section
  which is discussed in the Data Analyses subsection

4.16 Proper Nouns and Trade Names

Capitalize

- proper nouns and adjectives and words used as proper nouns. Proper adjectives that have acquired a common meaning are not capitalized; consult *Merriam-Webster's Collegiate Dictionary* (2005) for guidance.

  Freudian slip
  Wilks's lambda
  Greco-Latin square

  but

  eustachian tube
  cesarean section

- names of university departments if they refer to a specific department within a specific university and complete names of academic courses if they refer to a specific course.

  Department of Sociology, University of Washington
  Psychology 101
  Developmental Psychopathology

  but

  a sociology department
  an introductory psychology course

- trade and brand names of drugs, equipment, and food.

  Elavil [*but* amitriptyline hydrochloride]
  Hunter Klockounter
  Plexiglas
  Purina Monkey Chow
  Xerox

Do not capitalize names of laws, theories, models, statistical procedures, or hypotheses.

the empirical law of effect
parallel distributed processing model
associative learning model
a two-group *t* test

but

Gregory's theory of illusions [Retain uppercase in personal names.]
Fisher's *r* to *Z* transformation

4.17 Nouns Followed by Numerals or Letters

Capitalize nouns followed by numerals or letters that denote a specific place in a numbered series.

On Day 2 of Experiment 4
during Trial 5, the no-delay group performed
as shown in Table 2, Figure 3B, and Chapter 4
Grant AG02726 from the National Institute on Aging

Exception: Do not capitalize nouns that denote common parts of books or tables followed by numerals or letters.

page iv
row 3
column 5

Do not capitalize nouns that precede a variable.

trial *n* and item *x*

but

Trial 3 and Item b [The number and letter are not variables.]

4.18 Titles of Tests

Capitalize exact, complete titles of published and unpublished tests. Words such as *test* or *scale* are not capitalized if they refer to subscales of tests.

Advanced Vocabulary Test
Minnesota Multiphasic Personality Inventory
Stroop Color–Word Interference Test
the authors' Mood Adjective Checklist

but

MMPI Depression scale

Do not capitalize shortened, inexact, or generic titles of tests.

a vocabulary test   Stroop color test

4.19 Names of Conditions or Groups in an Experiment

Do not capitalize names of conditions or groups in an experiment.

> experimental and control groups
>
> participants were assigned to information and no-information conditions

but

> Conditions A and B [See section 4.17.]

4.20 Names of Factors, Variables, and Effects

Capitalize names of derived variables within a factor or principal components analysis. The words *factor* and *component* are not capitalized unless followed by a number (see section 4.17).

> Mealtime Behavior (Factor 4)
>
> Factors 6 and 7
>
> Component 1
>
> Big Five personality factors

Do not capitalize effects or variables unless they appear with multiplication signs. (Take care that you do not use the term *factor* when you mean *effect* or *variable,* for example, in an interaction or analysis of variance.)

> a small age effect
>
> the sex, age, and weight variables

but

> the Sex × Age × Weight interaction
>
> a 3 × 3 × 2 (Groups × Trials × Responses) design
>
> a 2 (methods) × 2 (item types)

Italics

4.21 Use of Italics

For specific use of italics in APA journals, see the guidelines listed below. In general, use italics infrequently.

Use italics for

- titles of books, periodicals, films, videos, TV shows, and microfilm publications.

> *The Elements of Style*
>
> *American Psychologist*

Exception: Words within the title of a book in text that would normally be italicized should be set in Roman type (this is referred to as *reverse italicization*).

A Stereotaxic Atlas of the Monkey Brain (Macaca Mulatta)
Dreaming by the Book: Freud's The Interpretation of Dreams *and the History of the Psychoanalytic Movement*

- genera, species, and varieties.

Macaca mulatta

- introduction of a new, technical, or key term or label (after a term has been used once, do not italicize it).

The term *backward masking*
box labeled *empty*

- a letter, word, or phrase cited as a linguistic example.

words such as *big* and *little*
the letter *a*
the meaning of *to fit tightly together*
a row of *Xs*

- words that could be misread.

the *small* group [meaning a designation, not group size]

- letters used as statistical symbols or algebraic variables.

Cohen's $d = 0.084$
$a/b = c/d$
SEM

- some test scores and scales.

Rorschach scores: *F+%*, *Z*
MMPI scales: *Hs*, *Pd*

- periodical volume numbers in reference lists.

American Psychologist, 26, 46–67

- anchors of a scale.

health ratings ranged from 1 (*poor*) to 5 (*excellent*)

Do not use italics for

- foreign phrases and abbreviations common in English (i.e., phrases found as main entries in *Merriam-Webster's Collegiate Dictionary,* 2005).

a posteriori   et al.

a priori   per se
ad lib   vis-à-vis

- chemical terms.

NaCl, LSD

- trigonometric terms.

sin, tan, log

- nonstatistical subscripts to statistical symbols or mathematical expressions.

F_{max}
$S_A + S_B$

- Greek letters.

β

- mere emphasis. (Italics are acceptable if emphasis might otherwise be lost; in general, however, use syntax to provide emphasis.)

Incorrect:

it is *important* to bear in mind that *this* process is *not* proposed as a *stage* theory of developments.

- letters used as abbreviations.

intertrial interval (ITI)

Abbreviations

4.22 Use of Abbreviations

To maximize clarity, use abbreviations sparingly. Although abbreviations are sometimes useful for long, technical terms in scientific writing, communication is usually garbled rather than clarified if, for example, an abbreviation is unfamiliar to the reader.

Overuse. Consider whether the space saved by abbreviations in the following sentence justifies the time necessary to master the meaning:

The advantage of the LH was clear from the RT data, which reflected high FP and FN rates for the RH.

Without abbreviations the passage reads as follows:

The advantage of the left hand was clear from the reaction time data, which reflected high false-positive and false-negative rates for the right hand.

Underuse. Abbreviations introduced on first mention of a term and used fewer than three times thereafter, particularly in a long paper, may be difficult for a reader to remember, and you probably serve the reader best if you write them out each time. In the following example, however, a standard abbreviation for a long, familiar term eases the reader's task:

> Patients at seven hospitals completed the MMPI–2.

Deciding whether to abbreviate. In all circumstances other than in the reference list (see section 6.22) and in the abstract, you must decide whether (a) to spell out a given expression every time it is used in an article or (b) to spell it out initially and abbreviate it thereafter. For example, the abbreviations *L* for large and *S* for small in a paper discussing different sequences of reward (*LLSS* or *LSLS*) would be an effective and readily understood shortcut. In another paper, however, writing about the *L reward* and the *S reward* would be both unnecessary and confusing. In most instances, abbreviating experimental group names is ineffective because the abbreviations are not adequately informative or easily recognizable and may even be more cumbersome than the full name. In general, use an abbreviation only (a) if it is conventional and if the reader is more familiar with the abbreviation than with the complete form or (b) if considerable space can be saved and cumbersome repetition avoided. In short, use only those abbreviations that will help you communicate with your readers. Remember, they have not had the same experience with your abbreviations as you have.

4.23 Explanation of Abbreviations

Because the abbreviations that psychologists use in their daily writing may not be familiar to students or to readers in other disciplines or other countries, a term to be abbreviated must, on its first appearance, be written out completely and followed immediately by its abbreviation in parentheses. Thereafter, use the abbreviation in text without further explanation (do not switch between the abbreviated and written-out forms of a term).

> The results of studies of simple reaction time (RT) to a visual target have shown a strong negative relation between RT and luminance.

Explain abbreviations that appear in a figure in the caption or legend. Explain those that appear in a table either in the table title (if it includes words that are abbreviated in the table body; see section 5.12) or in the table note (see section 5.16). Explain an abbreviation that is used in several figures or tables in each figure or table in which the abbreviation is used. Avoid introducing abbreviations into figure captions or table notes if they do not appear in the figure or table. Standard abbreviations for units of measurement do not need to be written out on first use (see section 4.27).

4.24 Abbreviations Accepted as Words

APA Style permits the use of abbreviations that appear as word entries (i.e., that are not labeled *abbr*) in *Merriam-Webster's Collegiate Dictionary* (2005). Such abbreviations do not need explanation in text.

> IQ REM ESP AIDS HIV NADP ACTH

4.25 Abbreviations Used Often in APA Journals

Some abbreviations may not be in the dictionary but appear frequently in the journal for which you are writing. Although probably well understood by many readers, these abbreviations should still be explained when first used.

Minnesota Multiphasic Personality Inventory (MMPI)
conditional stimulus (CS)
intertrial interval (ITI)
consonant–vowel–consonant (CVC)
short-term memory (STM)
reaction time (RT)

Do not use the abbreviations *S, E,* or *O* for subject, experimenter, and observer.

4.26 Latin Abbreviations

Use the following standard Latin abbreviations only in parenthetical material; in non-parenthetical material, use the English translation of the Latin terms; in both cases, include the correct punctuation that accompanies the term:

cf.	compare	i.e.,	that is,
e.g.,	for example,	viz.,	namely,
, etc.	, and so forth	vs.	versus, against

Exception: Use the abbreviation *v.* (for *versus*) in references and text citations to court cases, whether parenthetical or not (see Appendix 7.1, section A7.03, Examples 1–8).

Exception: In the reference list and in text, use the Latin abbreviation *et al.,* which means *and others,* in nonparenthetical as well as parenthetical material.

4.27 Scientific Abbreviations

Units of measurement. Use abbreviations and symbols for metric and nonmetric units of measurement that are accompanied by numeric values (e.g., 4 cm, 30 s, 12 min, 18 hr, 45°). (See Table 4.4 for a list of some common abbreviations used for units of measurement.)

Do not repeat abbreviated units of measure when expressing multiple amounts:

16–30 kHz   0.3, 1.5, and 3.0 mg/dl

Write out abbreviations for units that are not accompanied by numeric values (e.g., measured in centimeters, several kilograms).

Units of time. To prevent misreading, do not abbreviate the following units of time, even when they are accompanied by numeric values:

day   week   month   year

Table 4.4. Common Abbreviations for Units of Measurement

Abbreviation	Unit of measurement	Abbreviation	Unit of measurement
A	ampere	m	meter
Å	angstrom	μm	micrometer
AC	alternating current	mA	milliampere
a.m.	ante meridiem	mEq	milliequivalent
°C	degree Celsius	meV	million electron volts
Ci	curie	mg	milligram
cm	centimeter	ml	milliliter
cps	cycles per second	mm	millimeter
dB	decibel (specify scale)	mM	millimolar
DC	direct current	mmHg	millimeters of mercury
deg/s	degrees per second	mmol	millimole
dl	deciliter	mol wt	molecular weight
°F	degree Fahrenheit	mph	miles per hour (include metric equivalent in parentheses)
g	gram	MΩ	megohm
g	gravity	N	newton
Hz	hertz	p.m.	post meridiem
in.	inch (include metric equivalent in parentheses)	ppm	parts per million
IQ	intelligence quotient	psi	pounds per square inch (include metric equivalent in parentheses)
IU	international unit	rpm	revolutions per minute
kg	kilogram	S	Siemens
km	kilometer	V	volt
kph	kilometers per hour	W	watt
kW	kilowatt		
L	liter		

Abbreviate the following units of time:

hr, hour
min, minute
ms, millisecond
ns, nanosecond
s, second

Chemical compounds. Chemical compounds may be expressed by common name or by chemical name. If you prefer to use the common name, provide the chemical name in parentheses on first mention in the Method section. Avoid expressing compounds with chemical formulas, as these are usually less informative to the reader and have a high likelihood of being typed or typeset incorrectly (e.g., aspirin or salicylic acid, *not* $C_9H_8O_4$). If names of compounds include Greek letters, retain the letters as symbols and do not write them out (e.g., β carotene, *not* beta carotene).

Long names of organic compounds are often abbreviated; if the abbreviation is listed as a word entry in *Merriam-Webster's Collegiate Dictionary* (2005; e.g., NADP for *nicotinamide adenine dinucleotide phosphate*), you may use it freely, without writing it out on first use.

Concentrations. If you express a solution as a percentage concentration instead of as a molar concentration, be sure to specify the percentage as a weight-per-volume ratio (wt/vol), a volume ratio (vol/vol), or a weight ratio (wt/wt) of solute to solvent. The higher the concentration is, the more ambiguous the expression as a percentage. Specifying the ratio is especially necessary for concentrations of alcohol, glucose, and sucrose. Specifying the salt form is also essential for precise reporting: *d*-amphetamine HCl or *d*-amphetamine SO_4 (note that expression of chemical name in combination with a formula is acceptable in this case).

12% (vol/vol) ethyl alcohol solution
1% (wt/vol) saccharin solution

Routes of administration. You may abbreviate a route of administration when it is paired with a number-and-unit combination. Preferred style for APA is no periods: icv = intracerebral ventricular, im = intramuscular, ip = intraperitoneal, iv = intravenous, sc = subcutaneous, and so on.

anesthetized with sodium pentobarbital (90 mg/kg ip)

but

the first of two subcutaneous injections (*not* sc injections)

4.28 Other Abbreviations

Use abbreviations for statistics as described in section 4.45. For information on the International System of Units (SI), go to the APA Style website (www.apastyle.org).

4.29 Plurals of Abbreviations

To form the plural of most abbreviations and statistical symbols, add *s* alone, but not italicized and without an apostrophe.

IQs Eds. vols. *M*s *p*s *n*s

Exception: Do not add an *s* to make abbreviations of units of measurement plural (e.g., 12 cm; see section 4.40).

Exception: To form the plural of the reference abbreviation p. (page), write pp.; do not add an *s*.

4.30 Abbreviations Beginning a Sentence

Never begin a sentence with a lowercase abbreviation (e.g., lb) or a symbol that stands alone (e.g., α). Begin a sentence with a capitalized abbreviation or acronym (e.g., U.S. or APA) or with a symbol connected to a word (e.g., β-Endorphins) only when necessary to avoid indirect and awkward writing. In the case of chemical compounds, capitalize the first letter of the word to which the symbol is connected; keep the locant, descriptor, or positional prefix (i.e., Greek, small capital, and italic letters and numerals) intact.

In running text:	*At beginning of sentence:*
L-methionine	L-Methionine
N,N'-dimethylurea	*N,N'*-Dimethylurea
γ-hydroxy-β-aminobutyric acid	γ-Hydroxy-β-aminobutyric acid

Numbers

The general rule governing APA Style on the use of numbers is to use numerals to express numbers 10 and above and words to express numbers below 10. Sections 4.31–4.34 expand on this rule and state exceptions and special usages.

4.31 Numbers Expressed in Numerals

Use numerals to express

a. numbers 10 and above. (*Exceptions:* See sections 4.33–4.34.)

12 cm wide	the 15th trial
the remaining 10%	13 lists
25 years old	105 stimulus words
10th-grade students	

b. numbers in the abstract of a paper or in a graphical display within a paper.

c. numbers that immediately precede a unit of measurement.

a 5-mg dose
with 10.54 cm of

d. numbers that represent statistical or mathematical functions, fractional or decimal quantities, percentages, ratios, and percentiles and quartiles.

multiplied by 5
3 times as many [proportion]

0.33 of the
more than 5% of the sample
a ratio of 16:1
the 5th percentile

e. numbers that represent time, dates, ages, scores and points on a scale, exact sums of money, and numerals as numerals.

1 hr 34 min
at 12:30 a.m.
2-year-olds
scored 4 on a 7-point scale

Exception: Use words for approximations of numbers of days, months, and years (e.g., about three months ago).

f. numbers that denote a specific place in a numbered series, parts of books and tables, and each number in a list of four or more numbers.

Grade 8 [*but* the eighth grade; see section 4.34]
Table 3
row 5

4.32 Numbers Expressed in Words

Use words to express

a. any number that begins a sentence, title, or text heading. (Whenever possible, reword the sentence to avoid beginning with a number.)

Forty-eight percent of the sample showed an increase; 2% showed no change.
Twelve students improved, and 12 students did not improve.

b. common fractions.

one fifth of the class
two-thirds majority

c. universally accepted usage.

the Twelve Apostles
Five Pillars of Islam

4.33 Combining Numerals and Words to Express Numbers

Use a combination of numerals and words to express back-to-back modifiers.

2 two-way interactions
ten 7-point scales

A combination of numerals and words in these situations increases the clarity and readability of the construction. In some situations, however, readability may suffer; in such a case, spell out both numbers.

Correct:

first two items

Incorrect:

1st two items
first 2 items

4.34 Ordinal Numbers

Treat ordinal numbers as you would cardinal numbers (see sections 4.31–4.33).

Ordinal	**Cardinal base**
second-order factor	two orders
the fourth graders	four grades
the first item of the 75th trial	one item, 75 trials
the first and third groups	one group, three groups

4.35 Decimal Fractions

Use a zero before the decimal point with numbers that are less than 1 when the statistic can exceed 1.

0.23 cm
Cohen's $d = 0.70$
0.48 s

Do not use a zero before a decimal fraction when the statistic cannot be greater than 1 (e.g., correlations, proportions, and levels of statistical significance).

$r(24) = -.43$, $p = .028$

The number of decimal places to use in reporting the results of experiments and data analytic manipulations of the data should be governed by the following general principle: Round as much as possible while keeping prospective use and statistical precision in mind. As a general rule, fewer decimal digits are easier to comprehend than more digits; therefore, in general, it is better to round to two decimal places or to rescale the measurement (in which case effect sizes should be presented in the same metric). For instance, a difference in distances that must be carried to four decimals to be seen when scaled in meters can be more effectively illustrated in millimeters, which would require only a few decimal digits to illustrate the same difference. As a rule, when properly scaled, most data can be effectively presented with two decimal digits of accuracy. Report correlations, proportions, and inferential statistics such as t, F, and χ^2 to two decimals.

When reporting p values, report exact p values (e.g., $p = .031$) to two or three decimal places. However, report p values less than .001 as $p < .001$. The tradition of reporting p values in the form $p < .10$, $p < .05$, $p < .01$, and so forth, was appropriate in a time when only limited tables of critical values were available. However, in tables the "$p <$" notation may be necessary for clarity (see section 5.16).

4.36 Roman Numerals

If Roman numerals are part of an established terminology, do not change to Arabic numerals; for example, use Type II error. Use Arabic, not Roman, numerals for routine seriation (e.g., Step 1).

4.37 Commas in Numbers

Use commas between groups of three digits in most figures of 1,000 or more.

Exceptions:

page numbers	page 1029
binary digits	00110010
serial numbers	290466960
degrees of temperature	3071 °F
acoustic frequency designations	2000 Hz
degrees of freedom	*F*(24, 1000)

4.38 Plurals of Numbers

To form the plurals of numbers, whether expressed as figures or as words, add *s* or *es* alone, without an apostrophe.

fours and sixes   1950s   10s and 20s

Metrication

4.39 Policy on Metrication

APA uses the metric system in its journals. All references to physical measurements, where feasible, should be expressed in metric units. The metric system outlined in this section is based, with some exceptions, on the International System of Units (SI), which is an extension and refinement of the traditional metric system and is supported by the national standardizing bodies in many countries, including the United States.

In preparing manuscripts, use metric units if possible. If you use instruments that record measurements in nonmetric units, you may report the nonmetric units but also report the established SI equivalents in parentheses immediately after the nonmetric units.

> The rods were spaced 19 mm apart. [Measurement was made in metric units.]
> The rod was 3 ft (0.91 m) long. [Measurement was made in nonmetric units and converted to the rounded SI equivalent.]

4.40 Style for Metric Units

Abbreviation. Use the metric symbol (see International System [SI] Base and Supplementary Units and other resources on metrication at www.apastyle.org) to express a metric unit when it appears with a numeric value (e.g., 4 m). When a metric unit does not appear with a numeric value, spell out the unit in text (e.g., measured in meters) and use the metric symbol in column and headings of tables to conserve space (e.g., lag in ms).

Capitalization. Use lowercase letters when writing out full names of units (e.g., meter, nanometer), unless the name appears in capitalized material or at the beginning of a sentence.

For the most part, use lowercase letters for symbols (e.g., cd), even in capitalized material. Symbols derived from the name of a person usually include uppercase letters (e.g., Gy), as do symbols for some prefixes that represent powers of 10: exa (E), peta (P), tera (T), giga (G), and mega (M). (See Table 4.4 for more examples.)

Use the symbol *L* for liter when it stands alone (e.g., 5 L, 0.3 mg/L) because a lowercase *l* may be misread as the numeral one (use lowercase *l* for fractions of a liter: 5 ml, 9 ng/dl).

Plurals. Make full names of units plural when appropriate.

> meters

Do not make symbols or abbreviations of units plural.

> 3 cm, *not* 3 cms

Periods. Do not use a period after a symbol, except at the end of a sentence.

Spacing. Use a space between a symbol and the number to which it refers, except for measures of angles (e.g., degrees, minutes, and seconds).

> 4.5 m, 12 °C, but 45° angle

Compound units. Use a centered dot between the symbols of a compound term formed by the multiplication of units.

> Pa • s

Use a space between full names of units of a compound unit formed by the multiplication of units; do not use a centered dot.

> pascal second

Statistical and Mathematical Copy

APA Style for presenting statistical and mathematical copy reflects (a) standards of content and form agreed on in the field and (b) the requirements of clear communication.

4.41 Selecting Effective Presentation

Statistical and mathematical copy can be presented in text, in tables, and in figures. Detailed discussions of principles for the generation of tables, figures, and graphs can be found in Chapter 5. In deciding which approach to take, a general rule that might prove useful is

- if you need to present three or fewer numbers, first try using a sentence;
- if you need to present four to 20 numbers, first consider using a well-prepared table; and
- if you have more than 20 numbers, a graph is often more useful than a table.

Select the mode of presentation that optimizes understanding of the data by the reader. Detailed displays that allow fine-grained understanding of a data set may be more appropriate to include in online supplemental archives (see section 2.13) than in the print version of an article. Tables, figures, charts, and other graphics should be prepared with the understanding that if the manuscript is accepted, they are to be published at the editor's discretion. In any case, be prepared to submit tables and figures of complex statistical and mathematical material if an editor requests them.

4.42 References for Statistics

Do not give a reference for statistics in common use; this convention applies to most statistics used in journal articles. Do give a reference when (a) less common statistics are used, especially those that have appeared so recently that they can be found only in journals; (b) a statistic is used in an unconventional or a controversial way; or (c) the statistic itself is the focus of the article.

4.43 Formulas

Do not give a formula for a statistic in common use; do give a formula when the statistic or mathematical expression is new, rare, or essential to the manuscript. Presentation of equations is described in sections 4.47–4.48.

4.44 Statistics in Text

When reporting inferential statistics (e.g., t tests, F tests, χ^2 tests, and associated effect sizes and confidence intervals), include sufficient information to allow the reader to fully understand the analyses conducted. The data supplied, preferably in the text but possibly in an online supplemental archive depending on the magnitude of such data arrays, should allow the reader to confirm the basic reported analyses (e.g., cell means, standard deviations, sample sizes, and correlations) and should enable the interested reader to construct some effect-size estimates and confidence intervals beyond those supplied in the paper per se. In the case of multilevel data, present summary statistics for each level of aggregation. What constitutes sufficient information depends on the analytic approach reported.

For immediate recognition, the omnibus test of the main effect of sentence format was statistically significant, $F(2, 177) = 6.30$, $p = .002$, est $\omega^2 = .07$. The one-degree-of-freedom contrast of primary interest (the mean difference between Conditions 1 and 2) was also statistically significant at the specified .05 level, $t(177) = 3.51$, $p < .001$, $d = 0.65$, 95% CI [0.35, 0.95].

High-school GPA statistically predicted college mathematics performance, $R^2 = .12$, $F(1, 148) = 20.18$, $p < .001$, 95% CI [.02, .22]. The four-subtest battery added to this prediction, $R^2 = .21$, $\Delta R^2 = .09$, $F(4, 144) = 3.56$, $p = .004$, 95% CI [.10, .32]. Most important, when the two preceding variables were statistically accounted for, the college mathematics placement examination also explained unique variance in students' college mathematics performance, $R^2 = .25$, $\Delta R^2 = .04$, $F(1, 143) = 7.63$, $p = .006$, 95% CI [.13, .37].

If you present descriptive statistics in a table or figure, you do not need to repeat them in text, although you should (a) mention the table in which the statistics can be found and (b) emphasize particular data in the narrative when they help in interpretation of the findings.

When enumerating a series of similar statistics, be certain that the relation between the statistics and their referents is clear. Words such as *respectively* and *in order* can clarify this relationship.

Means (with standard deviations in parentheses) for Trials 1 through 4 were 2.43 (0.50), 2.59 (1.21), 2.68 (0.39), and 2.86 (0.12), respectively.

When reporting confidence intervals, use the format 95% CI [LL, UL], where LL is the lower limit of the confidence interval and UL is the upper limit.

When a sequence of confidence intervals is repeated in a series or within the same paragraph and the level of confidence (e.g., 95%) has remained unchanged, and the meaning is clear, you do not need to repeat the 95% CI. Every report of a confidence interval must clearly state the level of confidence. A sentence might then read, in part,

95% CIs [5.62, 8.31], [−2.43, 4.31], and [−4.29, −3.11], respectively

When a confidence interval follows reporting of a point estimate, the units of measurement should not be repeated:

$M = 30.5$ cm, 99% CI [18.0, 43.0]

4.45 Statistical Symbols

When using a statistical term in the narrative, use the term, not the symbol. For example, use

The means were

not

The *M*s were

Symbols for population versus sample statistics. Population parameters are usually represented by Greek letters. Most estimators are represented by italicized Latin letters. For example, the population correlation would be represented as ρ, and the estimator would be represented as *r*. [Est(ρ) and $\hat{\rho}$ are also acceptable]. Some test statistics are represented by italicized Latin letters (e.g., *t* and *F*), and a few are represented by Greek letters (e.g., Γ).

Symbols for number of subjects. Use an uppercase, italicized *N* to designate the number of members in the total sample (e.g., $N = 135$) and a lowercase, italicized *n* to designate the number of members in a limited portion of the total sample (e.g., $n = 30$).

Symbol for percentage. Use the symbol for percent only when it is preceded by a numeral. Use the word *percentage* when a number is not given.

found that 18% of the rats

determined the percentage of rats

Exception: In table headings and figure legends, use the symbol % to conserve space.

Standard, boldface, and italic type. Statistical symbols and mathematical copy in manuscripts are prepared with three different typefaces: standard, **boldface,** and *italic*. The same typeface is used in text, tables, and figures.

Greek letters, subscripts, and superscripts that function as identifiers (i.e., are not variables) and abbreviations that are not variables (e.g., log, GLM, WLS) are set in standard typeface.

μ_{girls}, α, β_{i}

Symbols for vectors and matrices are set in boldface.

V, **Σ**

All other statistical symbols are set in italic type.

N, M_x, df, SSE, MSE, t, F

On occasion, an element may serve as both an abbreviation and a symbol (e.g., *SD*); in those cases, use the typeface that reflects the function of element (see Table 4.5).

Identifying letters and symbols. As with all aspects of manuscript preparation, take care to ensure that there are no ambiguities that could lead to errors in the final production steps, particularly with mathematical and statistical symbols, non-English characters, and complex alignments (e.g., subscripts and superscripts). Avoid misunderstandings and corrections by preparing mathematical copy carefully.

4.46 Spacing, Alignment, and Punctuation

Space mathematical copy as you would space words: $a{+}b{=}c$ is as difficult to read as *wordswithoutspacing*. Instead, type $a + b = c$.

Align signs and symbols carefully. Use the subscript and superscript features in your word-processing software. In most cases, type subscripts first and then super-

Table 4.5. Statistical Abbreviations and Symbols

Abbreviation/symbol	Definition
English character set	
a	In item response theory, the slope parameter
AIC	Akaike information criterion
ANCOVA	Analysis of covariance
ANOVA	Analysis of variance
b, b_i	In regression and multiple regression analyses, estimated values of raw (unstandardized) regression coefficients; in item response theory, the difficulty-severity parameter
b^*, b_i^*	Estimated values of standardized regression coefficients in regression and multiple regression analyses
BIC	Bayesian information criterion
CAT	Computerized adaptive testing
CDF	Cumulative distribution function
CFA	Confirmatory factor analysis
CI	Confidence interval
d	Cohen's measure of sample effect size for comparing two sample means
d'	Discriminability, a measure of sensitivity in signal detection theory
df	Degrees of freedom
DIF	Differential item functioning
EFA	Exploratory factor analysis
EM	Expectation maximization
ES	Effect size
f	Frequency
f_e	Expected frequency
f_o	Observed frequency
F	F distribution, Fisher's F ratio
$F(\nu_1, \nu_2)$	F with ν_1 and ν_2 degrees of freedom
F_{crit}	Critical value for statistical significance in an F test
F_{max}	Hartley's test of homogeneity of variance
FIML	Full information maximum likelihood
g	Hedges's measure of effect size
GLM	Generalized linear model

Table 4.5. Statistical Abbreviations and Symbols (continued)

Abbreviation/symbol	Definition
GLS	Generalized least squares
H_0	Null hypothesis, hypothesis under test
H_1 (or H_a)	Alternative hypothesis
HLM	Hierarchical linear model(ing)
HSD	Tukey's honestly significant difference
IRT	Item response theory
k	Coefficient of alienation; number of studies in a meta-analysis; number of levels in an experimental design or individual study
k^2	Coefficient of nondetermination
KR20	Kuder–Richardson reliability index
LGC	Latent growth curve
LL	Lower limit (as of a CI)
LR	Likelihood ratio
LSD	Least significant difference
M (or $\bar{X}$)	Sample mean, arithmetic average
MANOVA	Multivariate analysis of variance
MANCOVA	Multivariate analysis of covariance
MCMC	Markov chain Monte Carlo
Mdn	Median
MLE	Maximum likelihood estimator, maximum likelihood estimate
MS	Mean square
MSE	Mean square error
n	Number of cases (generally in a subsample)
N	Total number of cases
ns	Not statistically significant
OLS	Ordinary least squares
OR	Odds ratio
p	Probability; probability of a success in a binary trial
p_{rep}	The probability a replication would give a result with the same sign as the original result
PDF	Probability density function
q	Probability of a failure in a binary trial, $1 - p$
Q	Test of homogeneity of effect sizes
r	Estimate of the Pearson product–moment correlation coefficient

Table 4.5. Statistical Abbreviations and Symbols (continued)

Abbreviation/symbol	Definition
$r_{ab.c}$	The partial correlation of *a* and *b* with the effect of *c* removed
$r_{a(b.c)}$	The part (or semipartial) correlation of *a* and *b* with the effect of *c* removed from *b*
r^2	Coefficient of determination; measure of strength of relationship; estimate of the Pearson product–moment correlation squared
r_b	Biserial correlation
r_{pb}	Point biserial correlation
r_s	Spearman rank order correlation
R	Multiple correlation
R^2	Multiple correlation squared; measure of strength of association
RMSEA	Root mean square error of approximation
s	Sample standard deviation (denominator $\sqrt{n-1}$)
S	Sample variance–covariance matrix
S^2	Sample variance (biased estimator) – denominator n
s^2	Sample variance (unbiased) – denominator $n - 1$
SD	Standard deviation
SE	Standard error
SEM	Standard error of measurement; standard error of the mean
SEM	Structural equation modeling
SS	Sum of squares
t	Student's *t* distribution; a statistical test based on the Student *t* distribution; the sample value of the *t*-test statistic
T_k	Generic effect size estimate
T^2	Hotelling's multivariate test for the equality of the mean vector in two multivariate populations
U	The Mann–Whitney test statistic
UL	Upper limit (as of a CI)
V	Pillai–Bartlett multivariate trace criterion; Cramér's measure of association in contingency tables
w_k	Fixed effects weights
w_{k^*}	Random effects weights
W	Kendall's coefficient of concordance and its estimate
WLS	Weighted least squares
z	A standardized score; the value of a statistic divided by its standard error

Table 4.5. Statistical Abbreviations and Symbols (continued)

Abbreviation/symbol	Definition
Greek character set	
α	In statistical hypothesis testing, the probability of making a Type I error; Cronbach's index of internal consistency (a form of reliability)
β	In statistical hypothesis testing, the probability of making a Type II error ($1 - \beta$ denotes statistical power); population values of regression coefficients (with appropriate subscripts as needed)
Γ	Goodman–Kruskal's index of relationship
δ	Population value of Cohen's effect size; noncentrality parameter in hypothesis testing and noncentral distributions
ε^2	Measure of strength of relationship in analysis of variance
Δ	Increment of change
η^2	Measure of strength of relationship (eta squared)
θ_k	Generic effect size in meta analysis
Θ	Roy's multivariate test criterion
κ	Cohen's measure of agreement corrected for chance agreement
λ	Element of a factor loading matrix
λ	Goodman–Kruskal measure of predictability
Λ	Wilks's multivariate test criterion
μ	Population mean; expected value
ν	Degrees of freedom
ρ	Population product–moment correlation
ρ_I	Population intraclass correlation
σ	Population standard deviation
σ^2	Population variance
Σ	Population variance–covariance matrix
τ	Kendall's rank-order correlation coefficient; Hotelling's multivariate trace criterion
ϕ	Standard normal probability density function
Φ	Measure of association in contingency tables; standard normal cumulative distribution function
χ^2	The chi-square distribution; a statistical test based on the chi-square distribution; the sample value of the chi-square test statistic
Ψ	In statistical hypothesis testing, a statistical contrast

Table 4.5. Statistical Abbreviations and Symbols (continued)

Abbreviation/symbol	Definition
ω^2	Strength of a statistical relationship
Mathematical symbols	
$\lvert a \rvert$	Absolute value of *a*
Σ	Summation

Note. Some forms are used as both abbreviations and symbols. Use the abbreviation form when referring to the concept and the symbol form when specifying a numeric value. As a rule, the symbol form will be either a non-English letter or an italicized version of the English letter form. Most abbreviations can be turned into symbols (for use when reporting numerical estimates) by simply italicizing the abbreviation. In addition, it is acceptable to use the form est(θ) or $\hat{\theta}$ to indicate an estimator or estimate of the parameter θ.

scripts (x_a^2). However, place a superscript such as the symbol for prime right next to its letter or symbol (x'_a). Because APA prefers to align subscripts and superscripts one under the other (*stacking*) for ease of reading instead of setting one to the right of the other (*staggering*), that is how they are normally typeset. If subscripts and superscripts should not be stacked, so indicate in a cover letter or on the manuscript.

Equations

Punctuate all equations, whether they are in the line of text or displayed (i.e., typed on a new line), to conform to their place in the syntax of the sentence (see the period following Equation 3 in section 4.48). If an equation exceeds the column width of a typeset page (approximately 55 characters, including spaces, will fit on one line in most APA journals), the typesetter will break it. For long equations, indicate on the final version of the accepted manuscript where breaks would be acceptable.

4.47 Equations in Text

Place short and simple equations, such as $a = [(1 + b)/x]^{1/2}$, in the line of text. Equations in the line of text should not project above or below the line; for example, the equation above would be difficult to set in the line of text if it were in this form:

$$a = \sqrt{\frac{1+b}{x}}\ .$$

To present fractions in the line of text, use a slanted line (/) and appropriate parentheses, brackets, and braces: Use ( ) first, then [( )], and finally {[( )]}. Use parentheses and brackets to avoid ambiguity: Does $a/b + c$ mean $(a/b) + c$ or $a/(b + c)$?

4.48 Displayed Equations

Display simple equations if they must be numbered for later reference. Display all complex equations. Number all displayed equations consecutively, with the number in parentheses near the right margin of the page:

$$w_j \pm z_{1-\alpha/2}\hat{\sigma}_{w_j}. \tag{3}$$

When referring to numbered equations, write out the reference; for example, write *Equation 3* (do not abbreviate as *Eq. 3*), or write *the third equation.*

4.49 Preparing Statistical and Mathematical Copy

If possible, type all signs and symbols in mathematical copy. Supply as camera-ready copy any special symbols that cannot be produced by a word-processing program. Type fences (i.e., parentheses, brackets, and braces), uppercase and lowercase letters, punctuation, subscripts and superscripts, and all other elements exactly as you want them to appear in the published article. Follow the conventions for the use of symbols, equations, and reporting results presented in the earlier sections of this chapter.

5

Displaying Results

Since the last edition of the *Publication Manual*, few areas have been affected by technological developments more dramatically than the methods available for the display of results of experimentation and inquiry—tables, graphs, charts, maps, drawings, and photographs. Almost all displays are now the results of electronic manipulation of basic data—be it with word-processing programs, spreadsheet programs, statistical packages, or highly specialized software for creating digital images. These changes have greatly increased the flexibility that authors have for effectively displaying results.

Tables and figures enable authors to present a large amount of information efficiently and to make their data more comprehensible. Tables usually show numerical values or textual information (e.g., lists of stimulus words) arranged in an orderly display of columns and rows. A figure may be a chart, a graph, a photograph, a drawing, or any other illustration or nontextual depiction. At times the boundary between tables and figures may be unclear; however, tables are almost always characterized by a row–column structure. Any type of illustration other than a table is referred to as a *figure*.

In this chapter, we discuss the purposes that data displays can serve and provide guidance on designing and preparing data displays so that they communicate most effectively. We provide specific guidance on formatting and constructing tables and figures, along with a number of illustrative examples.

General Guidance on Tables and Figures

5.01 Purposes of Data Displays

Data displays can serve several purposes:

- **exploration:** the data contain a message, and you would like to learn what it is (exploratory data analysis and data mining techniques are examples of displays that are principally exploratory);

- **communication:** you have discovered the meaning contained in the data and want to tell others about it (this is the traditional purpose of most data displays in scientific documents);
- **calculation:** the display allows you to estimate some statistic or function of the data (nomographs are the archetype of this);
- **storage:** you can store data in a display for retrieval later, including the results of a study for later use in a meta-analysis (historically, this role has been fulfilled by tables, but figures sometimes serve this purpose more efficiently); and
- **decoration:** data displays attract attention, and you may choose to use them to make your manuscript more visually appealing (as in newspapers and other media reports).

In scientific publication, the communication function of graphical displays dominates; however, other features (e.g., storage) may be useful in a graphical representation.

5.02 Design and Preparation of a Data Display

The first step in preparing a display for submission is to determine the purposes of the display and the relative importance of those purposes. For example, the detail required for a storage display may conflict with the clarity required for a communicative one. Once you have decided on a display's hierarchy of purposes, choose the template best designed for its primary purpose—the *canonical form* of a display. Such a display (e.g., a scatterplot) has shown itself to be flexible (it works for many kinds of data), robust (it works reasonably well even when it is not exactly suitable), and adaptive (it shows a capacity for adaptation to make it suitable). Further, the use of canonical forms simplifies the task of readers trying to make sense of a display because they can rely on past experience with the form.

The preparation of graphic materials requires careful attention to organization and content. Graphical elements need to be edited with the same care as the textual elements of a manuscript. Changes in text often demand changes in graphical elements, and failure to edit graphical materials and to sharpen the focus of the display is a major shortcoming in much scientific writing.

Design your graphical display with the reader in mind; that is, remember the communicative function of the display.

- Place items that are to be compared next to each other.
- Place labels so that they clearly abut the elements they are labeling.
- Use fonts that are large enough to be read without the use of magnification.
- Include all of the information needed to understand it within the graphical image—avoid novel abbreviations, use table notes, and label graphical elements.
- Keep graphical displays free of extraneous materials, no matter how decorative those materials may make the graphic look.

Communication is the primary purpose of the graphic. This does not mean, however, that well-designed, aesthetically pleasing graphics are not important. An attractive graphical display makes a scientific article a more effective communication device.

5.03 Graphical Versus Textual Presentation

Be selective in choosing how many graphical elements to include in your paper. First, a reader may have difficulty sorting through a large number of tables and figures and may lose track of your message. Second, a disproportionately large number of tables and figures compared with a small amount of text can cause problems with the layout of typeset pages; text that is constantly broken up with tables will be hard for the reader to follow. Third, graphical presentations are not always optimal for effective communication. For example, the results of many standard statistical significance tests can often be effectively presented in text:

> The one-way ANOVA, $F(1, 136) = 4.86$, $MSE = 3.97$, $p = .029$, $\eta^2 = .03$, demonstrated statistically significant differences between the two groups, as theory would dictate.

Information that used to be routinely presented in tables (e.g., analysis of variance [ANOVA] tables) is now routinely presented in text.

5.04 Formatting Tables and Figures

Most manuscripts are now submitted electronically; therefore, all the elements of the manuscript must be in electronic format. These elements may be produced in many different file formats (e.g., .doc, .jpg, .pps, .pdf), and any publisher may limit the formats it accepts. Most tables are constructed with the tables feature of the word-processing program used to generate the manuscript text. However, tables are sometimes cut and pasted from computer outputs (rarely recommended) or may be PDF images created from scans of tables prepared in other ways. When tables are prepared with standard word-processing programs, the text can be converted directly into typographic files, thereby lowering the probability of typesetting errors. Figures are generally submitted in a variety of formats, as is necessitated by the multiple ways in which they are produced. Often, figures such as graphs and charts are initially produced with presentation software such as Microsoft PowerPoint. Photographic elements are generally limited to specific image formats that allow for clear resolution of the image in its printed application. As a rule, figures are reproduced in the print version of articles as they are received from the author (following any editorial changes approved by the editor).

For publishers that offer online supplemental archives, carefully delineate the materials that will appear with the article from those that will be placed in the online supplemental archive (see section 2.13). Because of the relatively high cost of color reproduction, include it only when the color representation adds significantly to the understanding of the material. If color representation is not crucial for immediate understanding, you may consider placing it online as supplemental material.

5.05 Table and Figure Numbers

Number all tables and figures with Arabic numerals in the order in which they are first mentioned in text, regardless of whether a more detailed discussion of the table or figure occurs later in the paper. Do not use suffix letters to number tables and figures; that is, label them as Table 5, Table 6, and Table 7 or Figure 5, Figure 6, and Figure 7 instead of 5, 5a, and 5b. If the manuscript includes an appendix with tables or figures, identify those elements of the appendix with capital letters and Arabic numerals (e.g., Table A1 is the first table of Appendix A or of a sole appendix that is not labeled with a letter; Figure C2 is the second figure of Appendix C).

5.06 Permission to Reproduce Data Displays

If you reproduced or adapted a table, figure, questionnaire, or test item from a copyrighted source, you must obtain written permission for print and electronic reuse from the copyright holder and give credit in the table or figure caption to the original author and copyright holder. A number of commercial instruments—for example, intelligence tests and projective measures—are highly protected. Permission is required, and may be denied, to republish even one item from such instruments. Any reproduced table (or figure) or part thereof must be accompanied by a note at the bottom of the reprinted table (or in the figure caption) giving credit to the original author and to the copyright holder (see section 2.12 for the correct wording of copyright permission footnotes). For detailed information on copyright and permissions, see section 6.10.

Tables

When planning tables for inclusion in a manuscript, determine (a) the data readers will need to understand the discussion and (b) the data necessary to provide the "sufficient set of statistics" (see section 4.44) to support the use of the inferential methods used.

5.07 Conciseness in Tables

Limit the content of your tables to essential materials. Tables with surplus elements are less effective than lean tables. The principle of conciseness is relevant not only for text tables but also for tables to be placed in online supplemental archives. Although supplemental tables may be longer and more detailed than text tables, they must be directly and clearly related to the content of the article (see section 2.13). Tables should be integral to the text but should be designed so that they can be understood in isolation.

5.08 Table Layout

The basic components of a prototypical table are shown in Table 5.1, including the technical term, location, and definition of each element.

Table layout should be logical and easily grasped by the reader. Table entries that are to be compared should be next to one another. Following this principle, in general, different indices (e.g., means, standard deviations, sample sizes) should be segregated into different parts or lines of tables. Position variable and condition labels in close proximity to the values of the variable to facilitate comparison. Table 5.2 illustrates these principles.

All tables are meant to show something specific; for example, tables that communicate quantitative data are effective only when the data are arranged so that their meaning is obvious at a glance (Wainer, 1997). Often, the same data can be arranged in different ways to emphasize different features of the data. In Table 5.3, the same factor loading data are displayed in two different ways. The first example emphasizes the factor structure of the two test batteries by keeping the subscales of the batteries adjacent to each other. The second arrangement of the same data

Table 5.1. Basic Components of a Table

table number → Table X

table title → *Numbers of Children With and Without Proof of Parental Citizenship*

column spanner: heading that identifies the entries in two or more columns in the body of the table

decked heads: heading that is stacked, often to avoid repetition of words in column headings

stub head: heading that identifies the entries in leftmost column

column heads: heading that identifies the entries in just one column in the body of the table

table spanner: heading that covers the entire width of the body of the table, allowing for further divisions

	Girls		Boys	
Grade	With	Without	With	Without
		Wave 1		
3	280	240	281	232
4	297	251	290	264
5	301	260	306	221
Total	878	751	877	717
		Wave 2		
3	201	189	210	199
4	214	194	236	210
5	221	216	239	213
Total	636	599	685	622

Note. General notes to a table appear here, including definitions of abbreviations (see section 5.16).

[a]A specific note appears on a separate line below any general notes; subsequent specific notes are run in (see section 5.16).

*A probability note (*p* value) appears on a separate line below any specific notes; subsequent probability notes are run in (see section 5.16 for more details on content).

cell: point of intersection between a row and a column

stub or stub column: leftmost column of the table; usually lists the major independent or predictor variables

table spanner

table body: rows of cells containing primary data of the table

table note: three types of notes can be placed below the table, which can eliminate repetition from the body of the table

emphasizes the nature of the factors by grouping the subscales of the test batteries according to the pattern of the factor loadings. Which arrangement is better depends on your purpose.

5.09 Standard Forms

Some data tables have certain standard (canonical) forms. The advantage of using the canonical form is that the reader generally knows where to look in the table for certain kinds of information. In some situations, one may want to use a format other than

Table 5.2. Sample of Effective Table Layout

Table X

Proportion of Errors in Younger and Older Groups

	Younger			Older		
Level of difficulty	*n*	*M* (*SD*)	95% CI	*n*	*M* (*SD*)	95% CI
Low	12	.05 (.08)	[.02, .11]	18	.14 (.15)	[.08, .22]
Moderate	15	.05 (.07)	[.02, .10]	12	.17 (.15)	[.08, .28]
High	16	.11 (.10)	[.07, .17]	14	.26 (.21)	[.15, .39]

Note. CI = confidence interval.

the canonical table form to make a specific point or to stress certain relationships. The judicious use of nonstandard forms can be effective but must always be motivated by the special circumstances of the data array. When using nonstandard forms, make certain that labeling is extremely clear because most readers will assume that the canonical form is being used. Section 5.18 includes examples of standard tables for presenting several types of data.

5.10 Relation of Tables and Text

Discussing tables in text. An informative table supplements—rather than duplicates—the text. In the text, refer to every table and tell the reader what to look for. Discuss only the table's highlights; if you find yourself discussing every item of the table in the text, the table is unnecessary. Similarly, if additional tables are to be included in online supplemental archives, mention their existence only briefly in the print version of the article. Tables designated as supplemental materials must be accompanied by enough information to be completely understood on their own (see section 2.13).

Citing tables. In the text, refer to tables by their number:

> as shown in Table 8, the responses were provided by children with pretraining . . .

Do not write "the table above" (or below) or "the table on page 32," because the position and page number of a table cannot be determined until the pages are typeset.

5.11 Relation Between Tables

Consider combining tables that repeat data. Ordinarily, identical columns or rows of data should not appear in two or more tables. Be consistent in the presentations of all tables within a manuscript to facilitate comparisons. Use similar formats, titles, and headings, and use the same terminology throughout (e.g., *response time* or *reaction time*, not both).

Table 5.3. Sample Factor Loadings Table (With Rotation Method Specified)
The following table is formatted to emphasize the structure of the test batteries.

Table X

Factor Loadings for Exploratory Factor Analysis With Varimax Rotation of Personality Pathology Scales

Scale	Introversion	Emotional Dysregulation	Peculiarity
SPQ Constricted Affect	**.77**	.33	.21
Excessive Social Anxiety	**.43**	**.52**	.29
Ideas of Reference	−.08	.17	**.67**
No Friends	**.84**	.19	.13
Odd Beliefs	−.03	.13	**.50**
Odd Behavior	.23	.19	**.56**
Odd Speech	.15	.34	**.56**
Unusual Perceptions	.09	.14	**.76**
DAPP Submissiveness	.24	**.70**	.11
Cognitive Distortion	.26	**.70**	.36
Identity Problems	**.52**	**.58**	.16
Affective Lability	.11	**.73**	.34
Restricted Expression	**.69**	.31	.02
Passive Oppositionality	.25	**.70**	.12
Intimacy Problems	**.63**	.18	.03
Anxiousness	.24	**.83**	.18
Conduct Problems	.27	.10	.24
Suspiciousness	.39	.36	.23
Social Avoidance	**.59**	**.67**	.10
Insecure Attachment	.04	**.58**	.26
Self-Harm	.30	.38	.28
Chapman Magical Ideation	.12	.17	**.72**
Social Anhedonia	**.78**	.04	.26
Perceptual Aberrations	.12	.25	**.49**
Physical Anhedonia	**.61**	.05	−.15

Note. Factor loadings > .40 are in boldface. SPQ = Schizotypal Personality Questionnaire; DAPP = Dimensional Assessment of Personality Pathology—Basic Questionnaire.

(continued)

Table 5.3. Sample Factor Loadings Table (continued)
The following table is formatted to emphasize the structure of the factors.

Table X

Factor Loadings for Exploratory Factor Analysis With Varimax Rotation of Personality Pathology Scales

Scale	Introversion	Emotional Dysregulation	Peculiarity
SPQ No Friends	**.84**	.19	.13
Chapman Social Anhedonia	**.78**	.04	.26
SPQ Constricted Affect	**.77**	.33	.21
DAPP Restricted Expression	**.69**	.31	.02
DAPP Intimacy Problems	**.63**	.18	.03
Chapman Physical Anhedonia	**.61**	.05	–.15
DAPP Social Avoidance	**.59**	**.67**	.10
DAPP Identity Problems	**.52**	**.58**	.16
SPQ Excessive Social Anxiety	**.43**	**.52**	.29
DAPP Anxiousness	.24	**.83**	.18
DAPP Affective Lability	.11	**.73**	.34
DAPP Cognitive Distortion	.26	**.70**	.36
DAPP Passive Oppositionality	.25	**.70**	.12
DAPP Submissiveness	.24	**.70**	.11
DAPP Insecure Attachment	.04	**.58**	.26
DAPP Self-Harm	.30	.38	.28
SPQ Unusual Perceptions	.09	.14	**.76**
Chapman Magical Ideation	.12	.17	**.72**
SPQ Ideas of Reference	–.08	.17	**.67**
SPQ Odd Speech	.15	.34	**.56**
SPQ Odd Behavior	.23	.19	**.56**
SPQ Odd Beliefs	–.03	.13	**.50**
Chapman Perceptual Aberrations	.12	.25	**.49**
DAPP Suspiciousness	.39	.36	.23
DAPP Conduct Problems	.27	.10	.24

Note. Factor loadings > .40 are in boldface. SPQ = Schizotypal Personality Questionnaire; DAPP = Dimensional Assessment of Personality Pathology—Basic Questionnaire. Adapted from "A Dimensional Model of Personality Disorder: Incorporating *DSM* Cluster A Characteristics," by J. L. Tackett, A. L. Silberschmidt, R. F. Krueger, and S. R. Sponheim, 2008, *Journal of Abnormal Psychology, 117,* p. 457. Copyright 2008 by the American Psychological Association.

5.12 Table Titles

Give every table a brief but clear and explanatory title. The basic content of the table should be easily inferred from the title.

Too general:

Table 1

Relation Between College Majors and Performance [It is unclear what data are presented in the table.]

Too detailed:

Table 1

Mean Performance Scores on Test A, Test B, and Test C of Students With Psychology, Physics, English, and Engineering Majors [This duplicates information in the headings of the table.]

Good title:

Mean Performance Scores of Students With Different College Majors

Abbreviations that appear in the headings or the body of a table sometimes can be parenthetically explained in the table title.

Hit and False-Alarm (FA) Proportions in Experiment 2

Explain abbreviations that require longer explanations or that do not relate to the table title in a general note to the table (see section 5.16 and Table 5.2). Do not use a specific footnote to clarify an element of the title.

5.13 Table Headings

A table classifies related items and enables the reader to compare them. Data form the body of the table. Headings establish your organization of the data and identify the columns of data beneath them. Like a table title, a heading should be brief and should not be many more characters in length than the widest entry.

Poor:

Grade level
3
4
5

Better:

Grade
3
4
5

You may use standard abbreviations and symbols for nontechnical terms (e.g., *no.* for *number*, % for *percent*) and for statistics (e.g., *M*, *SD*, χ^2, or any other abbreviation in Table 4.4) in table headings without explanation. Abbreviations of technical terms, group names, and the like must be explained in the table title or in a note to the table (see section 5.12). Abbreviations may also be explained parenthetically following entries in the stub column.

Each column of a table must have a heading, including the *stub column* or *stub*, which is the leftmost column of the table (see Table 5.1 for illustration of technical terms). Subordination within the stub is easier to comprehend if you indent the stub items rather than create an additional column (e.g., Tables 5.4 and 5.5). The stub usually lists the major independent or predictor variables. In Table 5.1, for instance, the stub lists the grades. Number elements only when they appear in a correlation matrix (see Table 5.6) or if they are referred to by number in text.

All headings identify items below them, not across from them. The headings just above the body of the table (called *column heads* and *column spanners*) identify the entries in the vertical columns in the body of the table. A column head covers just one column; a column spanner covers two or more columns, each with its own column

Table 5.4. Sample Table With Detailed Specifications of Complex Experimental Designs

Table X

Summary of Experimental Designs

Group	Stage I	Stage II	Test
Experiment 1			
Block	A+	AB+ CD+	B vs. D
Unblock intensity	A+	AB**+** CD**+**	
Unblock number	A+	AB++ CD++	
Experiment 2	A+ C+	AB+	AD vs. BC
Experiment 3	A+ B**+** C+ D++		AD vs. BC A, B, C, D
Experiment 4a	A+ C+	AB**+**	AD vs. BC
Experiment 4b	A+ C+	AB++	AD vs. BC
Experiment 5	A+ C+	AB**+** CD++	AD vs. BC A, B, C, D

Note. A, B, C, and D were four conditioned stimuli: a clicker, tone, light, and flashing light, respectively (counterbalanced). + denotes a 0.4-mA shock unconditioned stimulus; ++ denotes two 0.4-mA shocks; **+** denotes a 0.8-mA unconditioned stimulus. Adapted from "Unblocking in Pavlovian Fear Conditioning," by L. Bradfield and G. P. McNally, 2008, *Journal of Experimental Psychology: Animal Behavior Processes, 34,* p. 259. Copyright 2008 by the American Psychological Association.

Table 5.5. Sample Table Display of a Sample's Characteristics

Table X

Individual and Family Characteristics as a Percentage of the Sample (Census Data in Parentheses)

Characteristic	Mother (n = 750)		Father (n = 466)		Child (n = 750)	
Self-identity						
Mexican	77.2		71.0		41.0	
Mexican American	22.8		29.0		59.0	
Nativity[a]						
Mexico	74.2	(38.2)	80.0	(44.2)	29.7	
United States	25.8	(61.8)	20.0	(55.8)	70.3	
Language preference[b]						
English	30.2	(52.7)	23.2	(52.7)	82.5	(70.0)
Spanish	69.8	(48.3)	76.8	(48.3)	17.5	(30.0)
Education level completed[a]						
8th grade or less	29.2	(30.7)	30.2	(33.4)		
Some high school	19.5	(20.9)	22.4	(22.6)		
12th grade	23.1	(22.5)	20.9	(20.7)		
Some college/vocational training	22.0	(19.2)	20.2	(17.1)		
Bachelor's or higher	6.2	(6.8)	6.2	(6.2)		
Employment status[c]						
Employed	63.6	(46.6)	96.6	(97.1)		
Unemployed	11.2	(3.5)	3.5	(2.9)		
Housewife	25.2					

Note. Adapted from "Sampling and Recruitment in Studies of Cultural Influences on Adjustment: A Case Study With Mexican Americans," by M. W. Roosa, F. F. Liu, M. Torres, N. A. Gonzales, G. P. Knight, and D. Saenz, 2008, *Journal of Family Psychology, 22,* p. 300. Copyright 2008 by the American Psychological Association.

[a]Census data are for all women or men and are not limited to parents or adults in our age group. [b]The most comparable census data for mothers and fathers are for all adults 18 and older and for children are for 15- to 17-year-olds. [c]Census data are for all women, not just mothers, whereas the male data are limited to husbands.

head. Headings stacked in this way are called *decked heads.* Often decked heads can be used to avoid repetition of words in column heads (see Table 5.1). If possible, do not use more than two levels of decked heads.

Incorrect:

Temporal lobe:	Left	Right

Wordy:

Left temporal lobe	Right temporal lobe

Correct:

Temporal lobe	
Left	Right

Table 5.6. Sample Table of Correlations in Which the Values for Two Samples Are Presented

Table X

Summary of Intercorrelations, Means, and Standard Deviations for Scores on the BSS, BDI, SAFE, and MEIM as a Function of Race

Measure	*1*	*2*	*3*	*4*	*M*	*SD*
1. BSS	—	.54*	.29*	−.23*	1.31	4.32
2. BDI	.54*	—	.34*	−.14*	8.33	7.76
3. SAFE	.19*	.30*	—	−.074	47.18	13.24
4. MEIM	−.09	−.11	−.08	—	47.19	6.26
M	1.50	9.13	39.07	37.78		
SD	3.84	7.25	13.17	7.29		

Note. Intercorrelations for African American participants ($n = 296$) are presented above the diagonal, and intercorrelations for European American participants ($n = 163$) are presented below the diagonal. Means and standard deviations for African American students are presented in the vertical columns, and means and standard deviations for European Americans are presented in the horizontal rows. For all scales, higher scores are indicative of more extreme responding in the direction of the construct assessed. BSS = Beck Suicide Scale; BDI = Beck Depression Inventory; SAFE = Societal, Attitudinal, Familial, and Environmental Acculturative Stress Scale; MEIM = Multigroup Ethnic Identity Measure. Adapted from "An Empirical Investigation of Acculturative Stress and Ethnic Identity as Moderators for Depression and Suicidal Ideation in College Students," by R. L. Walker, L. R. Wingate, E. M. Obasi, and T. E. Joiner, 2008, *Cultural Diversity and Ethnic Minority Psychology, 14,* p. 78. Copyright 2008 by the American Psychological Association.
*$p < .01$.

A few tables may require *table spanners* in the body of the table. These table spanners cover the entire width of the body of the table, allowing for further divisions within the table (see Tables 5.1 and 5.15). Also, table spanners can be used to combine two tables provided they have identical column heads.

Any item within a column should be syntactically as well as conceptually comparable with the other items in that column, and all items should be described by the column head:

Nonparallel:

Condition
Functional psychotic
Drinks to excess
Character disorder

Parallel:

Condition
Functional psychosis
Alcoholism
Character disorder

Stub heads, column heads, and column spanners should be singular unless they refer to groups (e.g., *Children*), but table spanners may be plural. Capitalize only the first letter of the first word of all headings (column heads, column spanners, stub

Table 5.7. Sample Table of Results of Fitting Mathematical Models

Table X

Estimates [and 95% Confidence Intervals] for the Parameters of the Simplified Conjoint Recognition Model for Experiment 5

	List condition				
Parameter	Target-first	Target-last	Control	$\Delta G^2_{(df=2)}$	*p*
a	.43 [.30, .57]	.28 [.16, .40]	.24 [.10, .38]	4.26	.12
b	.26 [.19, .32]	.27 [.21, .33]	.19 [.13, .24]	4.68	.10
G_t	.29 [.00, .63]	.38 [.14, .63]	.28 [.03, .53]	0.39	.82
G_r	.43 [.19, .67]	.70 [.55, .84]	.72 [.56, .88]	4.86	.09
V_t	.89 [.83, .94]	.81 [.75, .87]	.86 [.80, .91]	3.20	.20
V_r	$.72_a$ [61, .82]	$.05_b$ [.00, .42]	$.23_b$ [.00, .62]	20.89	<.01

Note. Parameter estimates in each row that share subscripts do not differ significantly. *a* = probability of guessing "target"; *b* = probability of guessing that an item is either a target or a related probe; G_t = probability of retrieving a target's gist trace given a target probe; G_r = probability of retrieving a target's gist trace given a related probe; V_t = probability of retrieving a target's verbatim trace given a target probe; V_r = probability of retrieving a target's verbatim trace given a related probe. Adapted from "A Simplified Conjoint Recognition Paradigm for the Measurement of Gist and Verbatim Memory," by C. Stahl and K. C. Klauer, 2008, *Journal of Experimental Psychology: Learning, Memory, and Cognition, 34,* p. 579. Copyright 2008 by the American Psychological Association.

heads, and table spanners) and word entries. Also, capitalize the first letter of each word of all proper nouns and the first word following a colon or em dash.

5.14 Table Body

Decimal values. The table body contains the data. Express numerical values to the number of decimal places that the precision of measurement justifies (see section 4.35), and if possible, carry all comparable values to the same number of decimal places.

Empty cells. If the point of intersection between a row and a column (called a *cell*) cannot be filled because data are not applicable, leave the cell blank. If a cell cannot be filled because data were not obtained or are not reported, insert a dash in that cell and explain the use of the dash in the general note to the table. By convention, a dash in the main diagonal position of a correlation matrix (see Table 5.6) indicates the correlation of an item with itself, which must be 1.00, and is simply replaced by the dash. If you need to explain that an element of a table is unavailable or inapplicable, use a specific note rather than a dash (see section 5.16).

Conciseness. Be selective in your presentation. Do not include columns of data that can be calculated easily from other columns:

Not concise:

	No. responses			
Participant	First trial	Second trial	Total	*M*
1	5	7	12	6

The example could be improved by giving either the number of responses per trial or the total number of responses, whichever is more important to the discussion, and by not including the column with the mean because its calculation is simple.

5.15 Confidence Intervals in Tables

When a table includes point estimates, for example, means, correlations, or regression slopes, it should also, where possible, include confidence intervals. You may report confidence intervals in tables either by using brackets, as in text (see section 4.10) and in Table 5.8, or by giving lower and upper limits in separate columns, as in Table 5.9. In every table that includes confidence intervals, state the confidence level, for example, 95%. It is usually best to use the same confidence level throughout a paper.

5.16 Table Notes

Tables may have three kinds of notes placed below the body of the table: general notes, specific notes, and probability notes.

A *general note* qualifies, explains, or provides information relating to the table as a whole and ends with an explanation of any abbreviations, symbols, and the like. Included within general notes would be any acknowledgments that a table is reproduced from another source. General notes are designated by the word *Note* (italicized) followed by a period. (See Tables 5.1 and 5.4, among others.)

> *Note*. Factor loadings greater than .45 are shown in boldface. M = match process; N = nonmatch process.

A *specific note* refers to a particular column, row, or cell. Specific notes are indicated by superscript lowercase letters (e.g., [a, b, c]). Within the headings and table body, order the superscripts from left to right and from top to bottom, starting at the top left.

Table notes, general or specific, apply only to that specific table and not to any other table. Begin each table's first footnote with a superscript lowercase *a* (see Table 5.5).

> [a]$n = 25$. [b]This participant did not complete the trials.

Table 5.8. Sample Table Including Confidence Intervals With Brackets

Table X

Weight Status, Body Dissatisfaction, and Weight Control Behaviors at Time 1 and Suicidal Ideation at Time 2

	Unadjusted[a]		Adjusted for demographic variables[b]	
Variable	*OR*	95% CI	*OR*	95% CI
Weight status				
Young men	0.97	[0.78, 1.21]	0.94	[0.75, 1.19]
Young women	1.06	[0.88, 1.26]	1.02	[0.85, 1.23]
Body dissatisfaction				
Young men	0.88	[0.50, 1.54]	0.99	[0.56, 1.75]
Young women	1.06	[0.77, 1.46]	1.02	[0.74, 1.42]
UWCB				
Young men	0.81	[0.54, 1.24]	0.77	[0.50, 1.19]
Young women	0.89	[0.65, 1.21]	0.93	[0.68, 1.27]
EWCB				
Young men	1.36	[0.55, 3.36]	1.73	[0.69, 4.37]
Young women	1.98	[1.34, 2.93]	2.00	[1.34, 2.99]

Note. OR = odds ratio; CI = confidence interval; UWCB = unhealthy weight control behaviors; EWCB = extreme weight control behaviors. Adapted from "Are Body Dissatisfaction, Eating Disturbance, and Body Mass Index Predictors of Suicidal Behavior in Adolescents? A Longitudinal Study," by S. Crow, M. E. Eisenberg, M. Story, and D. Neumark-Sztainer, 2008, *Journal of Consulting and Clinical Psychology, 76,* p. 890. Copyright 2008 by the American Psychological Association.
[a]Four weight-related variables entered simultaneously. [b]Adjusted for race, socioeconomic status, and age group.

A *probability note* indicates how asterisks and other symbols are used in a table to indicate *p* values and thus the results of tests of statistical hypothesis testing. For results of statistical significance testing in text and tables, report the exact probabilities to two or three decimal places (e.g., $p = .023$ as opposed to $p < .05$; see Table 5.7 and section 4.35). When displaying the result in graphical modes (including certain tables such as tables of correlation matrices), it may be difficult to follow this recommendation without making the graphic unruly. Therefore, when displaying results graphically, revert to reporting in the "$p <$" style if using exact probabilities would make it difficult to comprehend the graphic. When discussing the results in the text, use exact probabilities regardless of the display mode. Include a probability note only when relevant to specific data within the table.

If the "$p <$" style is required, asterisks indicate ranges of *p* values. Assign the same number of asterisks from table to table within your paper, such as $^{*}p < .05$, $^{**}p < .01$, and $^{***}p < .001$. Do not use any value smaller than $^{***}p < .001$.

Table 5.9. Sample Table Including Confidence Intervals With Upper and Lower Limits

Table X

Estimated Distance (cm) for Letter and Digit Stimuli

		95% CI	
Condition	*M* (*SD*)	*LL*	*UL*
Letters	14.5 (28.6)	5.4	23.6
Digits	31.8 (33.2)	21.2	42.4

Note. CI = confidence interval; *LL* = lower limit, *UL* = upper limit.

If you need to distinguish between one-tailed and two-tailed tests in the same table, use an asterisk for the two-tailed p values and an alternate symbol (e.g., dagger) for the one-tailed p values.

> *$p < .05$, two-tailed. **$p < .01$, two-tailed. †$p < .05$, one-tailed.
> ††$p < .01$, one-tailed.

To indicate statistically significant differences between two or more table entries—for example, means that are compared with procedures such as a Tukey test—use lowercase subscripts (see Table 5.7). Explain the use of the subscripts in the table note (see the following sample table notes).

> *Note.* Means sharing a common subscript are not statistically different at $\alpha = .01$ according to the Tukey HSD procedure.

Order the notes to a table in the following sequence: general note, specific note, probability note (see Table 5.1).

> *Note.* The participants . . . responses.
> [a]$n = 25$. [b]$n = 42$.
> *$p < .05$. **$p < .01$.

Each type of note begins flush left (i.e., no paragraph indentation) on a new line below the table. The first specific note begins flush left on a new line under the general note; subsequent specific notes are run in (lengthy specific notes may be set on separate lines when typeset). The first probability note begins flush left on a new line; subsequent probability notes are run in.

Notes can be useful for eliminating repetition from the body of a table. Certain types of information may be appropriate either in the table or in a note. To determine the placement of such material, remember that clearly and efficiently organized data enable the reader to focus on the data. Thus, if probability values or subsample sizes are numerous, use a column rather than many notes. Conversely, if a row or column contains few entries (or the same entry), eliminate the column by adding a note to the table:

Poor:

Group	n
Anxious	15
Depressed	15
Control	15

Better:

Group[a]
Anxious
Depressed
Control

[a]$n = 15$

5.17 Ruling of Tables

Limit the use of *rules* (i.e., lines) in a table to those that are necessary for clarity. Appropriately positioned white space can be an effective substitute for rules; for example, long, uninterrupted columns of numbers or words are more readable if a horizontal line of space is inserted after every fourth or fifth entry. In the manuscript, use spacing between columns and rows and strict alignment to clarify relationships within a table.

Tables may be submitted either single- or double-spaced. Consider the readability of the table during the review process in making your decision.

5.18 Presenting Data in Specific Types of Tables

Complex experimental designs can be summarized in compact tables, making the entire structure of the experiment clear without the need for lengthy textual descriptions (see Table 5.4).

Important characteristics of a sample can be concisely summarized in a well-organized table. Providing comparable census data can help the reader understand the generalizability of the results (see Table 5.5).

Key psychometric properties of the major variables can be easily summarized in a table (see Table 5.10). Clearly state the index of reliability (or other psychometric property) being used and the sample on which the reliability was based (if different from the study sample).

Table 5.11 shows one-degree-of-freedom within-subject contrasts within a larger set of effects, including both confidence intervals and effect sizes. In Table 5.6, note the compact, yet information-packed, form in which the intercorrelations among the variables for two different groups are presented in the same table—one group below the main diagonal, the other above the main diagonal. Means and standard deviations for the two groups are similarly positioned, with the Group 1 means and standard deviations given in the last two data columns and those for Group 2 in the last two data rows. Construction of a correlation matrix of this type not only is concise in terms of the amount of page space used but also makes the visual comparison of correlational elements much easier.

Clearly label the type of regression (e.g., hierarchical) and type of regression coefficients (raw or standardized) being reported (see Tables 5.12 and 5.13). For hierarchical and other sequential regressions, be sure to provide the increments of change (see section 4.44).

In model-comparison tables, ensure that the competing models are clearly identified and that the comparisons are clearly specified. Comparative fit indices can be useful for the reader (see Tables 5.14 and 5.15).

Table 5.10. Sample Table Display of Psychometric Properties of Key Outcome Variables

Table X

Psychometric Properties of the Major Study Variables

					Range		
Variable	*n*	*M*	*SD*	α	Potential	Actual	Skew
Dispositional affectivity							
Positive	560	3.27	0.77	.91	1–5	1.0–5.0	−0.36
Negative	563	2.26	0.79	.91	1–5	1.0–4.7	0.63
Social support							
Mother	160	4.17	1.08	.92	1–5	1.0–5.0	−1.54
Partner	474	4.03	1.19	.94	1–5	1.0–5.0	−1.26
Friend	396	4.37	0.89	.90	1–5	1.0–5.0	−1.94
Social conflict							
Mother	159	1.22	0.47	.81	1–5	1.0–3.6	3.07
Partner	471	1.40	0.79	.90	1–5	1.0–5.0	2.63
Friend	381	1.15	0.45	.79	1–5	1.0–5.0	5.27
Postabortion adjustment							
Distress	609	0.59	0.63	.90	0–4	0.0–3.0	1.56
Well-being	606	4.60	0.69	.85	1–6	2.3–6.0	−0.53

Note. The variation in *sample size* is due to the variation in the number of women who told a particular source about the abortion. Adapted from "Mixed Messages: Implications of Social Conflict and Social Support Within Close Relationships for Adjustment to a Stressful Life Event," by B. Major, J. M. Zubek, M. L. Cooper, C. Cozzarelli, and C. Richards, 1997, *Journal of Personality and Social Psychology, 76,* p. 1355. Copyright 1997 by the American Psychological Association.

The two illustrative samples in Table 5.3 demonstrate how table formatting can be varied depending on the emphasis desired. Tables may contain entries other than just numerals (e.g., text; see Table 5.16) as long as the basic row by column structure is maintained.

Table 5.11. Sample Table of One-Degree-of-Freedom Statistical Contrasts

Table X

Contrast of Time 1 With Time 2 For Exhaustion-Only Group That Changed Toward Burnout

	Time 1		Time 2				95% CI		Cohen's
Variable	*M*	*SD*	*M*	*SD*	*t*(34)	*p*	*LL*	*UL*	*d*
Workload	2.79	0.89	2.61	0.66	1.61	.12	–0.06	0.42	0.72
Control	3.60	0.83	3.13	1.18	1.91	.06	–0.05	0.98	0.85
Reward	3.58	0.82	3.26	0.62	1.68	.10	–0.08	0.70	0.75
Community	3.75	0.79	3.21	1.01	2.96	.006	0.16	0.92	1.32
Fairness	2.77	0.65	2.32	0.97	2.33	.03	0.05	0.85	1.04
Values	3.25	0.78	2.65	0.93	3.70	<.001	0.26	0.94	1.65
Exhaustion	3.16	0.96	3.62	0.95	–2.08	.05	–0.92	0.00	–0.93
Cynicism	0.92	0.38	3.30	1.05	–8.71	<.001	–2.95	–1.81	–3.89
Efficacy	4.54	1.08	4.38	1.25	0.51	.61	–0.49	0.80	0.23

Note. CI = confidence interval; *LL* = lower limit; *UL* = upper limit. Adapted from "Early Predictors of Job Burnout and Engagement," by C. Maslach and M. Leiter, 2008, *Journal of Applied Psychology, 93,* p. 509. Copyright 2008 by the American Psychological Association.

Table 5.12. Sample Regression Table

Table X

Predictors of Self-Reported Moral Behavior

Variable	Self-reported moral behavior		
		Model 2	
	Model 1 *B*	*B*	95% CI
Constant	3.192**	2.99**	[2.37, 3.62]
Gender	0.18*	0.17	[–0.00, 0.33]
Age	–0.06	–0.05	[–0.14, 0.03]
Social desirability bias	–0.08**	–0.08**	[–0.10, –0.05]
Moral identity internalization	–0.17**	–0.16**	[–0.26, –0.06]
Moral identity symbolization	0.07*	0.06	[–0.01, 0.12]
Perceptual moral attentiveness		0.07*	[0.00, 0.13]
Reflective moral attentiveness		–0.01	[–0.08, 0.06]
R^2	.29	.31	
F	19.07**	14.46**	
ΔR^2		.01	
ΔF		2.39	

Note. N = 242. CI = confidence interval. Adapted from "Moral Attentiveness: Who Pays Attention to the Moral Aspects of Life?" by S. J. Reynolds, 2008, *Journal of Applied Psychology, 93,* p. 1035. Copyright 2008 by the American Psychological Association.
*$p < .05$. **$p < .01$.

Table 5.13. Sample Hierarchical Multiple Regression Table

Table X

Hierarchical Multiple Regression Analyses Predicting Postabortion Positive Well-Being From Preabortion Social Support and Preabortion Social Conflict With Mother, Partner, and Friend

	Source of social support and social conflict					
	Mother		Partner		Friend	
Predictor	ΔR^2	β	ΔR^2	β	ΔR^2	β
Step 1	.13*		.10***		.10***	
Control variables[a]						
Step 2	.16***		.19***		.22***	
Positive affect		.31***		.32***		.35***
Negative affect		–.25***		–.27***		–.30***
Step 3	.02		.05***		.01*	
Social support		.17*		.17***		.08†
Social conflict		.09		–.08		–.06
Step 4	.01		.00		.00	
Social Support × Social Conflict		–.14		–.00		–.07
Total R^2	.32***		.33***		.34***	
n	153		455		373	

Note. Adapted from "Mixed Messages: Implications of Social Conflict and Social Support Within Close Relationships for Adjustment to a Stressful Life Event," by B. Major, J. M. Zubek, M. L. Cooper, C. Cozzarelli, and C. Richards, 1997, *Journal of Personality and Social Psychology, 72,* p. 1359. Copyright 1997 by the American Psychological Association.
[a]Control variables included age, race, education, marital status, religion, abortion history, depression history, and prior mental health counseling.
†$p < .10$. *$p < .05$. ***$p < .001$.

Table 5.14. Sample Model Comparison Table

Table X

Fit Indices for Nested Sequence of Cross-Sectional Models

Model	χ^2	NFI	PFI	χ^2_{diff}	NFI
1. Mobley's (1977) measurement model	443.18*	.92	.67		
2. Quit & search intentions	529.80*	.89	.69		
Difference between Model 2 and Model 1				86.61*	.03
3. Search intentions & thoughts of quitting	519.75*	.90	.69		
Difference between Model 3 and Model 1				76.57*	.02
4. Intentions to quit & thoughts of quitting	546.97*	.89	.69		
Difference between Model 4 and Model 1				103.78*	.03
5. One withdrawal cognition	616.97*	.87	.70		
Difference between Model 5 and Model 1				173.79*	.05
6. Hom, Griffeth, & Sallaro's (1984) structural model	754.37*	.84	.71		
Difference between Model 6 and Model 5				137.39*	.03
7. Structural null model	2,741.49*	.23	.27		
Difference between Model 7 and Model 6				1,987.13*	.61
8. Null model	3,849.07*				

Note. NFI = normed fit index; PFI = parsimonious fit index. Adapted from "Structural Equations Modeling Test of a Turnover Theory: Cross-Sectional and Longitudinal Analyses," by P. W. Hom and R. W. Griffeth, 1991, *Journal of Applied Psychology, 76,* p. 356. Copyright 1991 by the American Psychological Association.
$^*p < .05$.

Table 5.15. Sample Multilevel Model Table

Table X

Fixed Effects Estimates (Top) and Variance–Covariance Estimates (Bottom) for Models of the Predictors of Positive Parenting

Parameter	Model 1	Model 2	Model 3	Model 4	Model 5
			Fixed effects		
Intercept	12.51 (0.04)	12.23 (0.07)	12.23 (0.07)	12.23 (0.07)	12.64 (0.11)
Level 1 (child-specific)					
Age		–0.49* (0.02)	–0.48* (0.02)	–0.48* (0.02)	–0.48* (0.02)
Age^2		0.06* (0.01)	0.06* (0.01)	0.06* (0.01)	0.06* (0.01)
Negative affectivity		–0.56* (0.08)	–0.53* (0.08)	–0.57* (0.09)	–0.57* (0.09)
Girl		0.05 (0.05)	0.05 (0.05)	0.04 (0.05)	0.07 (0.05)
Not bio. mother		–0.34 (0.26)	–0.28 (0.26)	–0.28 (0.26)	–0.30 (0.28)
Not bio. father		–0.34* (0.10)	–0.31* (0.10)	–0.30* (0.10)	–0.29 (0.15)
Oldest sibling		0.38* (0.07)	0.37* (0.07)	0.37* (0.07)	0.36* (0.07)
Middle sibling		–0.36* (0.06)	–0.34* (0.06)	–0.35* (0.06)	–0.28* (0.06)
Level 2 (family)					
SES					0.18* (0.06)
Marital dissatisfaction					–0.43* (0.14)
Family size					–0.41* (0.08)
Single parent					0.09 (0.19)
All-girl sibship					–0.20 (0.13)
Mixed-gender sibship					–0.25* (0.10)
			Random parameters		
Level 2					
Intercept/intercept (σ^2_{a0})	5.13* (0.17)	4.87* (0.15)	4.92* (0.15)	4.86* (0.15)	4.79* (0.14)
Age/age (σ^2_{a1})			0.09* (0.01)	0.09* (0.01)	0.09* (0.01)

(continued)

Table 5.15. Sample Multilevel Model Table (continued)

Parameter	Model 1	Model 2	Model 3	Model 4	Model 5
Age/intercept (σ^2_{a10})			–0.04 (0.03)	–0.05 (0.03)	–0.05 (0.03)
Neg. affect/neg. affect (σ^2_{a3})				1.51* (0.46)	1.51* (0.46)
Neg. affect/ intercept (σ^2_{a30})				–0.03 (0.20)	–0.02 (0.20)
Neg. affect/ age (σ^2_{a31})				0.00 (0.05)	–0.00 (0.05)
Level 1					
Intercept/ intercept (w_0)	3.80* (0.08)	2.74* (0.06)	2.30* (0.07)	2.19* (0.07)	2.18* (0.07)
–2*log likelihood	38,369.7	37,001.9	36,919.6	36,899.8	36,849.4

Note. Standard errors are in parentheses. Not bio. mother = not living with the biological mother; Not bio. father = not living with the biological father; SES = socioeconomic status; Neg. affect = negative affectivity. Adapted from "The Role of the Shared Family Context in Differential Parenting," by J. M. Jenkins, J. Rasbash, and T. G. O'Connor, 2003, *Developmental Psychology, 39,* p. 104. Copyright 2003 by the American Psychological Association.
$^*p < .05$.

Table 5.16. Sample Word Table

Table X

Inductively Developed Thematic Categories

Category	Thematic category	Key terms	Characteristic Level 3 responses
Family traditionalism			Q1. How "should" husbands wives, and children act? What is the "right way" to act? What are certain family members supposed to do?
F1	Macho privilege	Man, woman, say, house OR mother	The husband is the one who gives "orders." The wife never says what she feels. The children should "obey," no matter what.
F2	Family trust and respect	Respect OR trust OR work OR help	Always share everything equally and there should be respect among everyone/ between couples and children.
F3	Family unity	Family OR unity	Above all, there should be family unity.
F4	Values traditions	Tradition OR continue OR important	If she is a true believer, she should always participate in the traditions.
Rural lifestyle			Q2. Many "traditional" people like Maria believe that life in a small rural town is better than life in a big city. Please tell me some of these beliefs.
R1	Small town life is better	Small town OR everybody knows each other	Because there is so much violence in the big city. . . . You know your town and people and you trust each other like family.
R2	Big city opportunities	Live OR believe OR big cities OR better	Better to live in a big city because there are more jobs and educational opportunities.
R3	Rural tranquility	Life OR less stress OR rural	I agree that life in a small town is better because in a small town life is more peaceful.
			There is less gang activity and overall life is more peaceful.
R4	It depends	It depends OR more opportunities OR the city	Sometimes it is true that rural life is better. However, it's also true that a big city can help you or can destroy you; that depends on you.

Note. Adapted from "Traditions and Alcohol Use: A Mixed-Methods Analysis," by F. G. Castro and K. Coe, 2007, *Cultural Diversity and Ethnic Minority Psychology, 13,* p. 276. Copyright 2007 by the American Psychological Association.

5.19 Table Checklist

The following checklist may help ensure that the data in your table are effectively presented and conform to the style rules presented in this chapter.

Table Checklist

- ☐ Is the table necessary?
- ☐ Does it belong in the print version of the article, or can it go in an online supplemental file?
- ☐ Are all comparable tables in the manuscript consistent in presentation?
- ☐ Is the title brief but explanatory?
- ☐ Does every column have a column head?
- ☐ Are all abbreviations explained, as well as special use of italics, parentheses, dashes, boldface, and special symbols?
- ☐ Are the notes in the following order: general note, specific note, probability note?
- ☐ Are all vertical rules eliminated?
- ☐ Are confidence intervals reported for all major point estimates? Is the confidence level—for example, 95%—stated, and is the same level of confidence used for all tables and throughout the paper?
- ☐ If statistical significance testing is used, are all probability level values correctly identified? Are asterisks attached to the appropriate table entries only when needed (as opposed to stating exact probabilities)? When used, is a probability level assigned the same number of asterisks in all tables in the same paper?
- ☐ If all or part of a copyrighted table is reproduced or adapted, do the table notes give full credit to the copyright owner? Have you received written permission for reuse (in print and electronic form) from the copyright holder and sent a copy of that written permission to the journal editor with the final version of your paper?
- ☐ Is the table referred to in text?

Figures

5.20 Principles of Figure Use and Construction

There are many different types of figures; however, certain principles are the same for all figure types. The first consideration is the information value of the figure in the context of the paper in which it is to appear. If the figure does not add substantively to the understanding of the paper or duplicates other elements of the paper, it should not be included. A second consideration is whether a figure is the best way to communicate the information. In some cases (particularly when quantitative information is being conveyed), a table may offer more precision than, say, a graph. A third consideration is the degree to which the figure can be produced in a way that captures the essential information features desired without visually distracting detail. When considering inclusion of a figure, always remember that the information value of the figure must dominate other decisions. If you focus on the principle of information value, other questions—for example, use of color, use of photographic images, or magnitude of cropping of a picture—should be relatively easy to resolve.

As with other elements of a manuscript, you may wish to consider placing some figures in online supplemental materials archives when those are available. Figures placed in online supplemental materials archives are those that would enrich the understanding of the material presented in the print version of the article but are not essential to the basic understanding of the material. You might want also to include materials that cannot be displayed in print format, such as video clips. As with other online supplemental materials, figures must be able to be understood on their own (see section 2.13). Therefore label them clearly and use detailed legends.

5.21 Types of Figures

Many types of figures can be used to present data to the reader. Sometimes the choice of which type to use will be obvious; at other times it will not. The more common types of figures used are described next.

- *Graphs* typically display the relationship between two quantitative indices or between a continuous quantitative variable (usually displayed as the *y*-axis) and groups of subjects displayed along the *x*-axis.
- *Charts* generally display nonquantitative information such as the flow of subjects through a process, for example, flow charts.
- *Maps* generally display spatial information.
- *Drawings* show information pictorially.
- *Photographs* contain direct visual representations of information.

Although these are general prototypes, there are many variations and versions of each, and the distinctions among many of them are not clear. Computer-generated images can be made to seem as if they are life-reflecting photographs, and photographs can be engineered to look more like drawings. Whenever photographic images are changed in a way that their basic information is modified, you must disclose the manipulation (see section 5.29).

Figures can be effectively used to illustrate complex theoretical formulations (see Figure 5.1) or to represent a theory graphically through a set of path models (see Figure 5.2). They can also show the sampling and flow of subjects through a randomized clinical trial or other experiment (see Figure 5.3) or the flow of participants in a survey study (see Figure 5.4). Figures can be used to illustrate the results of a one-way design with error bars representing precision of the resulting estimates (see Figure 5.5) or empirical results from a complex multivariate model (see Figure 5.6). They can also show details concerning the kinds of responses being gathered and scoring methods (see Figure 5.7) as well as details of an experimental laboratory set-up (see Figure 5.8) and an experimental procedure (see Figure 5.9).

Figure 5.1. Complex Theoretical Formulations

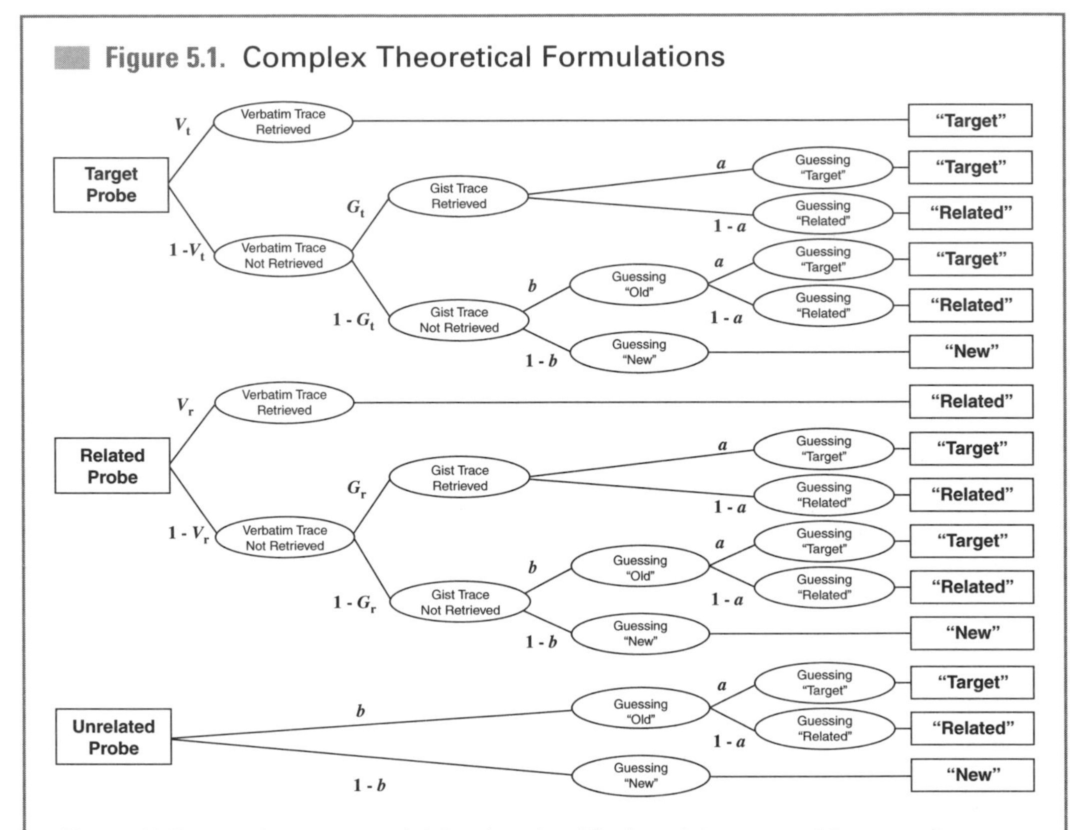

Figure X. Processing tree model for the simplified conjoint recognition paradigm. Rectangles on the left denote probe type, rectangles on the right denote responses. They are connected by branches of the processing tree that represent the combination of cognitive processes postulated by the model. V_t = probability of retrieving a target's verbatim trace given a target probe; V_r = probability of retrieving a target's verbatim trace given a related probe; G_t = probability of retrieving a target's gist trace given a target probe; G_r = probability of retrieving a target's gist trace given a related probe; b = probability of guessing that an item is either a target or a related probe; a = probability of guessing "target." Adapted from "A Simplified Conjoint Recognition Paradigm for the Measurement of Gist and Verbatim Memory," by C. Stahl and K. C. Klauer, 2008, *Journal of Experimental Psychology: Learning, Memory, and Cognition, 34,* p. 573. Copyright 2008 by the American Psychological Association.

5.22 Standards for Figures

The standards for good figures are simplicity, clarity, continuity, and (of course) information value.

A good figure

- augments rather than duplicates the text,
- conveys only essential facts,
- omits visually distracting detail,
- is easy to read—its elements (type, lines, labels, symbols, etc.) are large enough to be read with ease,

Figure 5.2. Theory Through a Set of Path Models

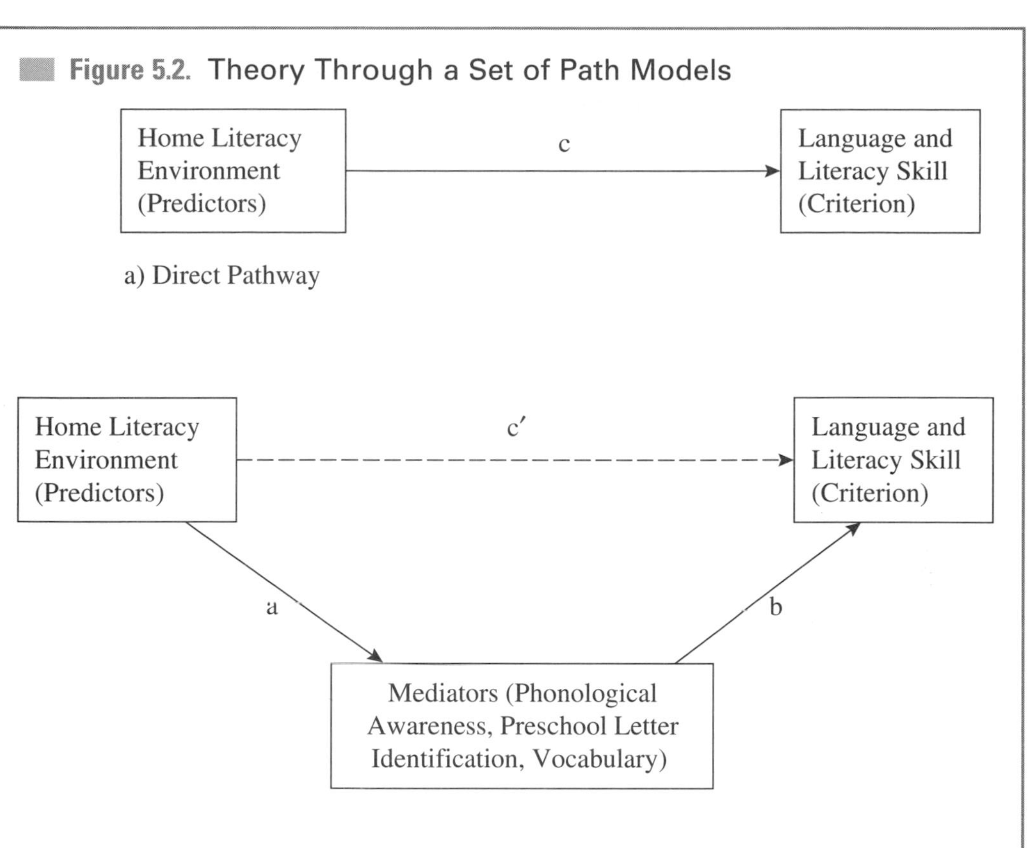

Figure X. Generic mediation model being tested (on the basis of Baron & Kenny, 1986). Adapted from "Preschool Home Literacy Practices and Children's Literacy Development: A Longitudinal Analysis," by M. Hood, E. Conlon, and G. Andrews, 2008, *Journal of Educational Psychology, 100,* p. 259. Copyright 2008 by the American Psychological Association.

- is easy to understand—its purpose is readily apparent,
- is consistent with and in the same style as similar figures in the same article, and
- is carefully planned and prepared.

Be certain in figures of all types that

- lines are smooth and sharp,
- typeface is simple (sans serif) and legible,
- units of measure are provided,
- axes are clearly labeled, and
- elements within the figure are labeled or explained.

Be certain, for instance, to distinguish between error bars and confidence intervals. When using confidence intervals, clearly specify the size of the interval (e.g., 95%);

Figure 5.3. Sampling and Flow of Subjects Through a Randomized Clinical Trial or Other Experiment

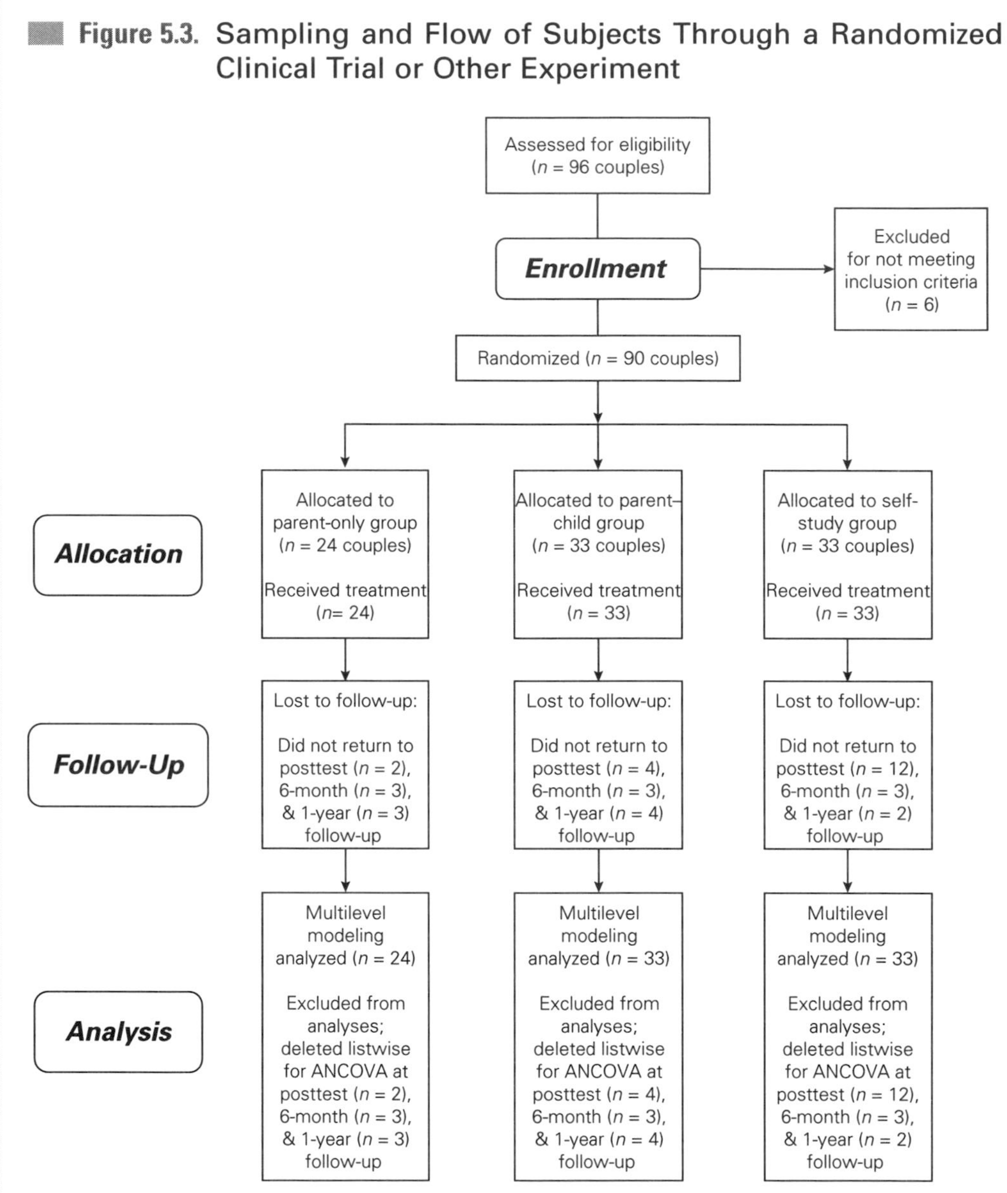

Figure X. Participant flow chart following Consolidated Standards of Reporting Trials guidelines. ANCOVA = analysis of covariance. Adapted from "Evaluating a Brief Prevention Program for Improving Marital Conflict in Community Families," by E. M. Cummings, W. B. Faircloth, P. M. Mitchell, J. S. Cummings, and A. C. Schermerhorn, 2008, *Journal of Family Psychology, 22,* p. 196. Copyright 2008 by the American Psychological Association.

Figure 5.4. Flow of Participants in a Survey Study

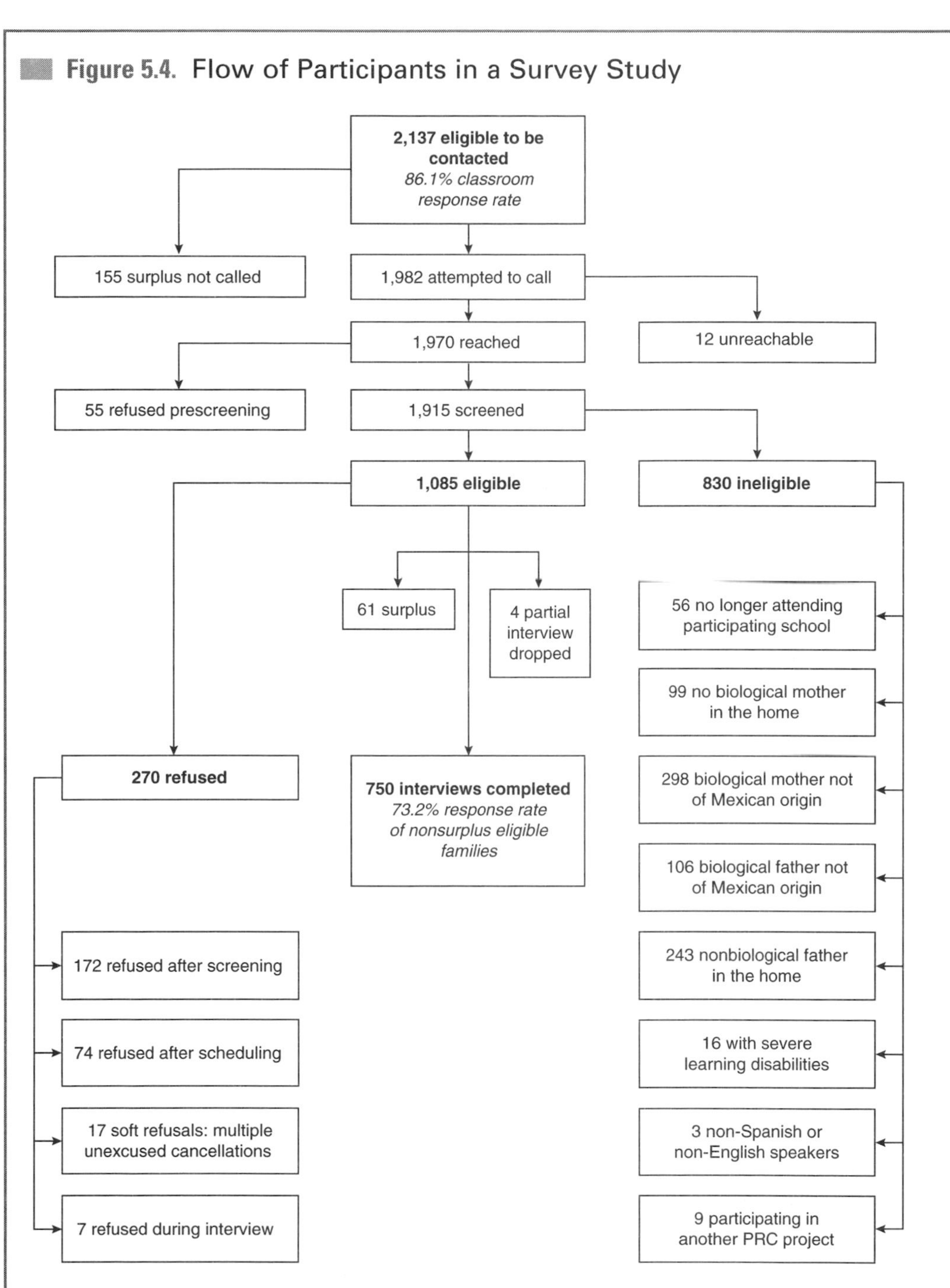

Figure X. Response rate throughout the recruitment and interviewing processes. PRC = Prevention Research Center. Adapted from "Sampling and Recruitment in Studies of Cultural Influences on Adjustment: A Case Study With Mexican Americans," by M. W. Roosa, F. F. Liu, M. Torres, N. A. Gonzales, G. P. Knight, and D. Saenz, 2008, *Journal of Family Psychology, 22,* p. 299. Copyright 2008 by the American Psychological Association.

Figure 5.5. Results of One-Way Design Using Error Bars to Represent Precision of the Resulting Estimates

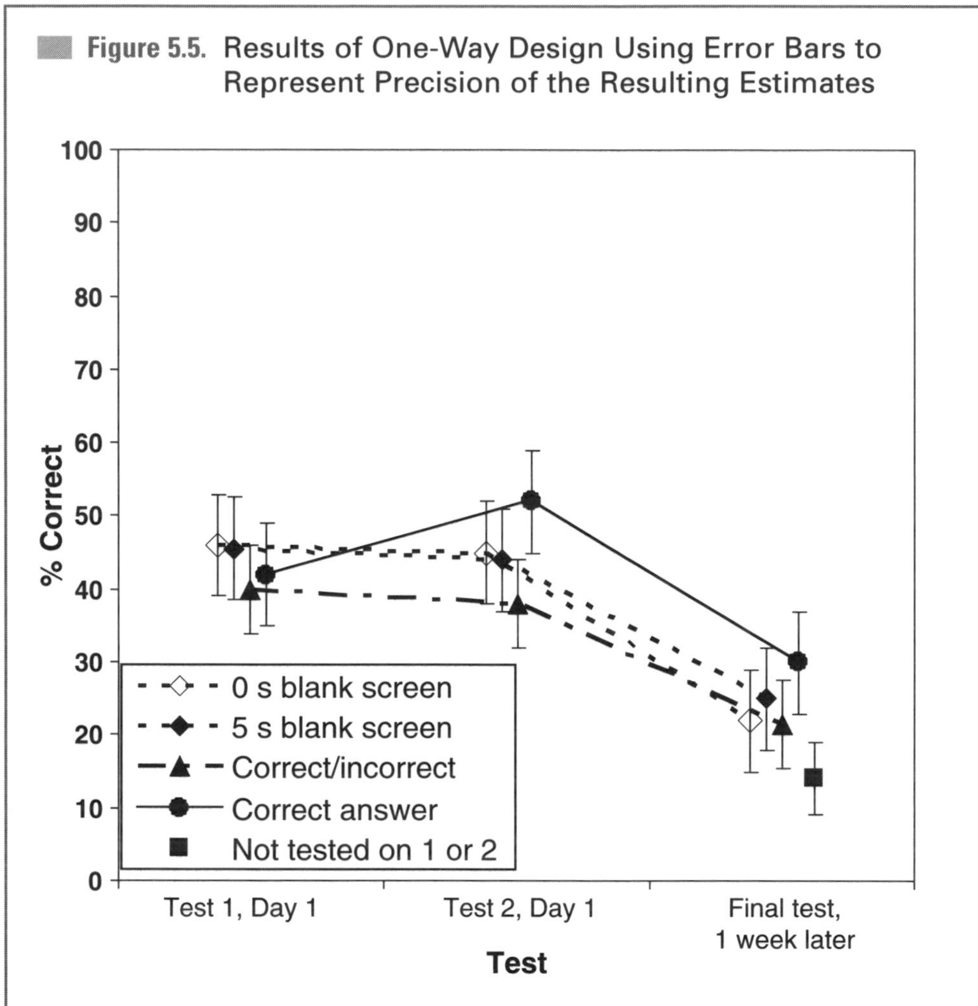

Figure X. Accuracy in Experiment 1 for each type of feedback and for each test. Error bars represent standard errors. Points are offset horizontally so that error bars are visible. Adapted from "When Does Feedback Facilitate Learning of Words?" by H. Pashler, N. J. Cepeda, J. T. Wixted, and D. Rohrer, 2005, *Journal of Experimental Psychology: Learning, Memory, and Cognition, 31,* p. 5. Copyright 2005 by the American Psychological Association.

when using error bars, provide the label for the error (e.g., standard error of the mean). In addition, be sure in all figures that

- sufficient information is given in the legend to make the figure understandable on its own,
- symbols are easy to differentiate, and
- the graphic is large enough for its elements to be discernible.

In general, high-quality graphics software handles the technical aspects of constructing figures. However, do examine the resulting images to ensure that figure guidelines have been followed and make any adjustments that might be needed.

Figure 5.6. Empirical Results From a Complex Multivariate Model

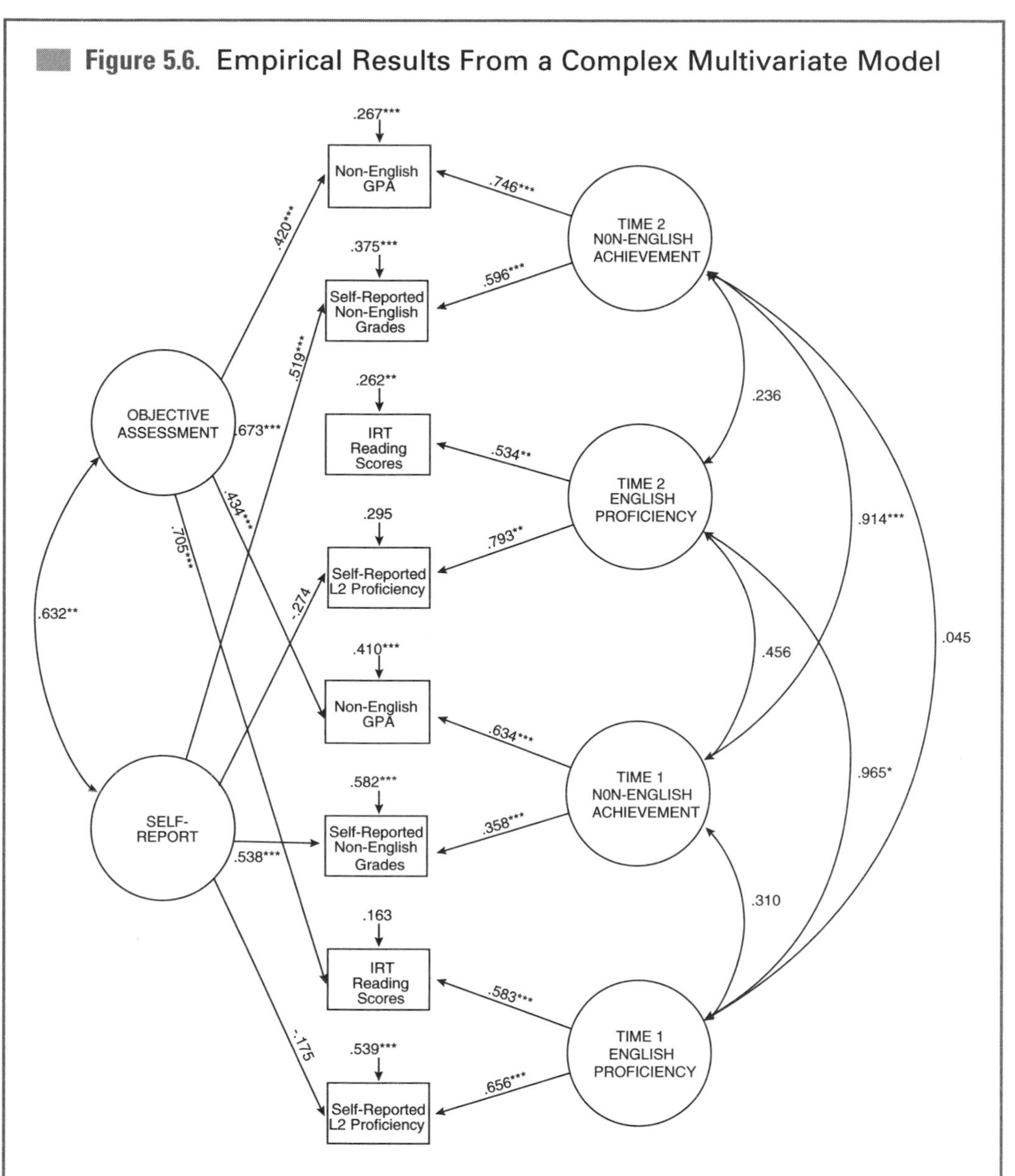

Figure X. Multitrait–multimethod confirmatory factor analysis model of two correlated traits and two correlated methods across two measurement waves. Completely standardized robust maximum likelihood parameter estimates. The residual variance components (error variances) indicate the amount of unexplained variance. Thus, for each observed variable, R^2 = (1 – error variance). GPA = grade point average; IRT = item response theory; L2 = English. Adapted from "Native Language Proficiency, English Literacy, Academic Achievement, and Occupational Attainment in Limited-English-Proficient Students: A Latent Growth Modeling Perspective," by R. S. Guglielmi, 2008, *Journal of Educational Psychology, 100,* p. 329. Copyright 2008 by the American Psychological Association.
$*p < .05$. $**p < .01$. $***p < .001$.

Figure 5.7. Kinds of Responses Being Gathered and Scoring Methods

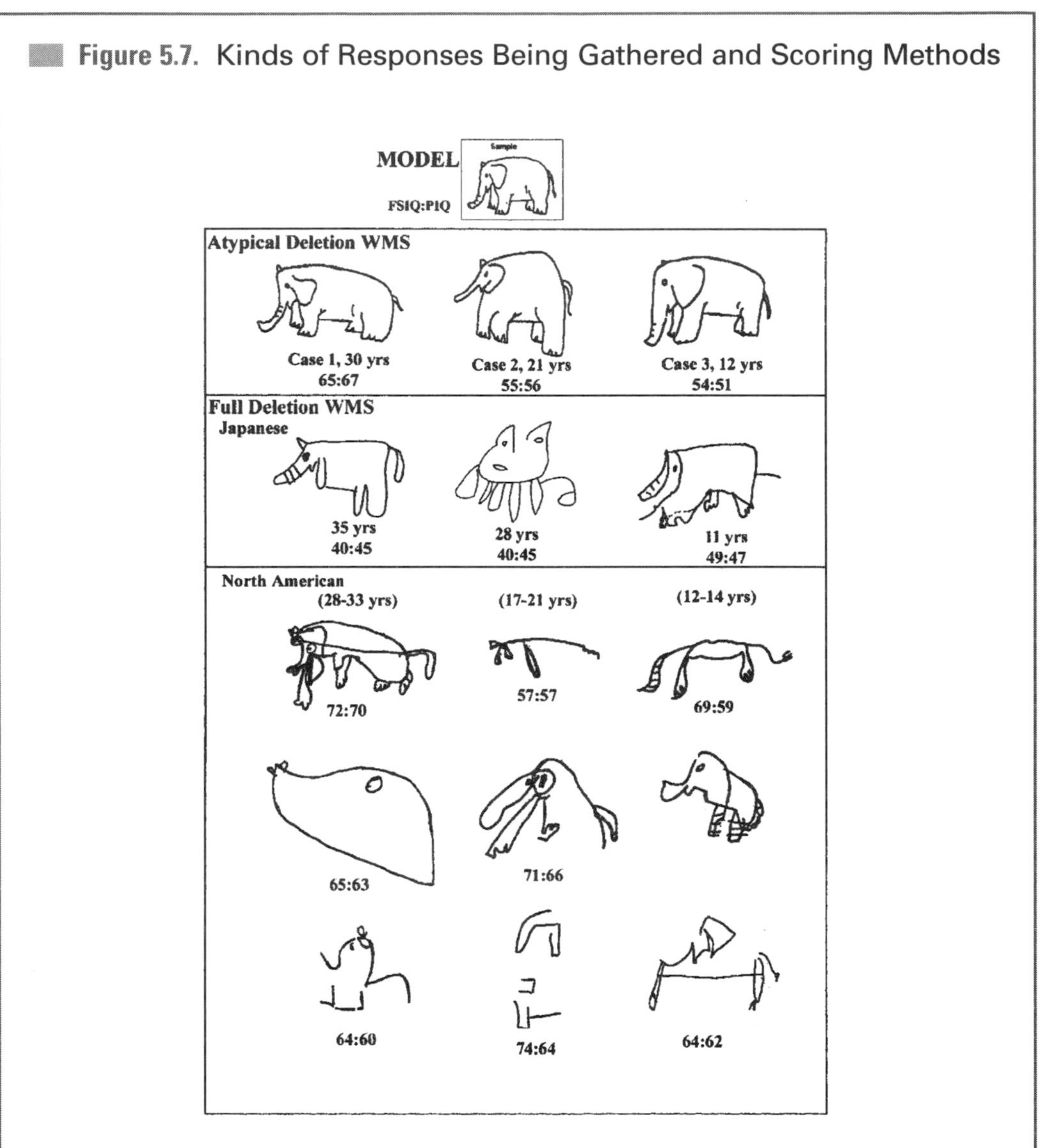

Figure X. Drawing copy task with elephant by smaller deletion cases (Cases 1, 2, and 3) and age and IQ-matched full deletion William syndrome cases. Adapted from "Williams Syndrome Deficits in Visual Spatial Processing Linked to GTF2IRD1 and GTF2I on Chromosome 7q11.23," by H. Hirota, R. Matsuoka, X.-N. Chen, L. S. Salandanan, A. Lincoln, F. E. Rose, . . . J. R. Korenberg, 2003, *Genetics in Medicine, 5,* p. 318. Copyright 2003 by American College of Medical Genetics. Reprinted with permission.

5.23 Figure Legends and Captions

A *legend* explains the symbols used in the figure; it is placed within the figure. A *caption* is a concise explanation of the figure that is placed directly below the figure and serves as the title of the figure.

Figure 5.8. Details of an Experimental Laboratory Set-Up

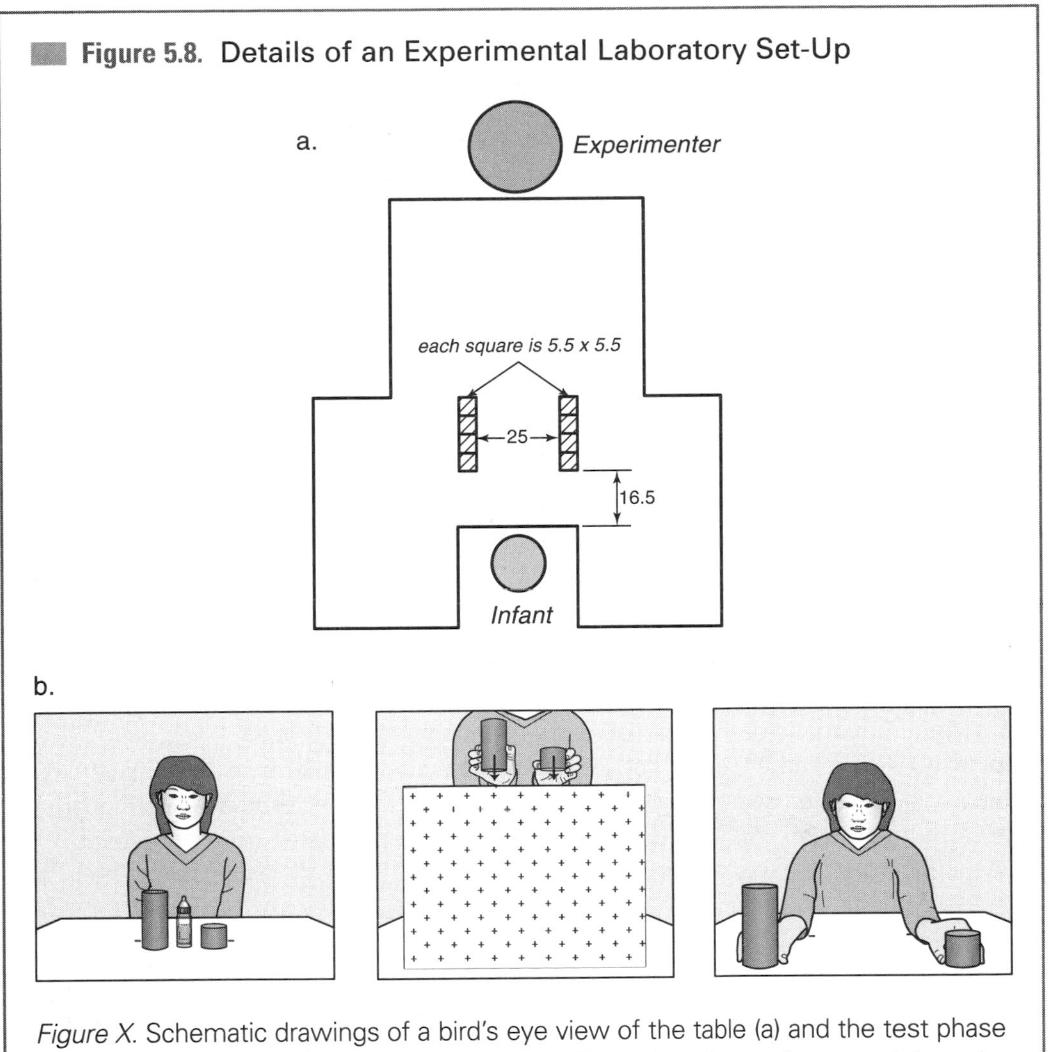

Figure X. Schematic drawings of a bird's eye view of the table (a) and the test phase of the choice task (b). Numbers represent the dimensions in centimeters. Adapted from "Visual Experience Enhances Infants' Use of Task-Relevant Information in an Action Task," by S.-h. Wang and L. Kohne, 2007, *Developmental Psychology, 43,* p. 1515. Copyright 2003 by the American Psychological Association.

Legends. The legend is an integral part of the figure; therefore, it should have the same kind and proportion of lettering that appear in the rest of the figure. Capitalize major words in the legend.

Captions. The caption serves both as an explanation of the figure and as a figure title; therefore, the figure itself should not include a title. The caption should be a brief but descriptive phrase. Compare the following captions.

Too brief:

Figure 3. Fixation duration.

Figure 5.9. Details of Experimental Procedure

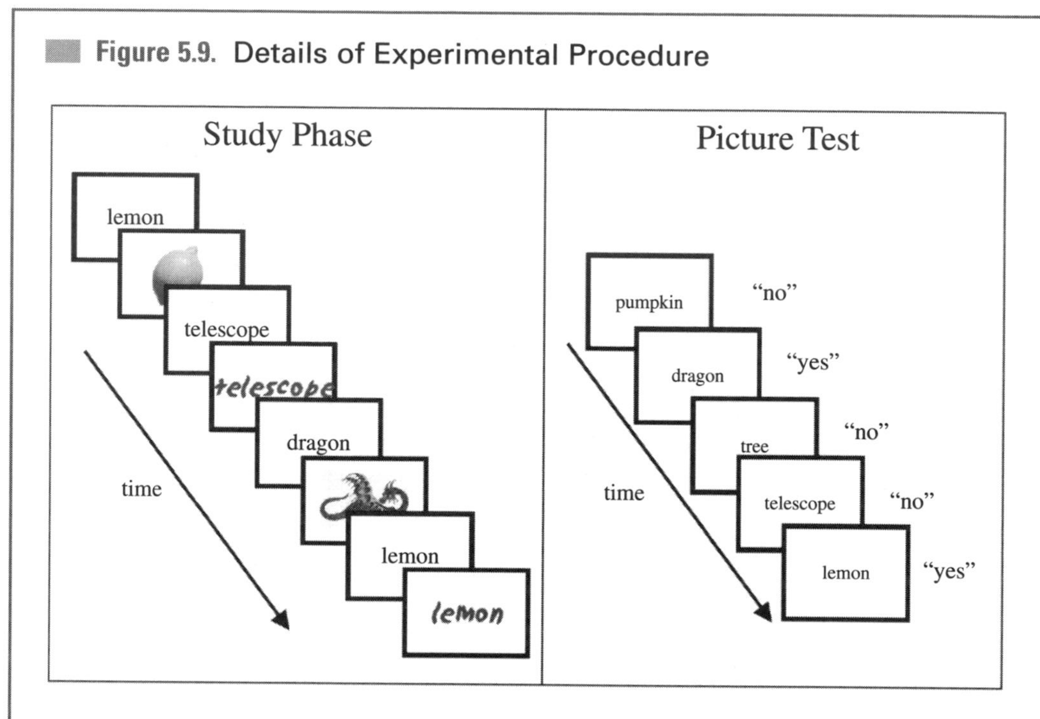

Figure X. Schematic of the criterial recollection task. At study, each black word was followed by the same word in red letters (depicted in italics) or by a colored picture. Black words were used at test as retrieval cues, under various retrieval instructions (picture test shown, with correct responses in quotes). Adapted from "Retrieval Monitoring and Anosognosia in Alzheimer's Disease," by D. A. Gallo, J. M. Chen, A. L. Wiseman, D. L. Schacter, and A. E. Budson, 2007, *Neuropsychology, 21,* p. 560. Copyright 2007 by the American Psychological Association.

Sufficiently descriptive:

> *Figure 3.* Fixation duration as a function of the delay between the beginning of eye fixation and the onset of the stimulus in Experiment 1.

After the descriptive phrase, add any information needed to clarify the figure: A reader should not have to refer to the text to decipher the figure's message. Always explain units of measurement, symbols, and abbreviations that are not included in the legend. If your graph includes error bars, explain whether they represent standard deviations, standard errors, confidence limits, or ranges; it is also helpful to display sample sizes. If statistically significant values are marked in the figure, explain the probability in the caption (follow the same system used for table notes; see section 5.16). Include within the caption any acknowledgment that a figure is reproduced from another source (see section 2.12).

Make certain that the symbols, abbreviations, and terminology in the caption and legend agree with the symbols, abbreviations, and terminology in the figure, in other figures in the article, and in the text.

5.24 Planning Figures

When planning a figure, consider the following guidelines:

- Parallel figures or figures of equal importance should be of equal size and scale.
- Like figures should be combined to facilitate comparisons between them. For example, two figures can be placed one above the other and treated as one figure. Two line graphs with identical axes might be combined horizontally and treated as one figure.
- A figure legend should be positioned within the borders of the figure (see Figure 5.5). Place labels for parts of a figure as close as possible to the components being identified.

5.25 Preparation of Figures

Figures intended for publication in scholarly journals should be computer generated using professional-level graphic software. Always check the file type requirements of the publisher to which you intend to submit your paper. Figures should be prepared at a resolution sufficient to produce high-quality images; appropriate resolution depends on figure type. Photographs (see section 5.29), for example, can be reproduced clearly at lower resolution than that needed for line art.

Image dimensions should be such that files can be easily transferred electronically. Avoid the use of three-dimensional and other effects (including color), except in rare instances in which they demonstrably enhance the presentation of your data. Individual publishers have stated policies with regard to color printing.

Size and proportion of elements. Each element must be large enough and sharp enough to be legible. Use a simple typeface (such as Arial, Futura, or Helvetica) with enough space between letters to avoid crowding. Letters should be clear, sharp, and uniformly dark and should be sized consistently throughout the figure. Type style affects legibility. For example, boldface type tends to thicken and become less readable. The size of lettering should be no smaller than 8 points and no larger than 14 points. As a general guideline, plot symbols should be about the size of a lowercase letter of an average label within the figure. Also consider the *weight* (i.e., size, density) of each element in a figure in relation to that of every other element, making the most important elements the most prominent. For example, curves on line graphs and outlines of bars on bar graphs should be bolder than axis labels, which should be bolder than the axes and tick marks.

Shading. Limit the number of different shadings used in a single graphic. If different shadings are used to distinguish bars or segments of a graph, choose shadings that are distinct (e.g., the best option to distinguish two sets of bars is no shading [open] and black [solid]). If more than three shadings are required, a table may be a better presentation of the data. Use computer-generated art in such a way as to maximize the clarity of the resulting graphic. And as always, keep it simple and clean looking.

Presenting Electrophysiological, Radiological, and Other Biological Data

The presentation of electrophysiological and radiological data presents special challenges because of both the complexity of the data and the lack of existence of a single convention for presentation of these types of data. The lack of a single, well-established standard for presentation requires that labeling of all aspects of the presentation be done clearly and completely (readers are referred to Devlin & Poldrack, 2007; Mildenberger, Eichenberg, & Martin, 2002; Picton et al., 2000; see also http://www.fmrimethods.org). Do not assume that readers will know the convention that you are following. In addition, most graphical and image-based representations of the basic data are highly processed, edited, and enhanced. The high level of processing of these forms of data makes it essential that the processing methods are clearly identified and that enhanced data (and the ensuing representation of such enhanced data) are clearly and openly identified.

In selecting data elements to present in the print version of the document, focus first on principles of clarity of representation, necessity for understanding, and coherence among representations. With the availability of online supplemental archives, carefully consider the readability of the text when deciding whether to include complex graphs and images in the text proper. When materials are better viewed in nonprint media or when images and graphics contain more information than can easily be comprehended in the usual print formats—for example, those that are greatly enhanced through the use of color or instances in which numerous images are needed to communicate the essential features of the study—consider the use of online supplemental archives for the presentation of the bulk of this information.

Many procedures used for the display of biologically related data use color, motion, or other display features not best rendered in black-and-white printing. In particular, fMRI images are typically coded in color, where color differences indicate activation differences. In the genetics area, gene staining results are often presented in color. Dynamical spread of brain activation can be displayed through color video clips. In the material that follows, we present print examples that are appropriate for black-and-white printing but also point to a number of examples (particularly those using color) that are included on the APA Style website (www.apastyle.org).

5.26 Electrophysiological Data

When presenting electrophysiological data, clear labeling is essential; for example, in the presentation of event-related brain potential data, it is essential that the direction of negativity (i.e., negative up or down) be indicated as well as the scale of the response. Information that is necessary for proper interpretation of the graphic, such as number or placement of electrodes, should accompany the graphic display. The graphic image and the points made in the text should be closely allied. Eliminate extraneous materials from graphic presentation (see Figure 5.10).

5.27 Radiological (Imaging) Data

When presenting brain images, clearly label each image. When axial or coronal sections are being displayed, clearly label which hemisphere is the left and which the right. When saggital slices are displayed, clearly indicate whether each slice is of the right or the left hemisphere. When slices are shown, show also an image that indicates where the slices were taken to help orient the reader. Specify the coordinate space in which the images have been normalized (e.g., Talairach, MNI).

Figure 5.10. Event-Related Brain Potential Data

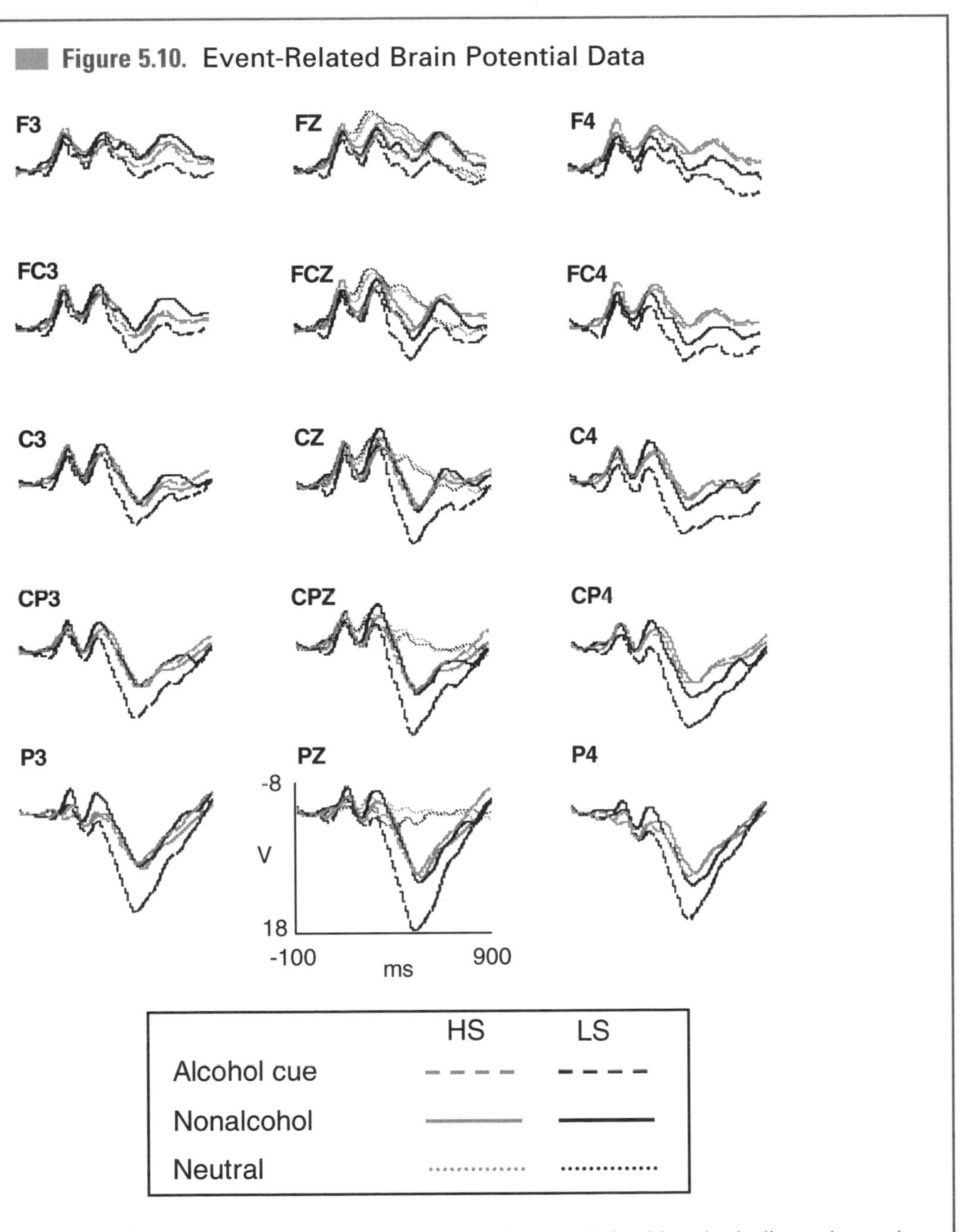

Figure X. Event-related brain potential waveforms elicited by alcoholic and nonalcoholic beverage cues as a function of sensitivity group. Waveforms elicited by frequent neutral (nontarget) images are presented for midline locations to illustrate the oddball effect in these data. Stimulus onset occurred at 0 ms. Electrodes are arrayed from most anterior (top) to most posterior (bottom) and from left to right as they were positioned on the scalp. HS = high alcohol sensitivity group; LS = low alcohol sensitivity group. Adapted from "Effects of Alcohol Sensitivity on P3 Event-Related Potential Reactivity to Alcohol Cues," by B. D. Bartholow, E. A. Henry, and S. A. Lust, 2007, *Psychology of Addictive Behaviors, 21,* p. 560. Copyright 2007 by the American Psychological Association.

Figure 5.11. Neuroimaging Data With Details of Processing Information

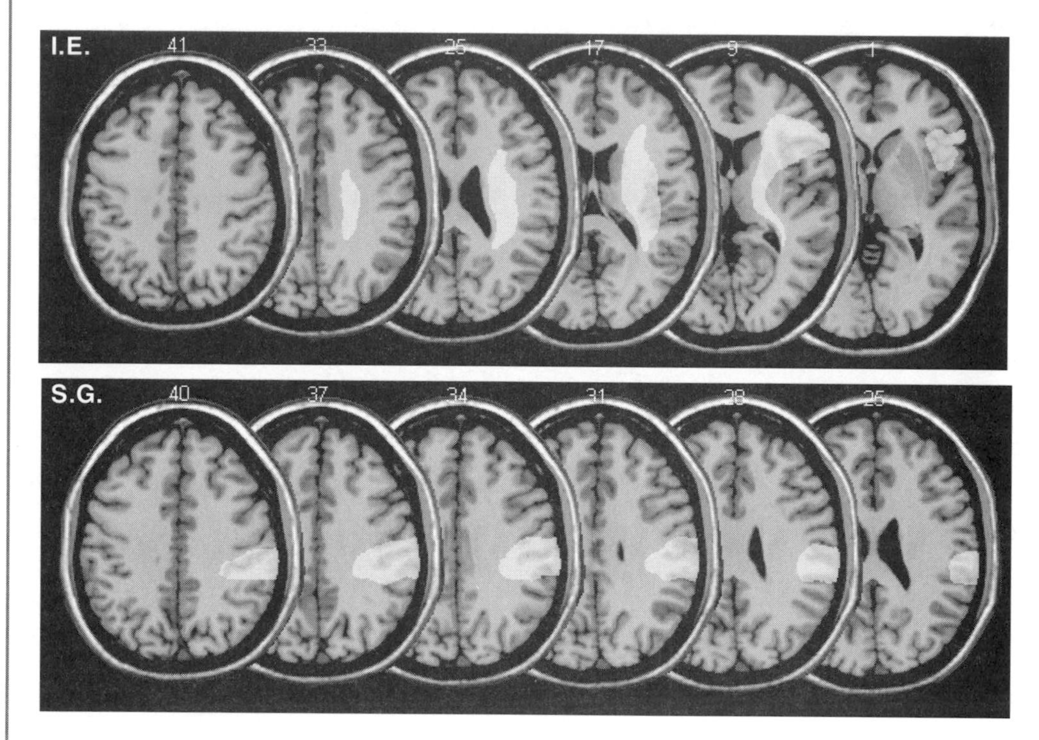

Figure X. Lesion maps for the two right hemisphere patients plotted onto a normal template brain using MRIcro software (Rorden & Brett, 2000). Affected regions (translucent white) are plotted onto axial slices, with numbers above each slice indicating *Z* coordinates in Talairach space. Adapted from "Central Perceptual Load Does Not Reduce Ipsilesional Flanker Interference in Parietal Extinction," by J. C. Snow and J. B. Mattingley, 2008, *Neuropsychology, 22,* p. 375. Copyright 2008 by the American Psychological Association.

Cutaway views of the brain that show activations interior to it can be useful if the cutaways clearly depict the tissue that has been excised. When activations are superimposed on a surface-rendered image of a brain, include a clear explanation of what activations are being shown, particularly with regard to the depth of the activation that has been brought to the surface; the use of flattened surface images may help make the data clearer. When using color, use it consistently in all representations within the document and clearly specify the color–scale mapping (see example at www.apastyle.org).

Neuroimaging data almost always require extensive postacquisition processing. Details of the processing methods should accompany their display (see Figure 5.11).

Photomicrographs are often used in cell-staining and other types of imaging studies. When preparing photomicrographs, include a scale bar and staining materials information in the figure caption.

5.28 Genetic Data

As with other displays of biological material, clear labeling enhances the display of genetic information such as deletion patterns—be they of the physical map variety (see Figure 5.12) or the photographic stain variety (see example at www.apastyle.org). Present information concerning locations, distances, markers, and identification methods with the figure. Genetic data displays often contain much information; careful editing of the image, and of its legend, can improve the communicative value of the figure.

5.29 Photographs

Photographic images are almost always submitted as digital files embedded in or attached to the electronic version of the manuscript. It is essential that these images be submitted at appropriate levels of resolution.

Because reproduction softens contrast and detail in photographs, starting with rich contrast and sharp prints will improve the final print version of the image. The camera view and the lighting should highlight the subject and provide high contrast; a light or dark background can provide even more contrast.

Photographs must be of professional quality and should be presented as black-and-white images, unless they include color-specific information relevant to the study (e.g., differently colored stimuli). Submit the image as a file type appropriate to the needs of the publication to which you are submitting. Do not submit color image files for figures intended for black-and-white printing; the transition from color to black and white for reproduction is unpredictable and can result in misleading images. It is the author's responsibility to ensure that the final representation is accurate. If color photos are necessary, consult your publication's instructions to authors for guidelines regarding color images.

Photographs usually benefit from cropping (i.e., eliminating what is not to be reproduced), just as careful editing of words can produce a more comprehensible text. Cropping recomposes the photo, eliminates extraneous detail, and centers the image. Before cropping, ensure that the image is straight (e.g., that vertical lines are truly vertical); use your software application to align the image if necessary. When used appropriately, these alterations can enhance and clarify the image and make it more useful

Figure 5.12. Display of Genetic Material—Physical Map

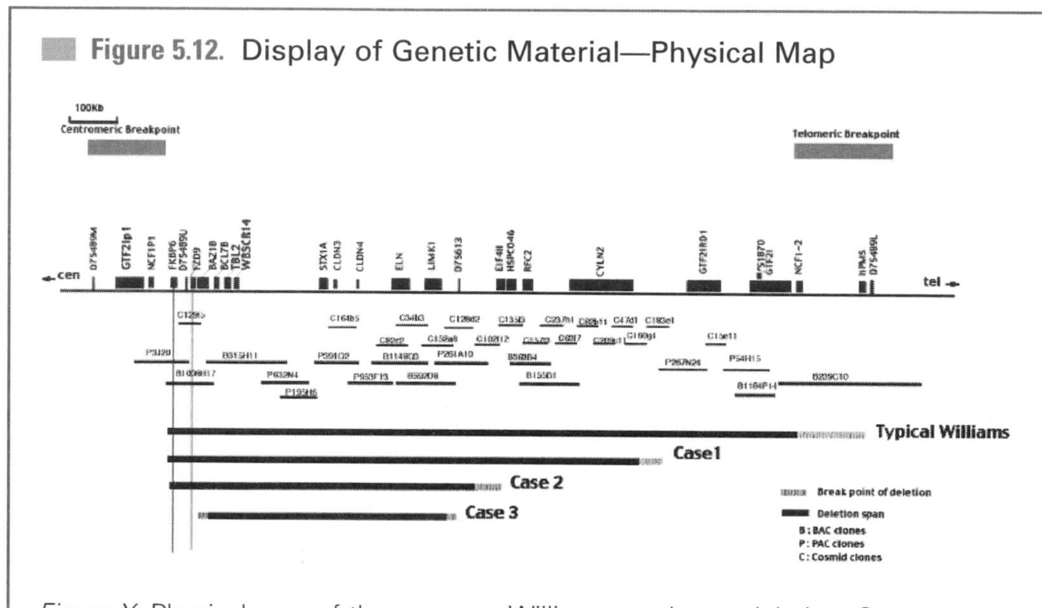

Figure X. Physical map of the common Williams syndrome deletion. Genes mapping in this region are represented by black boxes (names reading vertically). Bacterial artificial chromosomes, P1-derived artificial chromosomes, and cosmid clones spanning this region are indicated below the genes and are described in the Method section. The black horizontal lines depict the approximate size and extent of deletions in the three cases with atypical deletions and in typical subjects with Williams syndrome. Adapted from "Williams Syndrome Deficits in Visual Spatial Processing Linked to GTF2IRD1 and GTF2I on Chromosome 7q11.23," by H. Hirota, R. Matsuoka, X.-N. Chen, L. S. Salandanan, A. Lincoln, F. E. Rose, . . . J. R. Korenberg, 2003, *Genetics in Medicine, 5,* p. 315. Copyright 2003 by American College of Medical Genetics. Reprinted with permission.

as a means of scientific communication; they also help to protect the identity of individuals. However, the same technology can be used to deceive. Ethical principles of publication forbid any intentional misrepresentation of images in exactly the same way that fraudulent data manipulation is forbidden. When an image that might reasonably be thought to be a photographic image (as opposed to an image that is clearly a constructed image—a table, chart, cartoon, etc.) has been altered in a manner beyond simple cropping, clearly indicate in a note that accompanies the image that it has been altered.

If you photograph a person, obtain a signed release from that person to use the photograph. If you use a photograph from another source, try to obtain the original photograph because photographs of photographs do not print clearly. Obtain written permission for reuse (in both print and electronic form) from the copyright holder, and acknowledge the author and the copyright holder in the figure caption (see section 5.06; see also section 2.12). You may need to obtain permission from the photographer as well because professional photographs do not meet all the criteria of work for hire and are usually the property of the photographer.

5.30 Figure Checklist

The following checklist may be helpful in ensuring that your figure communicates most effectively and conforms to APA Style and formatting conventions.

Figure Checklist

- ☐ Is the figure necessary?
- ☐ Is the figure simple, clear, and free of extraneous detail?
- ☐ Is the figure title descriptive of the content of the figure?
- ☐ Are all elements of the figure clearly labeled?
- ☐ Are the magnitude, scale, and direction of grid elements clearly labeled?
- ☐ Are figures of equally important concepts prepared according to the same scale?
- ☐ Are all figures numbered consecutively with Arabic numerals?
- ☐ Are all figures mentioned in the text?
- ☐ Has written permission for print and electronic reuse been obtained? Is proper credit given in the figure caption?
- ☐ Have all substantive modifications to photographic images been disclosed?
- ☐ Are the figures being submitted in a file format acceptable to the publisher?
- ☐ Have the files been produced at a sufficiently high resolution to allow for accurate reproduction?

6

Crediting Sources

Scientific knowledge represents the accomplishments of many researchers over time. A critical part of the writing process is helping readers place your contribution in context by citing the researchers who influenced you. In this chapter, we provide the ground rules for acknowledging how others contributed to your work. We begin by describing the appropriate level of citation and offer a brief review of plagiarism and self-plagiarism. Next, we offer guidelines on formatting quoted material in text and information on seeking permission to reprint or adapt previously published material. This is followed by instruction on citing sources in text and a description of key elements of the reference list.

When to Cite

Cite the work of those individuals whose ideas, theories, or research have directly influenced your work. They may provide key background information, support or dispute your thesis, or offer critical definitions and data. Citation of an article implies that you have personally read the cited work. In addition to crediting the ideas of others that you used to build your thesis, provide documentation for all facts and figures that are not common knowledge. Figure 6.1 provides an example of the appropriate level of citation, adapted from an article in an APA journal.

The number of sources you cite in your work will vary by the intent of the article. For most articles, aim to cite one or two of the most representative sources for each key point. However, because the intent of a review article is to acquaint readers with all that has been written on a topic, authors of literature reviews typically include a more exhaustive list of citations.

Figure 6.1. Example of Appropriate Citation Level

Left-handers make up 8% to 13% of most human populations, with left-handedness more common in men than in women (Gilbert & Wysocki, 1992; McManus, 1991). Secondary school and university students engaged in "interactive" sports such as tennis and basketball are significantly more likely to be left-handed than those engaged in "noninteractive" sports such as swimming or rowing, or than those in the general population (Grouios, Tsorbatzoudis, Alexandris, & Barkoukis, 2000; Raymond et al., 1996). One possible explanation for this handedness bias is that left-handers are better than right-handers at some visuomotor tasks, as has been invoked to explain the left-handed bias among elite tennis players (Holtzen, 2000).

Note. Adapted from "Frequency-Dependent Performance and Handedness in Professional Baseball Players (*Homo sapiens*)," by E. D. Clotfelter, 2008, *Journal of Comparative Psychology, 122,* p. 68. Copyright 2008 by the American Psychological Association.

6.01 Plagiarism

As stated in Chapter 1, "Authors do not present the work of another as if it were their own work" (p. 16). Whether paraphrasing, quoting an author directly, or describing an idea that influenced your work, you must credit the source. To avoid charges of plagiarism, take careful notes as you research to keep track of your sources and cite those sources according to the guidelines presented in this chapter (see also section 1.10).

6.02 Self-Plagiarism

Whereas *plagiarism* refers to the practice of claiming credit for the words, ideas, and concepts of others, *self-plagiarism* refers to the practice of presenting one's own previously published work as though it were new. As noted in Chapter 1, "The core of the new document must constitute an original contribution to knowledge, and only the amount of previously published material necessary to understand that contribution should be included, primarily in the discussion of theory and methodology" (p. 16). Avoid charges of self-plagiarism by familiarizing yourself with the ethical standards regarding duplicate publication and the legal standards of fair use (see also section 1.10).

Quoting and Paraphrasing

6.03 Direct Quotation of Sources

Reproduce word for word material directly quoted from another author's work or from your own previously published work, material replicated from a test item, and verbatim instructions to participants. When quoting, always provide the author, year, and specific page citation or paragraph number for nonpaginated material (see section 6.05) in the text and include a complete reference in the reference list (see Citing References in Text, p. 174, for exceptions to this rule).

If the quotation comprises fewer than 40 words, incorporate it into text and enclose the quotation with double quotation marks. If the quotation appears in midsentence, end the passage with quotation marks, cite the source in parentheses immediately after the quotation marks, and continue the sentence. Use no other punctuation unless the meaning of the sentence requires such punctuation.

> Interpreting these results, Robbins et al. (2003) suggested that the "therapists in dropout cases may have inadvertently validated parental negativity about the adolescent without adequately responding to the adolescent's needs or concerns" (p. 541), contributing to an overall climate of negativity.

If the quotation appears at the end of a sentence, close the quoted passage with quotation marks, cite the source in parentheses immediately after the quotation marks, and end with a period or other punctuation outside the final parenthesis.

> Confusing this issue is the overlapping nature of roles in palliative care, whereby "medical needs are met by those in the medical disciplines; nonmedical needs may be addressed by anyone on the team" (Csikai & Chaitin, 2006, p. 112).

If the quotation comprises 40 or more words, display it in a freestanding block of text and omit the quotation marks. Start such a *block quotation* on a new line and indent the block about a half inch from the left margin (in the same position as a new paragraph). If there are additional paragraphs within the quotation, indent the first line of each an additional half inch. Double-space the entire quotation. At the end of a block quotation, cite the quoted source and the page or paragraph number in parentheses after the final punctuation mark.

> Others have contradicted this view:
>
>> Co-presence does not ensure intimate interaction among all group members. Consider large-scale social gatherings in which hundreds or thousands of people gather in a location to perform a ritual or celebrate an event.
>>
>> In these instances, participants are able to see the visible manifestation of the group, the physical gathering, yet their ability to make direct, intimate connections with those around them is limited by the sheer magnitude of the assembly. (Purcell, 1997, pp. 111–112)

Alternatively, if the quoted source is cited in the sentence introducing the block quote (e.g., "In 1997, Purcell contradicted this view . . ."), only the page or paragraph number is needed at the end of the quotation.

6.04 Paraphrasing Material

When paraphrasing or referring to an idea contained in another work, you are encouraged to provide a page or paragraph number, especially when it would help an interested reader locate the relevant passage in a long or complex text.

6.05 Direct Quotations of Online Material Without Pagination

Credit direct quotations of online material by giving the author, year, and page number in parentheses. Many electronic sources do not provide page numbers. If paragraph numbers are visible, use them in place of page numbers. Use the abbreviation *para.*

> Basu and Jones (2007) went so far as to suggest the need for a new "intellectual framework in which to consider the nature and form of regulation in cyberspace" (para. 4).

If the document includes headings and neither paragraph nor page numbers are visible, cite the heading and the number of the paragraph following it to direct the reader to the location of the quoted material.

> In their study, Verbunt, Pernot, and Smeets (2008) found that "the level of perceived disability in patients with fibromyalgia seemed best explained by their mental health condition and less by their physical condition" (Discussion section, para. 1).

In some cases in which no page or paragraph numbers are visible, headings may be too unwieldy to cite in full. Instead, use a short title enclosed in quotation marks for the parenthetical citation:

> "Empirical studies have found mixed results on the efficacy of labels in educating consumers and changing consumption behavior" (Golan, Kuchler, & Krissof, 2007, "Mandatory Labeling Has Targeted," para. 4).

(The heading was "Mandatory Labeling Has Targeted Information Gaps and Social Objectives.")

6.06 Accuracy of Quotations

Direct quotations must be accurate. Except as noted here and in sections 6.07 and 6.08, the quotation must follow the wording, spelling, and interior punctuation of the original source, even if the source is incorrect.

If any incorrect spelling, punctuation, or grammar in the source might confuse readers, insert the word *sic,* italicized and bracketed, immediately after the error in the quotation. (See sections 4.08 and 4.10 regarding the use of brackets in quotations.) Always check the manuscript copy against the source to ensure that there are no discrepancies.

6.07 Changes From the Source Requiring No Explanation

The first letter of the first word in a quotation may be changed to an uppercase or a lowercase letter. The punctuation mark at the end of a sentence may be changed to fit the syntax. Single quotation marks may be changed to double quotation marks and vice versa. Any other changes (e.g., italicizing words for emphasis or omitting words; see section 6.08) must be explicitly indicated.

6.08 Changes From the Source Requiring Explanation

Omitting material. Use three spaced ellipsis points (. . .) within a sentence to indicate that you have omitted material from the original source. Use four points to indicate any omission between two sentences. The first point indicates the period at the end of the first sentence quoted, and the three spaced ellipsis points follow. Do not use ellipsis points at the beginning or end of any quotation unless, to prevent misinterpretation, you need to emphasize that the quotation begins or ends in midsentence.

Inserting material. Use brackets, not parentheses, to enclose material such as an addition or explanation inserted in a quotation by some person other than the original author (see also the second example in section 4.10).

> "They are studying, from an evolutionary perspective, to what extent [children's] play is a luxury that can be dispensed with when there are too many other competing claims on the growing brain . . ." (Henig, 2008, p. 40).

Adding emphasis. If you want to emphasize a word or words in a quotation, italicize the word or words. Immediately after the italicized words, insert within brackets the words *emphasis added,* that is, [emphasis added] (see section 4.08, second example).

6.09 Citations Within Quotations

Do not omit citations embedded within the original material you are quoting. The works cited need not be included in the list of references (unless you happen to cite them as primary sources elsewhere in your paper).

> "In the United States, the American Cancer Society (2007) estimated that about 1 million cases of NMSC and 59,940 cases of melanoma would be diagnosed in 2007, with melanoma resulting in 8,110 deaths" (Miller et al., 2009, p. 209).

6.10 Permission to Quote, Reprint, or Adapt

You may need written permission from the owner of copyrighted work if you include lengthy quotations or if you include reprinted or adapted tables or figures. *Reprinting* indicates that the material is reproduced exactly as it appeared originally, without modifications, in the way in which it was intended. *Adaptation* refers to the modification of material so that it is suitable for a new purpose (e.g., paraphrasing or presenting an original theory or idea discussed in a long passage in a published article in a new way that suits your study; using part of a table or figure in a new table or figure in your manuscript). Requirements for obtaining permission to quote copyrighted material vary from one copyright owner to another; for example, APA policy permits authors to use, with some exceptions, a maximum of three figures or tables from a journal article or book chapter, single text extracts of fewer than 400 words, or a series of text extracts that total fewer than 800 words without requesting formal permission from APA. It is important to check with the publisher or copyright owner regarding specific requirements for permission to quote from or adapt copyrighted material.

It is the author's responsibility to find out whether permission is required from the copyright owner and to obtain it for both print and electronic reuse. APA cannot publish previously copyrighted material that exceeds the copyright holder's determination of "fair use" without permission.

If you must obtain written permission from the copyright owner, append a footnote to the quoted material with a superscript number, and in the footnote acknowledge permission from the owner of the copyright. Format the footnote as shown in Chapter 2, section 2.12.

Citing References in Text

References in APA publications are cited in text with an author–date citation system and are listed alphabetically in the reference list. This style of citation briefly identifies the source for readers and enables them to locate the source of information in the alphabetical reference list at the end of the article. Each reference cited in text must appear in the reference list, and each entry in the reference list must be cited in text. Make certain that each source referenced appears in both places and that the text citation and reference list entry are identical in spelling of author names and year.

However, two kinds of material are cited only in the text: references to classical works such as the Bible and the Qur'an, whose sections are standardized across editions, and references to personal communications (see sections 6.18 and 6.20). References in a meta-analysis are not cited in text unless they are also mentioned in the text (see section 6.26)

6.11 One Work by One Author

The author–date method of citation requires that the surname of the author (do not include suffixes such as *Jr.*) and the year of publication be inserted in the text at the appropriate point:

Kessler (2003) found that among epidemiological samples

Early onset results in a more persistent and severe course (Kessler, 2003).

If the name of the author appears as part of the narrative, as in the first example, cite only the year of publication in parentheses. Otherwise, place both the name and the year, separated by a comma, in parentheses (as in the second example). Even if the reference includes month and year, include only the year in the text citation. In the rare case in which both the year and the author are given as part of the textual discussion, do not add parenthetical information:

In 2003, Kessler's study of epidemiological samples showed that

Within a paragraph, when the name of the author is part of the narrative (as in the first example above), you need not include the year in subsequent nonparenthetical references to a study as long as the study cannot be confused with other studies cited in the article. Do include the year in all parenthetical citations:

Among epidemiological samples, Kessler (2003) found that early onset social anxiety disorder results in a more potent and severe course. Kessler also found. . . . The study also showed that there was a high rate of comorbidity with alcohol abuse or dependence and major depression (Kessler, 2003).

However, when both the name and the year are in parentheses (as in the second example above), include the year in subsequent citations within the paragraph:

Early onset results in a more persistent and severe course (Kessler, 2003). Kessler (2003) also found. . . .

6.12 One Work by Multiple Authors

When a work has two authors, cite both names every time the reference occurs in text. When a work has three, four, or five authors, cite all authors the first time the reference occurs; in subsequent citations, include only the surname of the first author followed by *et al.* (not italicized and with a period after *al*) and the year if it is the first citation of the reference within a paragraph.

Kisangau, Lyaruu, Hosea, and Joseph (2007) found [Use as first citation in text.]

Kisangau et al. (2007) found [Use as subsequent first citation per paragraph thereafter.]

Kisangau et al. found [Omit year from subsequent citations after first nonparenthetical citation within a paragraph. Include the year in subsequent citations if first citation within a paragraph is parenthetical. See section 6.11.]

Exception: If two references of more than three surnames with the same year shorten to the same form (e.g., both Ireys, Chernoff, DeVet, & Kim, 2001, and Ireys, Chernoff, Stein, DeVet, & Silver, 2001, shorten to Ireys et al., 2001), cite the surnames of the first authors and of as many of the subsequent authors as necessary to distinguish the two references, followed by a comma and *et al.*

Ireys, Chernoff, DeVet, et al. (2001) and Ireys, Chernoff, Stein, et al. (2001)

Precede the final name in a multiple-author citation in running text by the word *and*. In parenthetical material, in tables and captions, and in the reference list, join the names by an ampersand (&):

as Kurtines and Szapocznik (2003) demonstrated

as has been shown (Jöreskog & Sörbom, 2007)

When a work has six or more authors, cite only the surname of the first author followed by *et al.* (not italicized and with a period after *al*) and the year for the first and subsequent citations. (See section 6.27 and Example 2 in Chapter 7 for how to cite works with more than six authors in the reference list.) If two references with six or more authors shorten to the same form, cite the surnames of the first authors and of as many of the subsequent authors as necessary to distinguish the two references, followed by a comma and *et al.* For example, suppose you have entries for the following references:

Kosslyn, Koenig, Barrett, Cave, Tang, and Gabrieli (1996)

Kosslyn, Koenig, Gabrieli, Tang, Marsolek, and Daly (1996)

In text you would cite them, respectively, as

Kosslyn, Koenig, Barrett, et al. (1996) and Kosslyn, Koenig, Gabrieli, et al. (1996)

Table 6.1 illustrates the basic citation styles. Exceptions and citation styles that do not work in the tabular format are discussed in text or included as part of the example references.

6.13 Groups as Authors

The names of groups that serve as authors (e.g., corporations, associations, government agencies, and study groups) are usually spelled out each time they appear in a text citation. The names of some group authors are spelled out in the first citation and abbreviated thereafter. In deciding whether to abbreviate the name of a group author, use the general rule that you need to give enough information in the text citation for the reader to locate the entry in the reference list without difficulty. If the name is long and cumbersome and if the abbreviation is familiar or readily understandable, you may abbreviate the name in the second and subsequent citations. If the name is short or if the abbreviation would not be readily understandable, write out the name each time it occurs (see examples in Table 6.1).

6.14 Authors With the Same Surname

If a reference list includes publications by two or more primary authors with the same surname, include the first author's initials in all text citations, even if the year of publication differs. Initials help the reader to avoid confusion within the text and to locate the entry in the list of references (see section 6.25 for the order of appearance in the reference list).

References:

Light, I. (2006). *Deflecting immigration: Networks, markets, and regulation in Los Angeles.* New York, NY: Russell Sage Foundation.

Light, M. A., & Light, I. H. (2008). The geographic expansion of Mexican immigration in the United States and its implications for local law enforcement. *Law Enforcement Executive Forum Journal, 8,* 73–82.

Text Cites:

Among studies, we review M. A. Light and Light (2008) and I. Light (2006).

6.15 Works With No Identified Author or With an Anonymous Author

When a work has no identified author, cite in text the first few words of the reference list entry (usually the title) and the year. Use double quotation marks around the title of an article, a chapter, or a web page and italicize the title of a periodical, a book, a brochure, or a report:

on free care ("Study Finds," 2007)

the book *College Bound Seniors* (2008)

Table 6.1. Basic Citation Styles

Type of citation	First citation in text	Subsequent citations in text	Parenthetical format, first citation in text	Parenthetical format, subsequent citations in text
One work by one author	Walker (2007)	Walker (2007)	(Walker, 2007)	(Walker, 2007)
One work by two authors	Walker and Allen (2004)	Walker and Allen (2004)	(Walker & Allen, 2004)	(Walker & Allen, 2004)
One work by three authors	Bradley, Ramirez, and Soo (1999)	Bradley et al. (1999)	(Bradley, Ramirez, & Soo, 1999)	(Bradley et al., 1999)
One work by four authors	Bradley, Ramirez, Soo, and Walsh (2006)	Bradley et al. (2006)	(Bradley, Ramirez, Soo, & Walsh, 2006)	(Bradley et al., 2006)
One work by five authors	Walker, Allen, Bradley, Ramirez, and Soo (2008)	Walker et al. (2008)	(Walker, Allen, Bradley, Ramirez, & Soo, 2008)	(Walker et al., 2008)
One work by six or more authors	Wasserstein et al. (2005)	Wasserstein et al. (2005)	(Wasserstein et al.,2005)	(Wasserstein et al., 2005)
Groups (readily identified through abbreviation) as authors	National Institute of Mental Health (NIMH, 2003)	NIMH (2003)	(National Institute of Mental Health [NIMH], 2003)	(NIMH, 2003)
Groups (no abbreviation) as authors	University of Pittsburgh (2005)	University of Pittsburgh (2005)	(University of Pittsburgh, 2005)	(University of Pitts-burgh, 2005)

Treat references to legal materials like references to works with no author; that is, in text, cite materials such as court cases, statutes, and legislation by the first few words of the reference and the year (see Appendix 7.1 for the format of text citations and references for legal materials).

When a work's author is designated as "Anonymous," cite in text the word *Anonymous* followed by a comma and the date:

(Anonymous, 1998)

In the reference list, an anonymous work is alphabetized by the word *Anonymous* (see section 6.25).

6.16 Two or More Works Within the Same Parentheses

Order the citations of two or more works within the same parentheses alphabetically in the same order in which they appear in the reference list (including citations that would otherwise shorten to *et al.*).

Arrange two or more works by the same authors (in the same order) by year of publication. Place in-press citations last. Give the authors' surnames once; for each subsequent work, give only the date.

Training materials are available (Department of Veterans Affairs, 2001, 2003)

Past research (Gogel, 1990, 2006, in press)

Identify works by the same author (or by the same two or more authors in the same order) with the same publication date by the suffixes *a, b, c,* and so forth, after the year; repeat the year. The suffixes are assigned in the reference list, where these kinds of references are ordered alphabetically by title (of the article, chapter, or complete work).

Several studies (Derryberry & Reed, 2005a, 2005b, in press-a; Rothbart, 2003a, 2003b)

List two or more works by different authors who are cited within the same parentheses in alphabetical order by the first author's surname. Separate the citations with semicolons.

Several studies (Miller, 1999; Shafranske & Mahoney, 1998)

Exception: You may separate a major citation from other citations within parentheses by inserting a phrase, such as *see also*, before the first of the remaining citations, which should be in alphabetical order:

(Minor, 2001; see also Adams, 1999; Storandt, 2007)

6.17 Secondary Sources

Use secondary sources sparingly, for instance, when the original work is out of print, unavailable through usual sources, or not available in English. Give the secondary source in the reference list; in text, name the original work and give a citation for the secondary source. For example, if Allport's work is cited in Nicholson and you did not read Allport's work, list the Nicholson reference in the reference list. In the text, use the following citation:

Allport's diary (as cited in Nicholson, 2003).

6.18 Classical Works

When a date of publication is inapplicable, such as for some very old works, cite the year of the translation you used, preceded by *trans.*, or the year of the version you used, followed by *version.* When you know the original date of publication, include it in the citation.

(Aristotle, trans. 1931)

James (1890/1983)

Reference list entries are not required for major classical works, such as ancient Greek and Roman works or classical religious works; simply identify in the first citation in the text the version you used. Parts of classical works (e.g., books, chapters, verses, lines, cantos) are numbered systematically across all editions, so use these numbers instead of page numbers when referring to specific parts of your source:

1 Cor. 13:1 (Revised Standard Version)
(Qur'an 5:3–4)

6.19 Citing Specific Parts of a Source

To cite a specific part of a source, indicate the page, chapter, figure, table, or equation at the appropriate point in text. Always give page numbers for quotations (see section 6.03). Note that *page,* but not *chapter,* is abbreviated in such text citations:

(Centers for Disease Control and Prevention, 2005, p. 10)
(Shimamura, 1989, Chapter 3)

For guidance on citing electronic sources that do not provide page numbers, see section 6.05.

See section 6.18 for citing parts of classical works.

6.20 Personal Communications

Personal communications may be private letters, memos, some electronic communications (e.g., e-mail or messages from nonarchived discussion groups or electronic bulletin boards), personal interviews, telephone conversations, and the like. Because they do not provide recoverable data, personal communications are not included in the reference list. Cite personal communications in text only. Give the initials as well as the surname of the communicator, and provide as exact a date as possible:

T. K. Lutes (personal communication, April 18, 2001)
(V.-G. Nguyen, personal communication, September 28, 1998)

Use your judgment in citing other electronic forms as personal communications; online networks currently provide a casual forum for communicating, and what you cite should have scholarly relevance.

Some forms of personal communication are recoverable, and these should be referenced as archival materials. See section 7.10 for templates, descriptions, and examples of archival sources in the reference list.

6.21 Citations in Parenthetical Material

In a citation that appears in parenthetical text, use commas, not brackets, to set off the date:

(see Table 3 of U.S. Department of Labor, 2007, for complete data)

Reference List

The reference list at the end of a journal article provides the information necessary to identify and retrieve each source. Choose references judiciously and include only the sources that you used in the research and preparation of the article. APA journals and other journals using APA Style generally require reference lists, not bibliographies.[1] APA requires that the reference list be double-spaced and that entries have a hanging indent. Because a reference list includes only references that document the article and provide recoverable data, do not include in the list personal communications, such as letters, memoranda, and informal electronic communications. Instead, cite personal communications only in text (see section 6.20 for format).

6.22 Construction of an Accurate and Complete Reference List

Because one purpose of listing references is to enable readers to retrieve and use the sources, reference data must be correct and complete. Each entry usually contains the following elements: author, year of publication, title, and publishing data—all the information necessary for unique identification and library search. The best way to ensure that information is accurate and complete is to check each reference carefully against the original publication. Give special attention to spelling of proper names and of words in foreign languages, including accents or other special marks, and to completeness of journal titles, years, volume and issue numbers, page numbers, and electronic retrieval data. Authors are responsible for all information in their reference lists. Accurately prepared references help establish your credibility as a careful researcher.

Abbreviations. Acceptable abbreviations in the reference list for parts of books and other publications include the following:

Abbreviation	Book or publication part
ed.	edition
Rev. ed.	Revised edition
2nd ed.	second edition
Ed. (Eds.)	Editor (Editors)
Trans.	Translator(s)
n.d.	no date
p. (pp.)	page (pages)
Vol.	Volume (as in Vol. 4)
Vols.	Volumes (as in Vols. 1–4)
No.	Number
Pt.	Part
Tech. Rep.	Technical Report
Suppl.	Supplement

Arabic numerals. Although some volume numbers of books and journals are given in Roman numerals, APA journals use Arabic numerals (e.g., Vol. 3, not Vol. III) because they use less space and are easier to comprehend than Roman numerals. A Roman numeral that is part of a title should remain Roman (e.g., *Attention and Performance XIII*).

[1]Note that a *reference list* cites works that specifically support a particular article. In contrast, a *bibliography* cites works for background or for further reading and may include descriptive notes.

6.23 Consistency

Consistency in reference style is important, especially in light of evolving technologies in database indexing, such as automatic indexing by database crawlers. These computer programs use algorithms to capture data from primary articles as well as from the article reference list. If reference elements are out of order or incomplete, the algorithm may not recognize them, lowering the likelihood that the reference will be captured for indexing. With this in mind, follow the general formats for placement of data and use the electronic reference guidelines detailed in this chapter to decide which data are necessary to allow readers to access the sources you used.

6.24 Using the Archival Copy or Version of Record

When using information and data retrieved online, check to see whether you are citing the appropriate version of your reference source. In-progress and final versions of the same work might coexist on the Internet, which can present challenges in determining which version is most current and most authoritative. In most cases, it is best to cite the archival version or version of record, which has been peer-reviewed and may provide additional links to online supplemental material. If the most current version available was an advance release version at the time that you originally cited it, recheck the source and update its publication status as close as possible to the publication date of your work (see section 6.32).

6.25 Order of References in the Reference List

The principles for arranging entries in a reference list are described next. You may also find it helpful to look at the reference list in Chapter 2 in the sample manuscript and at reference lists in journals that are published in APA Style.

Alphabetizing names. Arrange entries in alphabetical order by the surname of the first author followed by initials of the author's given name, and use the following rules for special cases:

- Alphabetize by the author's surname. This surname/given name formula is commonly used in Western countries but is less commonly used in many Eastern countries. If you are uncertain about the proper format for a name, check with the author for the preferred form or consult the author's previous publication for the commonly used form (e.g., Chen Zhe may publish under Zhe Chen in the United States).
- Alphabetize letter by letter. When alphabetizing surnames, remember that "nothing precedes something": Brown, J. R., precedes Browning, A. R., even though *i* precedes *j* in the alphabet.

Singh, Y., precedes Singh Siddhu, N.
López, M. E., precedes López de Molina, G.
Ibn Abdulaziz, T., precedes Ibn Nidal, A. K. M.
Girard, J.-B., precedes Girard-Perregaux, A. S.
Villafuerte, S. A., precedes Villa-Lobos, J.
Benjamin, A. S., precedes ben Yaakov, D.

- Alphabetize the prefixes M', Mc, and Mac literally, not as if they were all spelled *Mac*. Disregard the apostrophe: MacArthur precedes McAllister, and MacNeil precedes M'Carthy.
- Alphabetize entries with numerals chronologically (e.g., Macomber, J., II, precedes Macomber, J., III).

Order of several works by the same first author. When ordering several works by the same first author, give the author's name in the first and all subsequent references, and use the following rules to arrange the entries:

- One-author entries by the same author are arranged by year of publication, the earliest first:

  Upenieks, V. (2003).
  Upenieks, V. (2005).

- One-author entries precede multiple-author entries beginning with the same surname (even if the multiple-author work was published earlier):

  Alleyne, R. L. (2001).
  Alleyne, R. L., & Evans, A. J. (1999).

- References with the same first author and different second or third authors are arranged alphabetically by the surname of the second author or, if the second author is the same, the surname of the third author, and so on:

  Boockvar, K. S., & Burack, O. R. (2007).
  Boockvar, K. S., Carlson LaCorte, H., Giambanco, V., Friedman, B., & Siu, A. (2006).
  Hayward, D., Firsching, A., & Brown, J. (1999).
  Hayward, D., Firsching, A., & Smigel, J. (1999).

- References with the same authors in the same order are arranged by year of publication, the earliest first:

  Cabading, J. R., & Wright, K. (2000).
  Cabading, J. R., & Wright, K. (2001).

- References by the same author (or by the same two or more authors in the same order) with the same publication date are arranged alphabetically by title (excluding *A* or *The*).

Exception: If the references with the same authors published in the same year are identified as articles in a series (e.g., Part 1 and Part 2), order the references in the series order, not alphabetically by title.

Place lowercase letters—*a, b, c,* and so forth—immediately after the year, within the parentheses:

Baheti, J. R. (2001a). Control . . .
Baheti, J. R. (2001b). Roles of . . .

Order of several works by different first authors with the same surname. Arrange works by different authors with the same surname alphabetically by first initial:

Mathur, A. L., & Wallston, J. (1999).
Mathur, S. E., & Ahlers, R. J. (1998).

Note: Include initials with the surname of the first author in text citations (see section 6.14).

Order of works with group authors or with no authors. Occasionally, a work will have as its author an agency, association, or institution, or it will have no author at all.

Alphabetize group authors, such as associations or government agencies, by the first significant word of the name. Full official names should be used (e.g., American Psychological Association, not APA). A parent body precedes a subdivision (e.g., University of Michigan, Department of Psychology).

If, and only if, the work is signed "Anonymous," begin the entry with the word *Anonymous* spelled out, and alphabetize the entry as if Anonymous were a true name.

If there is no author, move the title to the author position, and alphabetize the entry by the first significant word of the title.

Treat legal references like references with no author; that is, alphabetize legal references by the first significant item in the entry (word or abbreviation). See Appendix 7.1 for the format of references for legal materials and ways to cite them in the text.

6.26 References Included in a Meta-Analysis

If the number of articles contributing studies to the meta-analysis is relatively small (e.g., about 50 or fewer), they should appear in the reference list with an asterisk included to identify them. If the number of articles in the meta-analysis exceeds 50, then the references to the articles should be placed in a list and submitted as an online supplemental archive. In this second case, if an article is mentioned in the text and is included in the meta-analysis, it should be cited both in the reference list and in the supplemental materials.

Add the following statement before the first reference entry: *References marked with an asterisk indicate studies included in the meta-analysis.* The in-text citations to studies selected for meta-analysis are not preceded by asterisks.

Bandura, A. J. (1977). *Social learning theory.* Englewood Cliffs, NJ: Prentice Hall.

*Bretschneider, J. G., & McCoy, N. L. (1968). Sexual interest and behavior in healthy 80- to 102-year-olds. *Archives of Sexual Behavior, 14,* 343–350.

Reference Components

In general, a reference should contain the author name, date of publication, title of the work, and publication data. The following sections (6.27–6.31) describe these components. Detailed notes on style accompany the description of each element, and example numbers given in parentheses correspond to examples in Chapter 7 in sections 7.01–7.11.

6.27 Author and Editor Information

Authors.

- Invert all authors' names; give surnames and initials for up to and including seven authors (e.g., Author, A. A., Author, B. B., & Author, C. C.). When authors number eight or more, include the first six authors' names, then insert three ellipses, and add the last author's name (see Chapter 7, Example 2). In text, follow the citation guidelines in section 6.12.
- If the reference list includes different authors with the same surname and first initial, the authors' full first names may be given in brackets:

  Janet, P. [Paul]. (1876). La notion de la personnalité [The notion of personality]. *Revue Scientifique, 10,* 574–575.

  Janet, P. [Pierre]. (1906). The pathogenesis of some impulsions. *Journal of Abnormal Psychology, 1,* 1–17.

  In text:

  (Paul Janet, 1876)

  (Pierre Janet, 1906)

- If an author's first name is hyphenated, retain the hyphen and include a period after each initial (Lamour, J.-B., for Jean-Baptiste Lamour).
- Use commas to separate authors, to separate surnames and initials, and to separate initials and suffixes (e.g., Jr. and III; see Chapter 7, Example 24); with two to seven authors, use an ampersand (&) before the last author.
- Spell out the full name of a group author (e.g., Royal Institute of Technology; National Institute of Mental Health; see Chapter 7, Examples 31, 32, 35, 68). In a reference to a work with a group author (e.g., study group, government agency, association, corporation), a period follows the author element.

- If authors are listed with the word *with,* include them in the reference in parentheses: Bulatao, E. (with Winford, C. A.). The text citation, however, refers to the primary author only.
- In a reference to a work with no author, move the title to the author position, before the date of publication (see Chapter 7, Examples 9, 30, 71). A period follows the title.

Editors.

- In a reference to an edited book, place the editors' names in the author position, and enclose the abbreviation *Ed.* or *Eds.* in parentheses after the last editor's name. The period follows the parenthetical abbreviation (Eds.).
- In a reference to a chapter in an edited book, invert the chapter authors' names as noted above but do not invert book editors' names.
- The name of the book editor should be preceded by the word *In.* Provide initials and surnames for all editors (for substantial reference works with a large editorial board, naming the lead editor followed by *et al.* is acceptable).

  Author, A. A. (2008). Title of chapter. In E. E. Editor (Ed.), *Title of book* (pp. xx–xx). Location: Publisher.

- For a book with no editor, simply include the word *In* before the book title.

6.28 Publication Date

- Give in parentheses the year the work was published (for unpublished or informally published works, give the year the work was produced).
- For magazines, newsletters, and newspapers, give the year and the exact date of the publication (month or month and day), separated by a comma and enclosed in parentheses (see Chapter 7, Examples 7–11). If the date is given as a season, give the year and the season, separated by a comma and enclosed in parentheses.
- For papers and posters presented at meetings, give the year and month of the meeting, separated by a comma and enclosed in parentheses.
- Write *in press* in parentheses for articles that have been accepted for publication but that have not yet been published (see Chapter 7, Example 6). Do not give a date until the article has actually been published. (To reference a paper that is still in progress, under review, or being revised, see Chapter 7, Example 59.)
- If no date is available, write *n.d.* in parentheses.
- For several volumes in a multivolume work or several letters from the same collection, express the date as a range of years from earliest to latest (see Chapter 7, Examples 23 and 65).
- For archival sources, indicate an estimated date that is reasonably certain but not stated on the document by using *ca.* (circa) and enclose the information in square brackets (see Chapter 7, Example 67).
- Finish the element with a period after the closing parenthesis.

6.29 Title

Article or chapter title. Capitalize only the first word of the title and of the subtitle, if any, and any proper nouns; do not italicize the title or place quotation marks around it. Finish the element with a period.

Mental and nervous diseases in the Russo-Japanese war: A historical analysis.

Periodical title: Journals, newsletters, magazines. Give the periodical title in full, in uppercase and lowercase letters. Italicize the name of the periodical.

Social Science Quarterly

Nonperiodical title: Books and reports.

- Capitalize only the first word of the title and of the subtitle, if any, and any proper nouns; italicize the title.
- Enclose additional information given on the publication for its identification and retrieval (e.g., edition, report number, volume number) in parentheses immediately after the title. Do not use a period between the title and the parenthetical information; do not italicize the parenthetical information.

Development of entry-level tests to select FBI special agents (Publication No. FR-PRD-94–06).

- If a volume is part of a larger, separately titled series or collection, treat the series and volume titles as a two-part title (see Chapter 7, Example 24).
- Finish the element with a period.

Nonroutine information in titles. If nonroutine information is important for identification and retrieval, provide it in brackets immediately after the title and any parenthetical information. Capitalize the first letter of the notation. Brackets indicate a description of form, not a title. Here are some of the more common notations that help identify works:

Notation

[Letter to the editor]

[Special issue]

[Special section]

[Monograph]

[Abstract]

[Audio podcast]

[Data file]

[Brochure]

[Motion picture]

[Lecture notes]

[CD]

[Computer software]

[Video webcast]

[Supplemental material]

6.30 Publication Information

Periodicals: Journals, newsletters, magazines.

- Give the volume number after the periodical title; italicize it. Do not use *Vol.* before the number.
- Include the journal issue number (if available) along with the volume number if the journal is paginated separately by issue (see Chapter 7, Examples 3, 7, 8). Give the issue number in parentheses immediately after the volume number; do not italicize it. Give inclusive page numbers on which the cited material appears.
- Finish the element with a period.

Social Science Quarterly, 84, 508–525.

- Periodical publisher names and locations are generally not included in references, in accordance with long practice.

Nonperiodicals: Books and reports

- Give the location (city and state or, if outside of the United States, city and country) where the publisher is located as noted on the title page for books; reports; brochures; and other separate, nonperiodical publications.

- If the publisher is a university and the name of the state or province is included in the name of the university, do not repeat the name in the publisher location.
- The names of U.S. states and territories are abbreviated in the reference list and in the Method section (suppliers' locations); use the official two-letter U.S. Postal Service abbreviations. To cite locations outside the United States, spell out the city and the country names. However, if you are publishing outside the United States or for an international readership, check your institution's or publisher's specific style guidelines for writing out or abbreviating state, province, territory, and country names.
- Use a colon after the location.
- Give the name of the publisher in as brief a form as is intelligible. Write out the names of associations, corporations, and university presses, but omit superfluous terms, such as *Publishers, Co.,* and *Inc.,* which are not required to identify the publisher. Retain the words *Books* and *Press.*
- If two or more publisher locations are given in the book, give the location listed first or, if specified, the location of the publisher's home office.
- When the author is also the publisher, use *Author* to indicate the publisher.
- Finish the element with a period.

New York, NY: McGraw-Hill.
Washington, DC: Author.
Newbury Park, CA: Sage.
Pretoria, South Africa: Unisa.

6.31 Electronic Sources and Locator Information

Since this manual was last updated, electronic journal publishing has gone from being the exception to the rule. Publishing in the online environment has greatly increased the efficiency of publication processes and has contributed to a more vibrant and timely sharing of research results. However, the electronic dissemination of information has also led to a number of new publishing models. Unedited articles can now be disseminated on the Internet in advance of publication. Links to supplementary material such as long data sets and videos can be embedded in electronic articles and made accessible with a simple click. Corrections that were formerly noted in a subsequent journal issue can now be made with no fanfare as a simple update to online files. All of these circumstances have called for new ways of tracking digital information.

In this new environment, some former models for referencing material no longer apply. It is not always clear how to distinguish the advance online version of an article from the final published version or how to determine which is the "version of record" (see section 6.24). Moreover, readers may be consulting the electronic version with supplemental material or the print version of the same article without supplemental material. In the ephemeral world of the web, article links are not always robust.

In general, we recommend that you include the same elements, in the same order, as you would for a reference to a fixed-media source and add as much electronic retrieval information as needed for others to locate the sources you cited. We discuss next some key elements of the electronic retrieval process, beginning with some general information about uniform resource locators (URLs) and digital object identifiers

(DOIs) and ending with formatting guidance for citing publication data from electronic sources.

Understanding a URL. The URL is used to map digital information on the Internet. The components of a URL are as follows:

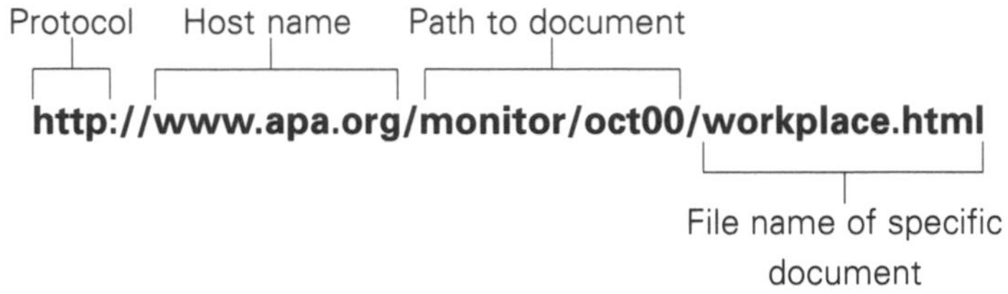

Protocol Host name Path to document

http://www.apa.org/monitor/oct00/workplace.html

File name of specific document

Protocol indicates what method a web browser (or other type of Internet software) should use to exchange data with the file server on which the desired document resides. The protocols recognized by most browsers are hypertext transfer protocol (HTTP), hypertext transfer protocol secure (HTTPS), and file transfer protocol (FTP). In a URL, the protocol is followed by a colon and two forward slashes (e.g., http://).

Host or *domain name* identifies the server on which the files reside. On the web, it is often the address for an organization's home page (e.g., http://www.apa.org is the address for APA's home page). Although many domain names start with "www," not all do (e.g., http://journals.apa.org is the home page for APA's electronic journals, and http://members.apa.org is the entry page to the members-only portion of the APA site). The domain name is not case sensitive; for consistency and ease of reading, always type it in lowercase letters.

The domain name extension (in the preceding example, ".org") can help you determine the appropriateness of the source for your purpose. Different extensions are used depending on what entity hosts the site. For example, the extensions ".edu" and ".org" are for educational institutions and nonprofit organizations, respectively; ".gov" and ".mil" are used for government and military sites, respectively; and ".com" and ".biz" are used for commercial sites. Domain name extensions may also include a country code (e.g., ".ca" for Canada or ".nz" for New Zealand). The rest of the address indicates the directory path leading to the desired document.

All content on the Internet is prone to being moved, restructured, or deleted, resulting in broken hyperlinks and nonworking URLs in the reference list. In an attempt to resolve this problem, scholarly publishers have begun assigning a DOI to journal articles and other documents.

The DOI system. Developed by a group of international publishers, the DOI System provides a means of persistent identification for managing information on digital networks (see http://www.doi.org/). The DOI System is implemented through registration agencies such as CrossRef, which provides citation-linking services for the scientific publishing sector. According to their mission statement, CrossRef is dedicated "to enable easy identification and use of trustworthy electronic content by promoting the cooperative development and application of a sustainable infrastructure" (http://www.crossref.org/).

CrossRef's participants have developed a system that provides two critical functions. First, they assign each article a "unique identifier and underlying routing system" that functions as a clearinghouse to direct readers to content, regardless of where the content resides (Kasdorf, 2003, p. 646). Second, they collaborate to use the DOI as an underlying linking mechanism "embedded" in the reference lists of electronic articles that allows click-through access to each reference. CrossRef currently has more than 2,600 participating publishers and scholarly societies.

The DOI as article identifier. A DOI is a unique alphanumeric string assigned by a registration agency (the International DOI Foundation) to identify content and provide a persistent link to its location on the Internet.

The publisher assigns a DOI when your article is published and made available electronically. All DOI numbers begin with a *10* and contain a prefix and a suffix separated by a slash. The prefix is a unique number of four or more digits assigned to organizations; the suffix is assigned by the publisher and was designed to be flexible with publisher identification standards. We recommend that when DOIs are available, you include them for both print and electronic sources.

The DOI is typically located on the first page of the electronic journal article, near the copyright notice (see Figure 6.2). The DOI can also be found on the database landing page for the article (see Figure 6.3).

The linking function of DOIs. The DOIs in the reference list function as links to the content you are referencing. The DOI may be hidden under a button labeled *Article*, *CrossRef*, *PubMed*, or another full-text vendor name (see Figure 6.4). Readers can then click on the button to view the actual article or to view an abstract and an opportunity to purchase a copy of the item. If the link is not live or if the DOI is referenced in a print publication, the reader can simply enter the DOI into the *DOI resolver* search field provided by the registration agency CrossRef.org and be directed to the article or a link to purchase it (see Figure 6.5). Locating the article online with the DOI will give you electronic access to any online supplemental archives associated with the article (see section 2.13 regarding supplemental materials).

6.32 Providing Publication Data for Electronic Sources

- For electronic versions based on a print source (as in PDF), give inclusive page numbers for the article cited. Use *pp.* before the page numbers in references to newspapers. See Chapter 7, Examples 1–3.

Figure 6.2. Location of Digital Object Identifier (DOI) in Journal Article

Journal of Experimental Psychology:
Learning, Memory, and Cognition
2008, Vol. 34, No. 3, 439-459

Copyright 2008 by the American Psychological Association
0278-7393/08/$12.00 DOI: 10.1037/0278-7393.34.3.439

How to Say No: Single- and Dual-Process Theories of Short-Term Recognition Tested on Negative Probes

Klaus Oberauer
University of Bristol

Three experiments with short-term recognition tasks are reported. In Experiments 1 and 2, participants decided whether a probe matched a list item specified by its spatial location. Items presented at study

Figure 6.3. Location of Digital Object Identifier for Article on Database Landing Page

Full Record Display

Unique Identifier
    2008-08834-010
Title
    A taxonomy of behavior change techniques used in interventions.
Publication Year
    2008
Language
    English
Author
    Abraham, Charles ; Michie, Susan
Email
    Abraham, Charles: s.c.s.abraham@sussex.ac.uk
Correspondence Address
    Charles Abraham, Department of Psychology, University of Sussex, Falmer, Brighton, England, BN1 9QG, s.c.s.abraham@sussex.ac.uk
Affiliation

Abraham, Charles	Department of Psychology, University of Sussex, Brighton, England
Michie, Susan	Department of Psychology, University College London, London, England

Source
    Health Psychology. Vol 27(3), May 2008, 379-387.
ISSN
    0278-6133 (Print); 1930-7810 (Electronic)
Publisher
    American Psychological Association: US
Other Publishers
    Lawrence Erlbaum Associates, US
Format Availability
    Electronic; Print
Format Covered
    Electronic
Publication Type
    Journal; Peer Reviewed Journal
Document Type
    Journal Article
Digital Object Identifier
    10.1037/0278-6133.27.3.379
Keywords
    behavior change; intervention; content; techniques; taxonomy; CONSORT
Index Terms
    *Behavior Change; *Health Promotion; *Intervention; *Taxonomies
Classification Codes
    3300 Health & Mental Health Treatment & Prevention
Population Group
    Human
Methodology
    0400 Empirical Study; 1800 Quantitative Study
Auxiliary Materials
    Other (Internet Available)
Release Date
    20080714

Figure 6.4. Example of Reference in Electronic Document With Digital Object Identifier Hidden Behind a Button

<ref>Hedges, L. V., & Vevea, J. L. (1998). Fixed- and random-effects models in meta-analysis. *Psychological Methods, 3,* 486<en>504. PsycINFO Article

- Provide the DOI, if one has been assigned to the content. Publishers who follow best practices publish the DOI prominently on the first page of an article. Because the DOI string can be long, it is safest to copy and paste whenever possible. Provide the alphanumeric string for the DOI exactly as published in the article. This is not a style issue but a retrieval issue.
- Use this format for the DOI in references: doi:xxxxxxx
- When a DOI is used, no further retrieval information is needed to identify or locate the content.
- If no DOI has been assigned to the content, provide the home page URL of the journal or of the book or report publisher. If you are accessing the article from a private

Figure 6.5. Digital Object Identifier Resolver

database, you may need to do a quick web search to locate this URL. Transcribe the URL correctly by copying it directly from the address window in your browser and pasting it into your working document (make sure the automatic hyphenation feature of your word processor is turned off).

- Do not insert a hyphen if you need to break a URL across lines; instead, break the URL before most punctuation (an exception would be http://). Do not add a period after the URL, to prevent the impression that the period is part of the URL. This is not a style issue but a retrieval issue.
- Test URLs in your references at each stage prior to the submission and/or publication of your work. If the document you are citing has moved, update the URL so that it points to the correct location. If the content is no longer available, substitute another source (i.e., the final version if you originally cited a draft) or drop it from the paper altogether.
- In general, it is not necessary to include database information. Journal coverage in a particular database may change over time; also, if using an aggregator such as EBSCO, OVID, or ProQuest (each of which contain many discipline-specific databases, such as PsycINFO), it may be unclear exactly which database provided the full text of an article.
- Some archival documents (e.g., discontinued journals, monographs, dissertations, or papers not formally published) can only be found in electronic databases such as ERIC or JSTOR. When the document is not easily located through its primary publishing channels, give the home or entry page URL for the online archive.
- Do not include retrieval dates unless the source material may change over time (e.g., Wikis).
- As with references to material in print or other fixed media, it is preferable to cite the final version (i.e., archival copy or version of record; see section 6.24).

7

Reference Examples

This chapter contains examples of references in APA Style. The examples are grouped into the following categories: periodicals; books, reference books, and book chapters; technical and research reports; meetings and symposia; doctoral dissertations and master's theses; reviews and peer commentary; audiovisual media; data sets, software, measurement instruments, and apparatus; unpublished and informally published works; archival documents and collections; and retrievable personal communications. In most categories, references to electronic or downloadable versions of each source type are integrated among references to print or other fixed media versions.

The most common kinds of references are illustrated here. Occasionally, however, you may need to use a reference for a source for which this chapter does not provide specific guidance. In such a case, choose the example that is most like your source and follow that format. Additional reference examples may be found on the APA Style website (www.apastyle.org). When in doubt, provide more information rather than less. Because one purpose of listing references is to enable readers to retrieve and use the sources, most entries contain the following elements: author, year of publication, title, and publishing or retrieval data—all the information necessary for unique identification and library search.

Following is an index to the reference examples that lists types of work referenced and variations of each reference element. The numbers after each index entry refer to the numbered reference examples. Appendix 7.1 at the end of this chapter includes templates and example references to legal materials.

Types and Variations

Periodicals

Books, Reference Books, and Book Chapters

Technical and Research Reports

Meetings and Symposia

Doctoral Dissertations and Master's Theses

Reviews and Peer Commentary

Audiovisual Media

Data Sets, Software, Measurement Instruments, and Apparatus

Unpublished and Informally Published Works

Archival Documents and Collections

Internet Message Boards, Electronic Mailing Lists, and Other Online Communities

Author Variations

Title Variations

Publication Information Variations

Examples by Type

7.01 Periodicals

Periodicals include items published on a regular basis such as journals, magazines, newspapers, and newsletters.

General reference form:

Author, A. A., Author, B. B., & Author, C. C. (year). Title of article. *Title of Periodical, xx,* pp–pp. doi:xx.xxxxxxxxxx

- Include the digital object identifier (DOI) in the reference if one is assigned (see section 6.31).
- If no DOI is assigned to the content and you retrieved it online, include the home page URL for the journal, newsletter, or magazine in the reference. Use this format: Retrieved from http://www.xxxxxxxx
- If each issue of a journal begins on page 1, give the issue number in parentheses immediately after the volume number.
- If you are citing an advance release version of the article, insert Advance online publication before the retrieval statement.
- Some journals offer supplemental material that is available only online. To reference this supplemental material, or any other nonroutine information that is important for identification and retrieval, include a description of the content in brackets following the title: [Letter to the editor], [Map], [Audio podcast].

1. Journal article with DOI

Herbst-Damm, K. L., & Kulik, J. A. (2005). Volunteer support, marital status, and the survival times of terminally ill patients. *Health Psychology, 24,* 225–229. doi:10.1037/0278-6133.24.2.225

2. Journal article with DOI, more than seven authors

Gilbert, D. G., McClernon, J. F., Rabinovich, N. E., Sugai, C., Plath, L. C., Asgaard, G., . . . Botros, N. (2004). Effects of quitting smoking on EEG activation and attention last for more than 31 days and are more severe with stress, dependence, DRD2 A1 allele, and depressive traits. *Nicotine and Tobacco Research, 6,* 249–267. doi:10.1080/14622200410001676305

- Use the following in-text citation: (Gilbert et al., 2004).
- When a reference has up to seven authors, spell out all authors' names in the reference list.

3. Journal article without DOI (when DOI is not available)

Sillick, T. J., & Schutte, N. S. (2006). Emotional intelligence and self-esteem mediate between perceived early parental love and adult happiness. *E-Journal of Applied Psychology, 2*(2), 38–48. Retrieved from http://ojs.lib.swin.edu.au/index.php/ejap

Light, M. A., & Light, I. H. (2008). The geographic expansion of Mexican immigration in the United States and its implications for local law enforcement. *Law Enforcement Executive Forum Journal, 8*(1), 73–82.

- Include the issue number if the journal is paginated by issue.
- If there is no DOI assigned and the reference was retrieved online, give the URL of the journal home page.
- No retrieval date is needed.

4. Journal article without DOI, title translated into English, print version

Guimard, P., & Florin, A. (2007). Les évaluations des enseignants en grande section de maternelle sont-elles prédictives des difficultés de lecture au cours préparatoire? [Are teacher ratings in kindergarten predictive of reading difficulties in first grade?]. *Approche Neuropsychologique des Apprentissages chez l'Enfant, 19,* 5–17.

- If the original version of a non-English article is used as the source, cite the original version. Give the original title and, in brackets, the English translation.
- If the English translation of a non-English article is used as the source, cite the English translation. Give the English title without brackets.

5. Journal article with DOI, advance online publication

Von Ledebur, S. C. (2007). Optimizing knowledge transfer by new employees in companies. *Knowledge Management Research & Practice.* Advance online publication. doi:10.1057/palgrave.kmrp.8500141

- This journal publishes four print issues per year but also offers individual articles online as soon as they are finalized. The content is assigned a DOI before it is assigned a volume, issue, or page numbers.
- If there is no DOI assigned and you retrieved the article electronically, give the URL of the journal home page.
- Definitions of *advance online publication* vary among journal publishers. Generally, the term refers to peer-reviewed work, but the content may not be copyedited or formatted for final production.
- Update your references close to the publication date of your work, and refer to final versions of your sources, if possible.

6. In-press article posted in a preprint archive

Briscoe, R. (in press). Egocentric spatial representation in action and perception. *Philosophy and Phenomenological Research.* Retrieved from http://cogprints.org/5780/1/ECSRAP.F07.pdf

- The exact URL is used because the article is informally published and not yet indexed on a journal website. Journal publishers that do not offer advance online publication may allow authors to post a version of their article online ahead of print in an outside repository, also called a *preprint archive.*
- Update your references close to the publication date of your work and refer to the final version of a work, if possible.

7. Magazine article

Chamberlin, J., Novotney, A., Packard, E., & Price, M. (2008, May). Enhancing worker well-being: Occupational health psychologists convene to share their research on work, stress, and health. *Monitor on Psychology, 39*(5), 26–29.

8. Online magazine article

Clay, R. (2008, June). Science vs. ideology: Psychologists fight back about the misuse of research. *Monitor on Psychology, 39*(6). Retrieved from http://www.apa.org/monitor/

9. Newsletter article, no author

Six sites meet for comprehensive anti-gang initiative conference. (2006, November/December). *OJJDP News @ a Glance.* Retrieved from http://www.ncjrs.gov/html/ojjdp/news_at_glance/216684/topstory.html

- The exact URL is helpful here because specific newsletter articles are difficult to locate from the government agency home page.
- Alphabetize works with no author by the first significant word in the title (in this case, "Six").
- In text, use a short title (or the full title if it is short) enclosed in quotation marks for the parenthetical citation: ("Six Sites Meet," 2006).

10. Newspaper article

Schwartz, J. (1993, September 30). Obesity affects economic, social status. *The Washington Post,* pp. A1, A4.

- Precede page numbers for newspaper articles with p. or pp.
- If an article appears on discontinuous pages, give all page numbers, and separate the numbers with a comma (e.g., pp. B1, B3, B5–B7).

11. Online newspaper article

Brody, J. E. (2007, December 11). Mental reserves keep brain agile. *The New York Times.* Retrieved from http://www.nytimes.com

- Give the URL of the home page when the online version of the article is available by search to avoid nonworking URLs.

12. Special issue or section in a journal

Haney, C., & Wiener, R. L. (Eds.). (2004). Capital punishment in the United States [Special issue]. *Psychology, Public Policy, and Law, 10*(4).

Greenfield, P., & Yan, Z. (Eds.). (2006). Children, adolescents, and the Internet [Special section]. *Developmental Psychology, 42,* 391–458.

- To cite an entire issue or special section of a journal, give the editors of the issue and the title of the issue.
- If the issue has no editors, move the issue title to the author position, before the year of publication, and end the title with a period. Alphabetize the reference entry by the first significant word in the title. In text, use a shortened title enclosed in quotation marks for the parenthetical citation: ("Capital Punishment," 2004).
- Provide the page range for special sections.
- To reference an article within a special issue, simply follow the format shown in Examples 1–4.

13. Monograph as part of journal issue

Ganster, D. C., Schaubroeck, J., Sime, W. E., & Mayes, B. T. (1991). The nomological validity of the Type A personality among employed adults [Monograph]. *Journal of Applied Psychology, 76,* 143–168. doi:10.1037/0021-9010.76.1.143

- For a monograph with an issue (or whole) number, include the issue number in parentheses followed by the serial number, for example, *58*(1, Serial No. 231).
- For a monograph bound separately as a supplement to a journal, give the issue number and supplement or part number in parentheses after the volume number, for example, *80*(3, Pt. 2).

14. Editorial without signature

Editorial: "What is a disaster" and why does this question matter? [Editorial]. (2006). *Journal of Contingencies and Crisis Management, 14,* 1–2.

15. Online-only supplemental material in a periodical

Marshall-Pescini, S., & Whiten, A. (2008). Social learning of nut-cracking behavior in East African sanctuary-living chimpanzees (*Pan troglodytes schweinfurthii*) [Supplemental material]. *Journal of Comparative Psychology, 122,* 186–194. doi:10.1037/0735-7036.122.2.186.supp

- The description of supplemental material or other nonroutine information (e.g., a letter to the editor, podcast, or map) is included in brackets to help the reader identify and retrieve the material.
- If no author is indicated, move the title and bracketed description to the author position.
- In text, use the following parenthetical citation (Marshall-Pescini & Whiten, 2008).

16. Abstract as original source

Woolf, N. J., Young, S. L., Fanselow, M. S., & Butcher, L. L. (1991). MAP-2 expression in cholinoceptive pyramidal cells of rodent cortex and hippocampus is altered by Pavlovian conditioning [Abstract]. *Society for Neuroscience Abstracts, 17,* 480.

Lassen, S. R., Steele, M. M., & Sailor, W. (2006). The relationship of school-wide positive behavior support to academic achievement in an urban middle school. *Psychology in the Schools, 43,* 701–712. Abstract retrieved from http://www.interscience.wiley.com

- Although it is preferable to cite the full text of an article, abstracts can be used as sources and included in the reference list.

17. Abstract as secondary source

Hare, L. R., & O'Neill, K. (2000). Effectiveness and efficiency in small academic peer groups. *Small Group Research, 31,* 24–53. Abstract retrieved from Sociological Abstracts database. (Accession No. 200010185)

- Although it is preferable to cite the full text of an article, abstracts can be used as sources and included in the reference list.
- Database names and abstract identifier (if applicable) may be given for material of limited circulation.

7.02 Books, Reference Books, and Book Chapters

This category includes books and reference books such as encyclopedias, dictionaries, and discipline-specific reference books (e.g., *Diagnostic and Statistical Manual of Mental Disorders*; see example at www.apastyle.org). It also includes books that are published in electronic form only, reference works and public domain books available online, and out-of-print books that may be available only in online repositories. When DOIs are assigned, use them as noted in the examples that follow.

For an entire book, use the following reference formats:

Author, A. A. (1967). *Title of work.* Location: Publisher.

Author, A. A. (1997). *Title of work.* Retrieved from http://www.xxxxxxx

Author, A. A. (2006). *Title of work.* doi:xxxxx

Editor, A. A. (Ed.). (1986). *Title of work.* Location: Publisher.

For a chapter in a book or entry in a reference book, use the following formats:

Author, A. A., & Author, B. B. (1995). Title of chapter or entry. In A. Editor, B. Editor, & C. Editor (Eds.), *Title of book* (pp. xxx–xxx). Location: Publisher.

Author, A. A., & Author, B. B. (1993). Title of chapter or entry. In A. Editor & B. Editor (Eds.), *Title of book* (pp. xxx–xxx). Retrieved from http://www.xxxxxxx

Author, A. A., & Author, B. B. (1995). Title of chapter or entry. In A. Editor, B. Editor, & C. Editor (Eds.), *Title of book* (pp. xxx–xxx). doi:xxxxxxxx

- If there are no page numbers, the chapter or entry title is sufficient.

For an entry in a reference work with no byline, use the following formats:

Title of entry. (1998). In A. Editor (Ed.), *Title of reference work* (xx ed., Vol. xx, pp. xxx–xxx). Location: Publisher.

Title of entry. (1998). In *Title of reference work* (xx ed., Vol. xx). Retrieved from http://www.xxxxxxxxx

- When the author and publisher are the same, use the word *Author* as the name of the publisher.
- Alphabetize books with no author or editor by the first significant word in the title. In the text citation, use a few words of the title, or the whole title if it is short, in place of an author name.
- Place information about editions, volume numbers, and page numbers (such as revised edition, volume number, or chapter page range) in parentheses following the title, with the period after the parentheses: (Rev. ed.) or (Vol. xx, pp. xxx–xxx). As with periodicals, for any nonroutine information that is important for identification and retrieval, place a description of content in brackets following the title: [Brochure].
- For major reference works with a large editorial board, you may list the name of the lead editor, followed by *et al.*
- For books or chapters available only online, the electronic retrieval statement takes the place of publisher location and name (see Examples 19–22, 24).

18. Entire book, print version

Shotton, M. A. (1989). *Computer addiction? A study of computer dependency.* London, England: Taylor & Francis.

19. Electronic version of print book

Shotton, M. A. (1989). *Computer addiction? A study of computer dependency* [DX Reader version]. Retrieved from http://www.ebookstore.tandf.co.uk /html/index.asp

Schiraldi, G. R. (2001). *The post-traumatic stress disorder sourcebook: A guide to healing, recovery, and growth* [Adobe Digital Editions version]. doi:10 .1036/0071393722

20. Electronic-only book

O'Keefe, E. (n.d.). *Egoism & the crisis in Western values.* Retrieved from http://www.onlineoriginals.com/showitem.asp?itemID=135

21. Electronic version of republished book

Freud, S. (1953). The method of interpreting dreams: An analysis of a specimen dream. In J. Strachey (Ed. & Trans.), *The standard edition of the complete psychological works of Sigmund Freud* (Vol. 4, pp. 96–121). Retrieved from http://books.google.com/books (Original work published 1900)

- In text, use the following citation: (Freud, 1900/1953).

22. Limited-circulation book or monograph, from electronic database

Thomas, N. (Ed.). (2002). *Perspectives on the community college: A journey of discovery* [Monograph]. Retrieved from http://eric.ed.gov/

- Database information may be given for items of limited circulation.

23. Several volumes in a multivolume work

Koch, S. (Ed.). (1959–1963). *Psychology: A study of science* (Vols. 1–6). New York, NY: McGraw-Hill.

- In text, use the following parenthetical citation: (Koch, 1959–1963).

24. Electronic version of book chapter in a volume in a series

Strong, E. K., Jr., & Uhrbrock, R. S. (1923). Bibliography on job analysis. In L. Outhwaite (Series Ed.), *Personnel Research Series: Vol. 1. Job analysis and the curriculum* (pp. 140–146). doi:10.1037/10762-000

- If the content has been assigned a DOI, give the DOI in the reference. No URL or database name is needed.
- In regularly published series with subtitles that change regularly, the series title is uppercase and the subtitle is lowercase, as in a book title.

25. Book chapter, print version

Haybron, D. M. (2008). Philosophy and the science of subjective well-being. In M. Eid & R. J. Larsen (Eds.), *The science of subjective well-being* (pp. 17–43). New York, NY: Guilford Press.

26. Book chapter, English translation, reprinted from another source

Piaget, J. (1988). Extracts from Piaget's theory (G. Gellerier & J. Langer, Trans.). In K. Richardson & S. Sheldon (Eds.), *Cognitive development to adolescence: A reader* (pp. 3–18). Hillsdale, NJ: Erlbaum. (Reprinted from *Manual of child psychology,* pp. 703–732, by P. H. Mussen, Ed., 1970, New York, NY: Wiley)

- If the English translation of a non-English work is used as the source, cite the English translation. Give the English title without brackets, followed by the translator's name in parentheses.
- In text, use the following parenthetical citation: (Piaget, 1970/1988).

27. Reference book

VandenBos, G. R. (Ed.). (2007). *APA dictionary of psychology.* Washington, DC: American Psychological Association.

28. Non-English reference book, title translated into English

Real Academia Española. (2001). *Diccionario de la lengua española* [Dictionary of the Spanish language] (22nd ed.). Madrid, Spain: Author.

- If a non-English reference work is used as the source, give the title in the original language and, in brackets, the English translation.

29. Entry in an online reference work

Graham, G. (2005). Behaviorism. In E. N. Zalta (Ed.), *The Stanford encyclopedia of philosophy* (Fall 2007 ed.). Retrieved from http://plato.stanford.edu/entries/behaviorism/

30. Entry in an online reference work, no author or editor

Heuristic. (n.d.). In *Merriam-Webster's online dictionary* (11th ed.). Retrieved from http://www.m-w.com/dictionary/heuristic

- If the online version refers to a print edition, include the edition number after the title.

7.03 Technical and Research Reports

Technical and research reports, like journal articles, usually cover original research but may or may not be peer reviewed. They are part of a body of literature sometimes referred to as *gray literature*, which "can serve a valuable supplementary role to formal publication, including additional resources, details, research methods and experimental techniques" ("Gray literature," 2006). Format references to technical and research reports as you would a book.

Author, A. A. (1998). *Title of work* (Report No. xxx). Location: Publisher.

- If the issuing organization assigned a number (e.g., report number, contract number, monograph number) to the report, give that number in parentheses immediately after the title.
- If you obtained a report from the U.S. Government Printing Office, list the publisher location and name as Washington, DC: Government Printing Office.
- For reports retrieved online, identify the publisher as part of the retrieval statement unless the publisher has been identified as the author: Retrieved from Agency name website: http://www.xxxxxxx

31. Corporate author, government report

U.S. Department of Health and Human Services, National Institutes of Health, National Heart, Lung, and Blood Institute. (2003). *Managing asthma: A guide for schools* (NIH Publication No. 02-2650). Retrieved from http://www.nhlbi.nih.gov/health/prof/lung/asthma/asth_sch.pdf

32. Corporate author, task force report filed online

American Psychological Association, Task Force on the Sexualization of Girls. (2007). *Report of the APA Task Force on the Sexualization of Girls.* Retrieved from http://www.apa.org/pi/wpo/sexualization.html

33. Authored report, from nongovernmental organization

Kessy, S. S. A., & Urio, F. M. (2006). *The contribution of microfinance institutions to poverty reduction in Tanzania* (Research Report No. 06.3). Retrieved from Research on Poverty Alleviation website: http://www.repoa.or.tz /documents_storage/Publications/Reports/06.3_Kessy_and_Urio.pdf

34. Report from institutional archive

McDaniel, J. E., & Miskel, C. G. (2002). *The effect of groups and individuals on national decisionmaking: Influence and domination in the reading policymaking environment* (CIERA Report 3-025). Retrieved from University of Michigan, Center for Improvement of Early Reading Achievement website: http://www.ciera.org/library/reports/inquiry-3/3-025/3-025.pdf

35. Issue brief

Employee Benefit Research Institute. (1992, February). *Sources of health insurance and characteristics of the uninsured* (Issue Brief No. 123). Washington, DC: Author.

- Use this form for issue briefs, working papers, and other corporate documents, with the appropriate document number for retrieval in parentheses.

7.04 Meetings and Symposia

Proceedings of meetings and symposia can be published in book or periodical form. To cite published proceedings from a book, use the same format as for a book or book chapter (see Example 39). To cite proceedings that are published regularly, use the same format as for a periodical (see Example 38). For contributions to symposia or for paper or poster presentations that have not been formally published, use the following templates.

Symposium:

Contributor, A. A., Contributor, B. B., Contributor, C. C., & Contributor, D. D. (Year, Month). Title of contribution. In E. E. Chairperson (Chair), *Title of symposium.* Symposium conducted at the meeting of Organization Name, Location.

Paper presentation or poster session:

Presenter, A. A. (Year, Month). *Title of paper or poster.* Paper or poster session presented at the meeting of Organization Name, Location.

- For symposium contributions and paper or poster presentations that have not been formally published, give the month and year of the symposium or meeting in the reference.

36. Symposium contribution

Muellbauer, J. (2007, September). Housing, credit, and consumer expenditure. In S. C. Ludvigson (Chair), *Housing and consumer behavior.* Symposium conducted at the meeting of the Federal Reserve Bank of Kansas City, Jackson Hole, WY.

37. Conference paper abstract retrieved online

Liu, S. (2005, May). *Defending against business crises with the help of intelligent agent based early warning solutions.* Paper presented at the Seventh International Conference on Enterprise Information Systems, Miami, FL. Abstract retrieved from http://www.iceis.org/iceis2005/abstracts_2005.htm

38. Proceedings published regularly online

Herculano-Houzel, S., Collins, C. E., Wong, P., Kaas, J. H., & Lent, R. (2008). The basic nonuniformity of the cerebral cortex. *Proceedings of the National Academy of Sciences, USA, 105,* 12593–12598. doi:10.1073/pnas.0805417105

39. Proceedings published in book form

Katz, I., Gabayan, K., & Aghajan, H. (2007). A multi-touch surface using multiple cameras. In J. Blanc-Talon, W. Philips, D. Popescu, & P. Scheunders (Eds.), *Lecture Notes in Computer Science: Vol. 4678. Advanced Concepts for Intelligent Vision Systems* (pp. 97–108). Berlin, Germany: Springer-Verlag. doi: 10.1007/978-3-540-74607-2_9

7.05 Doctoral Dissertations and Master's Theses

Doctoral dissertations and master's theses can be retrieved from subscription databases, institutional archives, and personal websites. If the work is retrieved from ProQuest Dissertations and Theses database (whose index and abstracting sources include *Dissertation Abstracts International* [*DAI*] and *Master's Theses International,* both published by University Microforms International, and *American Doctoral Dissertations*, published by Association of Research Libraries) or another published source, include this information in the reference.

For a doctoral dissertation or master's thesis available from a database service, use the following reference template:

Author, A. A. (2003). *Title of doctoral dissertation or master's thesis* (Doctoral dissertation or master's thesis). Retrieved from Name of database. (Accession or Order No.)

For an unpublished dissertation or thesis, use the following template:

Author, A. A. (1978). *Title of doctoral dissertation or master's thesis* (Unpublished doctoral dissertation or master's thesis). Name of Institution, Location.

- Italicize the title of a doctoral dissertation or master's thesis.
- Identify the work as a doctoral dissertation or master's thesis in parentheses after the title.

- If the paper is available through a database, give the accession or order number in parentheses at the end of the reference.

40. Master's thesis, from a commercial database

McNiel, D. S. (2006). *Meaning through narrative: A personal narrative discussing growing up with an alcoholic mother* (Master's thesis). Available from ProQuest Dissertations and Theses database. (UMI No. 1434728)

41. Doctoral dissertation, from an institutional database

Adams, R. J. (1973). *Building a foundation for evaluation of instruction in higher education and continuing education* (Doctoral dissertation). Retrieved from http://www.ohiolink.edu/etd/

42. Doctoral dissertation, from the web

Bruckman, A. (1997). *MOOSE Crossing: Construction, community, and learning in a networked virtual world for kids* (Doctoral dissertation, Massachusetts Institute of Technology). Retrieved from http://www-static.cc.gatech.edu /~asb/thesis/

43. Doctoral dissertation, abstracted in *DAI*

Appelbaum, L. G. (2005). Three studies of human information processing: Texture amplification, motion representation, and figure-ground segregation. *Dissertation Abstracts International: Section B. Sciences and Engineering, 65*(10), 5428.

44. Doctoral thesis, from a university outside the United States

Carlbom, P. (2000). *Carbody and passengers in rail vehicle dynamics* (Doctoral thesis, Royal Institute of Technology, Stockholm, Sweden). Retrieved from http://urn.kb.se/resolve?urn=urn:nbn:se:kth:diva-3029

7.06 Reviews and Peer Commentary

Reviews of books, motion pictures, and other information or entertainment products are published in a variety of venues, including periodicals, websites, and blogs. Some publications will print author responses to a reviewer's criticism or multiple reviews of the same product.

Reviewer, A. A. (2000). Title of review [Review of the book *Title of book*, by A. A. Author]. *Title of complete work, xx*, xxx–xxx.

- If the review is untitled, use the material in brackets as the title; retain the brackets to indicate that the material is a description of form and content, not a title.
- Identify the type of medium being reviewed in brackets (book, motion picture, television program, etc.).
- If the reviewed item is a book, include the author names after the title of the book, separated by a comma.
- If the reviewed item is a film, DVD, or other media, include the year of release after the title of the work, separated by a comma.

45. Review of a book

Schatz, B. R. (2000, November 17). Learning by text or context? [Review of the book *The social life of information*, by J. S. Brown & P. Duguid]. *Science, 290,* 1304. doi:10.1126/science.290.5495.1304

46. Review of a video

Axelman, A., & Shapiro, J. L. (2007). Does the solution warrant the problem? [Review of the DVD *Brief therapy with adolescents*, produced by the American Psychological Association, 2007]. *PsycCRITIQUES, 52*(51). doi:10.1037/a0009036

47. Review of a video game, no author

[Review of the video game *BioShock,* produced by 2K Games, 2007]. (n.d.). Retrieved from http://www.whattheyplay.com/products/bioshock-for-xbox-360/?fm=3&ob=1&t=0#166

48. Peer commentary on an article

Wolf, K. S. (2005). *The future for Deaf individuals is not that bleak* [Peer commentary on the paper "Decrease of Deaf potential in a mainstreamed environment" by K. S. Wolf]. Retrieved from http://www.personalityresearch.org/papers/hall.html#wolf

7.07 Audiovisual Media

Audiovisual media include motion pictures; audio or television broadcasts (including podcasts); and static objects such as maps, artwork, or photos.

For a motion picture, use the following format:

Producer, A. A. (Producer), & Director, B. B. (Director). (Year). *Title of motion picture* [Motion picture]. Country of Origin: Studio.

For a music recording, use the following format:

Writer, A. (Copyright year). Title of song [Recorded by B. B. Artist if different from writer]. On *Title of album* [Medium of recording: CD, record, cassette, etc.] Location: Label. (Date of recording if different from song copyright date)

- List the primary contributors in the author position and use parentheses to identify their contribution.
- For an episode from a television or radio series, use the same format as for a chapter in a book, but list the script writer and director in the author position and the producer in the editor position.

49. Video

American Psychological Association. (Producer). (2000). *Responding therapeutically to patient expressions of sexual attraction* [DVD]. Available from http://www.apa.org/videos/

50. Podcast

Van Nuys, D. (Producer). (2007, December 19). *Shrink rap radio* [Audio podcast]. Retrieved from http://www.shrinkrapradio.com/

51. Single episode from a television series

Egan, D. (Writer), & Alexander, J. (Director). (2005). Failure to communicate [Television series episode]. In D. Shore (Executive producer), *House.* New York, NY: Fox Broadcasting.

52. Music recording

lang, k.d. (2008). Shadow and the frame. On *Watershed* [CD]. New York, NY: Nonesuch Records.

- In text citations, include side and band or track numbers: "Shadow and the Frame" (lang, 2008, track 10).

53. Map retrieved online

Lewis County Geographic Information Services (Cartographer). (2002). Population density, 2000 U.S. Census [Demographic map]. Retrieved from http://www.co.lewis.wa.us/publicworks/maps/Demographics/census-pop-dens_2000.pdf

7.08 Data Sets, Software, Measurement Instruments, and Apparatus

This category includes raw data and tools that aid persons in performing a task such as data analysis or measurement. Reference entries are not necessary for standard software and programming languages, such as Microsoft Word or Excel, Java, Adobe Photoshop, and even SAS and SPSS. In text, give the proper name of the software, along with the version number. Do provide reference entries for specialized software or computer programs with limited distribution.

Rightsholder, A. A. (Year). Title of program (Version number) [Description of form]. Location: Name of producer.

or

Rightsholder, A. A. (Year). Title of program [Description of form]. Retrieved from http://xxxx

- Do not italicize the names of software, programs, or languages.
- Do italicize the title of a data set.
- If an individual has proprietary rights to the software, name him or her as the author; otherwise, treat such references as unauthored works.
- In parentheses immediately after the title, identify the version number, if any.
- In brackets immediately after the title or version number, identify the source as a computer program, language, software, and so forth. Do not use a period between the title and the bracketed material.

- Give the location and name of the organization that produced the work, if applicable, in the publisher position. If the program can be downloaded or ordered from the web, give this information in the publisher position.
- For an apparatus patent, use the legal reference format (see Appendix 7.1).

54. Data set

Pew Hispanic Center. (2004). *Changing channels and crisscrossing cultures: A survey of Latinos on the news media* [Data file and code book]. Retrieved from http://pewhispanic.org/datasets/

55. Measurement instrument

Friedlander, M. L., Escudero, V., & Heatherington, L. (2002). E-SOFTA: System for observing family therapy alliances [Software and training videos]. Unpublished instrument. Retrieved from http://www.softa-soatif.com/

56. Software

Comprehensive Meta-Analysis (Version 2) [Computer software]. Englewood, NJ: Biostat.

57. Apparatus

Eyelink II [Apparatus and software]. (2004). Mississauga, Ontario, Canada: SR Research.

7.09 Unpublished and Informally Published Works

Unpublished work includes work that is in progress, has been submitted for publication, or has been completed but not submitted for publication. This category also includes work that has not been formally published but is available on a personal or institutional website, an electronic archive such as ERIC, or a preprint archive.

Author, A. A. (Year). *Title of manuscript.* Unpublished manuscript [or "Manuscript submitted for publication," or "Manuscript in preparation"].

- If the work is available on an electronic archive, give this information at the end.
- Update your references frequently prior to publication of your work; refer to the final published version of sources when possible.

58. Unpublished manuscript with a university cited

Blackwell, E., & Conrod, P. J. (2003). *A five-dimensional measure of drinking motives.* Unpublished manuscript, Department of Psychology, University of British Columbia, Vancouver, Canada.

59. Manuscript in progress or submitted for publication

Ting, J. Y., Florsheim, P., & Huang, W. (2008). *Mental health help-seeking in ethnic minority populations: A theoretical perspective.* Manuscript submitted for publication.

- Do not give the name of the journal or publisher to which the manuscript has been submitted.
- Treat a manuscript *accepted* for publication but not yet published as an in-press reference (see Example 6).
- Use the same format for a draft or work in progress, but substitute the words Manuscript in preparation for the final sentence. Use the year of the draft you read (not *in preparation*) in the text citation.

60. Unpublished raw data from study, untitled work

Bordi, F., & LeDoux, J. E. (1993). [Auditory response latencies in rat auditory cortex]. Unpublished raw data.

61. Informally published or self-archived work

Mitchell, S. D. (2000). *The import of uncertainty.* Retrieved from http://philsci-archive.pitt.edu/archive/00000162/

This work was later published in a journal and would now be referenced as follows:

Mitchell, S. D. (2007). The import of uncertainty. *The Pluralist, 2*(1), 58–71.

62. Informally published or self-archived work, from ERIC

Kubota, K. (2007). *"Soaking" model for learning: Analyzing Japanese learning/teaching process from a socio-historical perspective.* Retrieved from ERIC database. (ED498566)

7.10 Archival Documents and Collections

Archival sources include letters, unpublished manuscripts, limited-circulation brochures and pamphlets, in-house institutional and corporate documents, clippings, and other documents, as well as such nontext materials as photographs and apparatus, that are in the personal possession of an author, form part of an institutional collection, or are stored in an archive such as the Archives of the History of American Psychology at the University of Akron or the APA Archives.

Author, A. A. (Year, Month Day). *Title of material.* [Description of material]. Name of Collection (Call number, Box number, File name or number, etc.). Name of Repository, Location.

- This general format may be modified for collections requiring more or less specific information to locate materials, for different types of collections, or for additional descriptive information (e.g., a translation of a letter). Authors may choose to list correspondence from their own personal collections, but correspondence from other private collections should be listed only with the permission of the collector.
- As with any reference, the purpose is to direct the reader to the source, despite the fact that only a single copy of the document may be available and the reader may have some difficulty actually seeing a copy.

- Include as much information as is needed to help locate the item with reasonable ease within the repository. For items from collections with detailed finding aids, the name of the collection may be sufficient; for items from collections without finding aids, more information (e.g., call number, box number, file name or number) may be necessary to help locate the item.
- If several letters are cited from the same collection, list the collection as a reference and provide specific identifying information (author, recipient, and date) for each letter in the in-text citations.
- Use square brackets to indicate information that does not appear on the document. Use question marks to indicate uncertainty regarding names and dates; use *ca.* (circa, not italicized) to indicate estimated dates (see Example 67).
- For interviews and oral histories, list the interviewee as the author. Include the interviewer's name in the description.
- If a publication of limited circulation is available in libraries, the reference may be formatted as usual for published material, without the archival source.

63. Letter from a repository

Frank, L. K. (1935, February 4). [Letter to Robert M. Ogden]. Rockefeller Archive Center (GEB series 1.3, Box 371, Folder 3877), Tarrytown, NY.

64. Letter from private collection

Zacharius, G. P. (1953, August 15). [Letter to William Rickel (W. Rickel, Trans.)]. Copy in possession of Hendrika Vande Kemp.

65. Collection of letters from an archive

Allport, G. W. (1930–1967). Correspondence. Gordon W. Allport Papers (HUG 4118.10). Harvard University Archives, Cambridge, MA.

In-text citations of specific letters:

(Allport, G. W., 1930–1967, Allport to E. G. Boring, March 1, 1939)

(Allport, G. W., 1930–1967, E. G. Boring to Allport, December 26, 1937)

- Note that Examples 63 and 65 refer to archival materials that can be recovered and thus include full reference list details that allow the reader to find them. Private letters and correspondence that are not easily retrievable are considered personal communications and are cited only in text (see section 6.20).

66. Unpublished papers, lectures from an archive or personal collection

Berliner, A. (1959). *Notes for a lecture on reminiscences of Wundt and Leipzig.* Anna Berliner Memoirs (Box M50). Archives of the History of American Psychology, University of Akron, Akron, OH.

67. Archival/historical source for which the author and/or date is known or is reasonably certain but not stated on the document

[Allport, A.?]. [ca. 1937]. *Marion Taylor today—by the biographer*. Unpublished manuscript, Marion Taylor Papers. Schlesinger Library, Radcliffe College, Cambridge, MA.

68. Archival source with corporate author

Subcommittee on Mental Hygiene Personnel in School Programs. (1949, November 5–6). *Meeting of Subcommittee on Mental Hygiene Personnel in School Programs*. David Shakow Papers (M1360). Archives of the History of American Psychology, University of Akron, Akron, OH.

69. Interview recorded and available in an archive

Smith, M. B. (1989, August 12). Interview by C. A. Kiesler [Tape recording]. President's Oral History Project, American Psychological Association. APA Archives, Washington, DC.

70. Transcription of a recorded interview, no recording available

Sparkman, C. F. (1973). *An oral history with Dr. Colley F. Sparkman/Interviewer: Orley B. Caudill*. Mississippi Oral History Program (Vol. 289), University of Southern Mississippi, Hattiesburg.

71. Newspaper article, historical, in an archive or personal collection

Psychoanalysis institute to open. (1948, September 18). [Clipping from an unidentified Dayton, OH newspaper]. Copy in possession of author.

72. Historical publication of limited circulation

Sci-Art Publishers. (1935). *Sci-Art Publications* [Brochure]. Cambridge, MA: Author. A. A. Roback Papers (HUGFP 104.50, Box 2, Folder "Miscellaneous Psychological Materials"). Harvard University Archives, Cambridge, MA.

73. Photographs

[Photographs of Robert M. Yerkes]. (ca. 1917–1954). Robert Mearns Yerkes Papers (Box 137, Folder 2292). Manuscripts and Archives, Yale University Library, New Haven, CT.

7.11 Internet Message Boards, Electronic Mailing Lists, and Other Online Communities

The Internet offers several options for people around the world to sponsor and join discussions devoted to particular subjects. These options include blogs, newsgroups, online forums and discussion groups, and electronic mailing lists. (The last are often referred to as *listservs*. However, LISTSERV is a trademarked name for a particular software program; *electronic mailing list* is the appropriate generic term.)

Author, A. A. (Year, Month Day). Title of post [Description of form]. Retrieved from http://www.xxxx

- If the author's full name is available, list the last name first followed by initials. If only a screen name is available, use the screen name.
- Provide the exact date of the posting.
- Follow the date with the subject line of the message (also referred to as the "thread"); do not italicize it. Provide a description of the message in brackets after the title.
- Include the information "Retrieved from" followed by the URL where the message can be retrieved. Include the name of the list to which the message was posted, if this information is not part of the URL.
- Provide the address for the archived version of the message.

74. Message posted to a newsgroup, online forum, or discussion group

Rampersad, T. (2005, June 8). Re: Traditional knowledge and traditional cultural expressions [Online forum comment]. Retrieved from http://www.wipo.int/roller/comments/ipisforum/Weblog/theme_eight_how_can_cultural#comments

75. Message posted to an electronic mailing list

Smith, S. (2006, January 5). Re: Disputed estimates of IQ [Electronic mailing list message]. Retrieved from http://tech.groups.yahoo.com/group/ForensicNetwork/message/670

76. Blog post

PZ Myers. (2007, January 22). The unfortunate prerequisites and consequences of partitioning your mind [Web log post]. Retrieved from http://scienceblogs.com/pharyngula/2007/01/the_unfortunate_prerequisites.php

A blog comment would be referenced as follows:

MiddleKid. (2007, January 22). Re: The unfortunate prerequisites and consequences of partitioning your mind [Web log comment]. Retrieved from http://scienceblogs.com/pharyngula/2007/01/the_unfortunate_prerequisites.php

- In the second example a screen name is used for the author name. The author has adopted a nickname, or screen name, to use when posting comments to this web log.

77. Video blog post

Norton, R. (2006, November 4). How to train a cat to operate a light switch [Video file]. Retrieved from http://www.youtube.com/watch?v=Vja83KLQXZs

Appendix 7.1: References to Legal Materials

Legal periodicals and APA journals differ in the placement and format of references. The main difference is that legal periodicals cite references in footnotes, whereas APA journals locate all references, including references to legal materials, in the reference list. For most references, use APA format as described in this chapter. References to legal materials, however, which include court decisions, statutes, other legislative materials, and various secondary sources, are more useful to the reader if they provide the information in the conventional format of legal citations. Some examples of references and citations to court cases, statutes, and other legislative materials appear in this appendix along with guidelines for their preparation. For more information on preparing these and other kinds of legal references, consult the latest edition of *The Bluebook: A Uniform System of Citation* (*Bluebook*; 18th ed., 2005), which is the source for the legal citation style that follows.

Ensure that your legal references are accurate and contain all of the information necessary to enable a reader to locate the material being referenced. Consult law librarians to verify that your legal references (a) contain the information necessary for retrieval and (b) reflect the current status of the legal authority cited to avoid the possibility of relying on a case that has been overturned on appeal or on legislation that has been significantly amended or repealed.

A7.01 General Forms

A reference form is provided in each of the following sections. For the most part, each reference form for statutes and other legislation includes (a) a popular or formal title or name of the legislation and (b) the citation, either to the published compilation of legislative materials where the legislation is codified (e.g., a specific numbered section of a specific volume of the *United States Code*), including the statutory compilation's publication date in parentheses, or the identifying label for the legislation assigned by the enacting body during the particular legislative session (e.g., a specific section of an act identified by its public law number).

A typical reference form for court decisions includes (a) the title or name of the case (usually one party vs. another); (b) the citation, usually to a volume and page of one of the various sets of books (called *reporters*, which usually contain decisions of courts in particular political divisions, or *jurisdictions*) where published cases can be found (e.g., the *Federal Reporter*, *Second Series*); and finally, (c) the precise jurisdiction of the court writing the decision (e.g., the New York Court of Appeals), in parentheses, including the date of the decision.

For both legislation and court decisions, the citation may be followed by certain additional descriptive information that pertains to the content of the legislation or court decision, the history of the legislation or court decision (e.g., later appeals of court decisions or later amendments to legislation), or other sources from which the legislation or court citation may be retrieved. Authors are encouraged to consult the *Bluebook* for the proper format for such additional information. Follow the *Bluebook* closely for correct abbreviation style. Some examples of the more common abbreviations that appear in APA journals are shown here.

Cong.	U.S. Congress
H.R.	House of Representatives

S.	Senate
Reg.	Regulation
Res.	Resolution
F.	*Federal Reporter*
F.2d	*Federal Reporter, Second Series*
F.3d	*Federal Reporter, Third Series*
F. Supp.	*Federal Supplement*
U.S.C.	*United States Code*
Cong. Rec.	*Congressional Record*
Fed. Reg.	*Federal Register*

A7.02 Text Citations of Legal Materials

Although the reference format for legal materials differs from that of other kinds of works cited in APA publications, the text citations are formed in the same way and serve the same purpose. As for works with no identified author (see section 6.15), give the first few words of the reference list entry and date; that is, give enough information in the text citation to enable the reader to locate the entry in the reference list quickly and easily. Examples of text citations and reference entries for specific kinds of legal materials are given in the following sections.

A7.03 Court Decisions (*Bluebook* Rule 10)

In text, cite the name of the case (italicized) and the year of the decision. If two or more years are given, cite those years as well. Court cases often have several years, each of which reflects a specific stage in the case's history. Giving only one date could give the impression that only a single point in the case's history is being cited or might mislead a reader as to the timing of the case.

Reference form for cases:

Name v. Name, Volume Source Page (Court Date).

Abbreviate the published source (if any), court, and date as specified in the *Bluebook*.

1. Sample reference list entry to a case

Lessard v. Schmidt, 349 F. Supp. 1078 (E.D. Wis. 1972).

Text citation:

Lessard v. Schmidt (1972)

(*Lessard v. Schmidt,* 1972)

Explanation: This decision was rendered by the federal district court for the Eastern District of Wisconsin in 1972. It appears in volume 349 of the *Federal Supplement* and starts on page 1078 of that volume.

2. Sample reference list entry to an appealed case

Durflinger v. Artiles, 563 F. Supp. 322 (D. Kan. 1981), *aff'd,* 727 F.2d 888 (10th Cir. 1984).

Text citation:

Durflinger v. Artiles (1981/1984)

Explanation: This decision was rendered by the federal district court for the District of Kansas in 1981. On appeal, the decision was affirmed by the 10th Circuit Court of Appeals in 1984. Consult the *Bluebook* for the proper forms to signal the various stages in a case's history.

Unpublished cases:

3. Sample reference to an unreported decision

Gilliard v. Oswald, No. 76-2109 (2d Cir. Mar. 16, 1977).

Explanation: The docket number and the court are provided. The opinion was announced on March 16, 1977. To cite to a particular page of a *slip opinion* (opinion that is not published in a case reporter but is separately printed), use the form slip op. at [page number].

Alternative: You may cite unreported cases found on electronic databases, such as LEXIS or Westlaw, instead of citing them to slip opinions. Give the name of the database, a record number if available, and enough information for the reader to find the case. Precede screen page numbers, if assigned, with an asterisk to distinguish them from the page number of the slip opinion; paragraph numbers, if assigned, should be preceded by a paragraph symbol.

With record number:

Dougherty v. Royal Zenith Corp., No. 88-8666, 1991 U.S. Dist. LEXIS 10807, at *2 (E.D. Pa. July 31, 1991).

With no record number:

Gustin v. Mathews, No. 76-7-C5 (D. Kan. Jan. 31, 1977) (LEXIS, Genfed library, Dist file).

Note: If the case is not available as a slip opinion or online, consult the *Bluebook* for other reference formats.

Court cases at the trial level:

4. Sample reference to a state trial court opinion

Casey v. Pennsylvania-American Water Co., 12 Pa. D. & C.4th 168 (C.P. Washington County 1991).

Explanation: This decision was rendered by the Court of Common Pleas in Washington County, Pennsylvania, in 1991. (The Court of Common Pleas is the name of most of the trial-level courts in Pennsylvania. In other states, the trial-level courts are called *superior courts* or *supreme courts*, which can be confusing because one usually thinks of the supreme court as the highest court in any particular jurisdiction and not as the lowest. Authors should check the *Bluebook* for a listing of each jurisdiction's particular court structure.) The decision can be located in *Pennsylvania District and County Reports, Fourth Series*, beginning on page 168 of that volume.

5. Sample reference to a federal district court opinion

Davis v. Monsanto Co., 627 F. Supp. 418 (S.D. W. Va. 1986).

Explanation: The opinion was rendered in the federal district court for the Southern District of West Virginia and was decided in 1986. It appears in volume 627 of the *Federal Supplement* and starts on page 418 of that volume.

Court cases at the appellate level:

6. Sample reference to a case appealed to a state supreme court

Compton v. Commonwealth, 239 Va. 312, 389 S.E.2d 460 (1990).

Explanation: This opinion was written by the Virginia Supreme Court in 1990. It can be found in volume 239 of the *Virginia Reports*, which publishes the state's supreme court decisions, starting on page 312. There is a parallel citation to volume 389 of the *South Eastern Reporter, Second Series*, starting on page 460. A reporter prints cases; the *South Eastern Reporter* is a regional reporter containing cases from several states in the southeastern section of the country.

7. Sample reference to a case appealed to a state court of appeals

Texas v. Morales, 826 S.W.2d 201 (Tex. Ct. App. 1992).

Explanation: This opinion was rendered by the Texas Court of Appeals in 1992 and can be found in volume 826 of the *South Western Reporter, Second Series*, starting on page 201.

8. Sample references to cases decided by the U.S. Supreme Court

Brown v. Board of Educ., 347 U.S. 483 (1954).

Maryland v. Craig, 110 S. Ct. 3160 (1990).

Explanation: Each of these cases was decided by the U.S. Supreme Court. The first citation is to the *United States Reports*. Such a citation is given when the appropriate volume of the *United States Reports* is available. The second citation is to the *Supreme Court Reporter.* Use this source when the volume of the *United States Reports* in which the case will appear has not yet been published.

A7.04 Statutes (*Bluebook* Rule 12)

In text, give the popular or official name of the act (if any) and the year of the act. In the reference list entry, include the source and section number of the statute, and in parentheses, give the publication date of the statutory compilation, which may be different from the year in the name of the act.

Reference form for statutes:

Name of Act, Volume Source § section number (year).

Abbreviate the source as specified in the *Bluebook*. A few states use chapter or article numbers instead of section numbers; use abbreviations or symbols as shown in the *Bluebook*.

9. Sample reference to a statute

Mental Health Systems Act, 42 U.S.C. § 9401 (1988).

Text citation:

Mental Health Systems Act (1988)

Mental Health Systems Act of 1988

10. Sample reference to a statute in a state code

Mental Care and Treatment Act, 4 Kan. Stat. Ann. §§ 59-2901-2941 (1983 & Supp. 1992).

Explanation: This Kansas act can be found in codified version between sections 2901 and 2941 in Chapter 59 of volume 4 of the 1983 edition of *Kansas Statutes Annotated*. Two amendments to the act and additional references are provided in the 1992 supplement for the *Kansas Statutes Annotated*. If you are discussing a particular provision of the law, cite the particular section in which the provision appeared (e.g., § 59-2903). *Ann.* stands for *Annotated*, which refers to the version of the Kansas statutory compilation containing summarized cases interpreting particular sections of the statute.

11. Sample reference to a statute in a federal code

Americans With Disabilities Act of 1990, 42 U.S.C.A. § 12101 *et seq.* (West 1993).

Explanation: This act can be located beginning at section 12101 of title 42 of the *United States Code Annotated*, which is the unofficial version of the *United States Code* (the official statutory compilation of the laws enacted by Congress). *Et seq.* is a Latin phrase meaning "and following" and is a shorthand way of showing that the act covers not just the initial section cited but also others that follow the initial section. The text in parentheses indicates that the *United States Code Annotated* is published by West Publishing and that 1993 is the publication date of the volume in which the cited sections can be found. Citing to U.S.C., U.S.C.A., or U.S.C.S. is the preferred method of citing legislation, because codified legislation is usually easier to work with and retrieve than is a session law, the form of legislation before it is codified. A session law citation is constructed as follows:

Americans With Disabilities Act of 1990, Pub. L. No. 101-336, § 2, 104 Stat. 328 (1991).

Explanation: The citation is to the version of the act in its uncodified form. The act was the 336th public law enacted by the 101st Congress. Section 2 is the particular section of the act cited (§ 2 happens to correspond to § 12101 of 42 U.S.C.A., which is where § 2 was ultimately codified). The text of the section cited can also be found in the official compilation of uncodified session laws, called *United States Statutes at Large* (abbreviated *Stat.*) at volume 104, p. 328. Volume 104 of the *United States Statutes at Large* was published in 1991.

A7.05 Legislative Materials (*Bluebook* Rule 13)

For testimony and hearings, bills and resolutions, and reports and documents, provide in text the title or number (or other descriptive information) and the date.

Form for testimony at federal hearings and for full hearings:

Title, xxx Cong. (date).

12. Sample reference for federal testimony

RU486: The import ban and its effect on medical research: Hearings before the Subcommittee on Regulation, Business Opportunities, and Energy, of the House Committee on Small Business, 101st Cong. 35 (1990) (testimony of Ronald Chesemore).

Text citation:

RU486: The Import Ban (1990)

(*RU486: The Import Ban,* 1990)

Explanation: This testimony was given before a subcommittee of the U.S. House of Representatives during the second session of the 101st Congress and can be located beginning on page 35 of the official pamphlet that documents the hearing. In the reference, always include the entire subject-matter title as it appears on the cover of the pamphlet, the bill number (if any), the subcommittee name (if any), and the committee name. If you are citing an entire hearing, certain adjustments to the citation should be made, as in Example 13.

13. Sample reference for a full federal hearing

Urban America's need for social services to strengthen families: Hearing before the Subcommittee on Human Resources of the Committee on Ways and Means, House of Representatives, 102d Cong. 1 (1992).

Text citation:

Urban America's Need (1992)

(*Urban America's Need,* 1992)

Explanation: This hearing was held in 1992 in the U.S. House of Representatives during the 102d Congress. The hearing begins on page 1 of the official pamphlet that was prepared after the hearing.

14. Form for unenacted federal bills and resolutions

Title [if relevant], bill or resolution number, xxx Cong. (year).

The number should be preceded by *H.R.* (House of Representatives) or *S.* (Senate), depending on the source of the unenacted bill or resolution.

Reference list entry:

S. 5936, 102d Cong. § 4 (1992).

Text citation:

Senate Bill 5936 (1992)

(S. 5936, 1992)

15. Sample references to unenacted federal bills

Equitable Health Care for Severe Mental Illnesses Act of 1993, H.R. 1563, 103d Cong. (1993).

Equitable Health Care for Severe Mental Illnesses Act of 1993, S. 671, 103d Cong. (1993).

Explanation: The first example is to a bill created in the U.S. House of Representatives during the 103d Congress; it was assigned the bill number 1563. The second example is the Senate's version of the same bill.

16. Form for enacted federal bills and resolutions

xx. Res. xxx, xxx Cong., Volume Source page (year) (enacted).

Reference list entry:

S. Res. 107, 103d Cong., 139 Cong. Rec. 5826 (1993) (enacted).

Text citation:

Senate Resolution 107 (1993)

(S. Res. 107, 1993)

Explanation: This resolution by the Senate is numbered 107 and is reported in volume 139 of the *Congressional Record* on page 5826. Note that enacted bills and joint resolutions are laws and should be cited as statutes. Enacted simple or concurrent resolutions should follow this format.

17. Form for federal reports (Rep.) and documents (Doc.)

xx. Rep. No. xx-xxx (year).

As with bills, report numbers should be preceded by *H.R.* or *S.* as appropriate. The report number is composed of the year of the Congress followed by a hyphen and the number of the report, and ending with the calendar year.

Reference list entry:

S. Rep. No. 102-114, at 7 (1991).

Text citation:

Senate Report No. 102-114 (1991)

(S. Rep. No. 102-114, 1991)

Explanation: This report was submitted to the Senate by the Senate Committee on Labor and Human Resources concerning the Protection and Advocacy for Mentally Ill Individuals Amendments Act of 1991. The reference is to material that starts on page 7 of that document.

A7.06 Administrative and Executive Materials (*Bluebook* Rule 14)

For rules and regulations, advisory opinions, and executive orders, provide in text the title or number (or other descriptive information) and the date.

18. Form for federal regulation

Title/Number, Volume Source § xxx (year).

Reference list entries:

FDA Prescription Drug Advertising Rule, 21 C.F.R. § 202.1 (2006).

Adoption and Foster Care Analysis and Reporting System, 73 Fed. Reg. 82,082 (proposed Jan. 11, 2008) (to be codified at 45 C.F.R. pt. 1355).

Text citations:

FDA Prescription Drug Advertising Rule (2006)

(Adoption and Foster Care Analysis and Reporting System, 2008)

Explanation: The first rule was codified in 2006 in volume 21 of the *Code of Federal Regulations* (the official regulatory code) as section 202.1. The second rule was proposed and published in the *Federal Register* before being officially codified; the parenthetical information is a cross-reference (indicated in the entry in the *Register*) to the section of the *Code of Federal Regulations* where the proposed rule will be codified.

19. Form for executive order

Exec. Order No. xxxxx, 3 C.F.R. Page (year).

Reference list entry:

Exec. Order No. 11,609, 3 C.F.R. 586 (1971–1975), *reprinted as amended in* 3 U.S.C. 301 app. at 404-07 (1994).

Text citation:

Executive Order No. 11,609 (1994)

(Executive Order No. 11,609, 1994)

Explanation: Executive orders are reported in title 3 of the *Code of Federal Regulations*; this one appears on page 586. Provide a parallel citation to the *United States Code* (U.S.C.) or, if U.S.C. is unavailable, to the *United States Code Service* (U.S.C.S.).

A7.07 Patents

In text, give the patent number and the issue date (not application date) of the patent. In the reference list entry, include the inventor(s) to whom the patent is issued and the official source from which the patent information can be retrieved.

Reference list entry:

Smith, I. M. (1988). *U.S. Patent No. 123,445.* Washington, DC: U.S. Patent and Trademark Office.

Text citation:

U.S. Patent No. 123,445 (1988)

(U.S. Patent No. 123,445, 1988)

Explanation: This patent was issued in 1988. I. M. Smith is the inventor who holds the patent right. The patent number is a unique identifying code given to every patent. In this reference example, the patent number represents a utility patent because there is no letter prefix. If this were a nonutility patent, such as a design patent (coded with a *D*), the patent number in the reference and citation would be D123,445.

8

The Publication Process

The author, editor, and publisher share responsibility for the ethical and efficient handling of a manuscript. This responsibility begins when the editor receives the manuscript and extends through the life of the published article. In this chapter, we describe the peer review process, focusing first on how editors evaluate manuscripts. Next, we delineate the author's responsibilities in four areas: (a) preparing the manuscript for submission, (b) attending to administrative and ethical responsibilities, (c) complying with publisher policy requirements, and (d) working with the publisher during the production process.[1]

Editorial Process

8.01 Peer Review

Scholarly journal articles are original, *primary* publications. This means that they have not been previously published, that they contribute to the archive of scientific knowledge, and that they have been reviewed by a panel of peers. The peer-reviewed literature in a field is built by individual contributions that together represent the accumulated knowledge of a field.

To ensure the quality of each contribution—that the work is original, valid, and significant—scholars in the subspecialties of a field carefully review submitted manuscripts. By submitting a manuscript to a peer-reviewed journal, an author implicitly consents to the circulation and discussion of the manuscript. During the review process, the manuscript is considered a confidential and privileged document, but publishers differ, so check the journal's instructions to authors (see section 1.14, for

[1]This chapter gives instructions to authors of journal articles. Authors and editors of book manuscripts should follow instructions given by the publisher's book production department. For information on dissertations and master's theses, see "Converting the Thesis or Dissertation Into an Article" on the APA Style website (www.apastyle.org).

a discussion of the ethical standards that have been established for manuscript reviewers).

The *editor* of each journal is responsible for the quality and content of the journal. Journal editors look for manuscripts that (a) contribute significantly to the content area covered by the journal, (b) communicate with clarity and conciseness, and (c) follow style guidelines. Journal editors are often assisted by *associate editors,* who assume responsibility for a specific content area of the journal or for a portion of the manuscripts submitted to the journal. For some journals, an associate editor may act as editor at all stages of the consideration of a manuscript (i.e., as an action editor), including communication with an author regarding acceptance, rejection, or required revision of a manuscript. *Consulting and advisory editors* and *ad hoc reviewers* review manuscripts and make recommendations to editors or to associate editors concerning the disposition of manuscripts. However, the editor has the final editorial authority and may make a decision other than that recommended by the reviewers.

The editor may accept or reject a manuscript outright, that is, before its review by an associate editor or by reviewers. More typically, however, the editor sends the manuscript to an associate editor or directly to reviewers.

Reviewers. An action editor usually seeks the assistance of several scholars in the content area of the submitted manuscript in arriving at an editorial decision. An action editor may solicit reviews from particular scholars for any number of reasons, including technical expertise, familiarity with a particular controversy, and balance of perspectives. Reviewers provide scholarly input into the editorial decision, but the decision is the action editor's alone to make.

Masked review. Journal editors, either routinely or at the author's request, may use masked review. In masked review, the identity of the author of a manuscript is concealed from reviewers during the review process. Consult the instructions to authors in the journals to which you submit your manuscripts to determine whether a journal routinely uses masked review or offers masked review to authors who request it. Authors are responsible for concealing their identities in manuscripts that are to receive masked review; for example, they should take extra care to format their manuscripts so their identities as document creators are not easily revealed. It is APA policy that authors' names will not be revealed to reviewers after the review process is complete without the consent of the authors. Further, the APA review process is masked in both directions; reviewer identities will not be revealed to authors unless the reviewer chooses to do so.

Timing of peer review. The period of review can vary, depending on both the length and complexity of the manuscript and the number of reviewers asked to evaluate it, but the review process typically takes approximately two to three months. After that time, the author can expect to be notified as to the status of the manuscript. It would be appropriate for an author to contact the editor if no communication has been received after more than three months.

8.02 Manuscript Acceptance or Rejection

Reviewers provide the editor with evaluations of a manuscript on the basis of their assessment of the scholarly quality of the manuscript, the importance of the novel contribution that the work might provide, and the appropriateness of the work to the particular journal. The decision to accept a manuscript, to reject it, or to invite a revision is the responsibility of the editor; the editor's decision may differ from the recommendation of any or all of the reviewers. Editors may generally choose one of three actions:

1. *Acceptance.* Once a manuscript is accepted, it enters into the production phase of publication. No further changes may be made by the author to the manuscript other than those recommended by the copyeditor. The author remains responsible for the completion of all associated paperwork (e.g., copyright transfers, disclosures, permissions). Failure to complete all required paperwork may result in retraction of the acceptance of a manuscript.
2. *Rejection.* A manuscript is usually rejected because (a) the work is seen as falling outside the coverage domain of the journal; (b) it contains such severe flaws of design, methodology, analysis, or interpretations that the editor questions the validity of the submission; or (c) it is judged as making a limited novel contribution to the field. At times, editors reject good manuscripts simply because they lack the space to publish all of the high-quality manuscripts that are submitted to the journal. A manuscript that has been rejected by a journal may not be revised and resubmitted to that same journal.

   If a manuscript is rejected and the author believes a pertinent point was overlooked or misunderstood by the reviewers, the author may appeal the editor's decision by contacting the editor. Those who feel their manuscripts are unfairly rejected by APA journals may appeal such decisions to the Chief Editorial Advisor.

3. *Rejection with invitation to revise and resubmit.* This category applies to a range of manuscripts that are judged to have a high potential for eventual publication in the journal but that are not yet ready for final acceptance. Manuscripts in this category range from those that the editor has judged to need substantial reworking (including the possibility that additional empirical data may need to be gathered, that entirely new experiments may need to be added, or that analyses need to be modified) to those that need only a small number of specific modifications. Some journals use a category labeled *conditional acceptance* for this latter level of revision. Rejection with invitation to revise and resubmit does not guarantee eventual publication of the paper by that journal. In many cases, this invitation is time bound; it does not extend across changes in editors.

   Most manuscripts need to be revised, and some manuscripts need to be revised more than once (revision does not guarantee acceptance). Initial revisions of a manuscript may reveal to the author or to the editor and reviewers deficiencies that were not apparent in the original manuscript, and the editor may request further revision to correct those deficiencies. During the review process, an editor may ask an author to supply material that supplements the manuscript (e.g., complex statistical tables, instructions to participants). As the manuscript moves through the review process, editors are free to solicit reviews from reviewers who were not among the initial set of reviewers.

   If the editor rejects a manuscript or returns it to the author for revision, the editor explains why the manuscript is rejected or why the revisions are required.

The editor does not have to provide the reviewers' comments to the author but frequently chooses to do so. Editors do not undertake major editorial revision of manuscripts. Authors are expected to attend to editors' detailed recommendations for revision; however, the content and style of the article remain the sole responsibility of the author. Slavish compliance with all recommendations of all reviewers may result in a manuscript that is difficult to comprehend, which is not the intent of the review process. When resubmitting a revised manuscript, authors are encouraged to enclose a cover letter explaining how they have responded to all the reviewers' comments (regardless of whether the authors agreed or disagreed with the comments).

Author Responsibilities

8.03 Preparing the Manuscript for Submission

The specific requirements for submitting a manuscript differ among journals. Therefore, before submitting a manuscript, refer to the journal's website. The journal's instructions to authors will tell you (a) the journal's area of coverage, that is, what kinds of manuscripts are appropriate for that journal; (b) the current editor's name and address; and (c) instructions for manuscript preparation and submission specific to that journal, including whether the journal routinely uses masked review.

Quality of presentation. The physical appearance of a manuscript can enhance or detract from it. A well-prepared manuscript encourages editors and reviewers to view your work as professional. In contrast, mechanical flaws sometimes lead reviewers to misinterpret content.

In this section, we describe the mechanical details of producing a manuscript that meets requirements for peer review and publication in a scholarly journal. Publishers will produce the typeset version of your article directly from your word-processing file, should your manuscript be accepted for publication. The instructions given in this chapter lay the groundwork for producing a usable electronic file.

Assistance in scientific writing in English. Scholars who are not experienced in scientific writing in English can be hindered in their publishing efforts by a lack of familiarity with idiomatic language usage. These individuals are urged to correct the problem by consulting with colleagues who are experienced writers in the English language. They may also wish to contact copyediting services that can help authors evaluate and correct their manuscripts. We highly recommend use of these services for those who consistently face obstacles in getting their work published.

Format. Formatting your manuscript according to the specifications described in this section enhances clarity and readability and facilitates peer reviews, copyediting, and typesetting.

Typeface. The use of a uniform typeface and font size enhances readability for the editor and allows the publisher to estimate the article length. The preferred typeface for APA publications is Times New Roman, with 12-point font size.

A *serif* typeface, "with short light lines projecting from the top or bottom of a main stroke of a letter" (*Chicago Manual of Style*, 2003, p. 837), is preferred for text because it improves readability and reduces eye fatigue. (A *sans serif* type may be used in figures, however, to provide a clean and simple line that enhances the visual presentation.) Do not use a compressed typeface or any settings in your word-processing software that decrease the spacing between letters or words. The default settings are normally acceptable.

Special characters. Special characters are accented letters and other diacriticals, Greek letters, math signs, and symbols. Type all special characters that you can, using the special character functions of your word-processing program.

Line spacing. Double-space between all text lines of the manuscript. Double-space after every line in the title, headings, footnotes, quotations, references, and figure captions. Although you may apply triple- or quadruple-spacing in special circumstances, such as immediately before and after a displayed equation, never use single-spacing or one-and-a-half spacing except in tables or figures.

Margins. Leave uniform margins of at least 1 in. (2.54 cm) at the top, bottom, left, and right of every page. Combined with a uniform typeface and font size, uniform margins enhance readability and provide a consistent gauge for estimating article length.

Line length and alignment. The length of each typed line is a maximum of 6½ in. (16.51 cm). Do not justify lines; that is, do not use the word-processing feature that adjusts spacing between words to make all lines the same length (flush with the margins). Instead, use the flush-left style, and leave the right margin uneven, or *ragged*. Do not divide words at the end of a line, and do not use the hyphenation function to break words at the ends of lines. Let a line run short rather than break a word at the end of a line.

Paragraphs and indentation. Indent the first line of every paragraph and the first line of every footnote. For consistency, use the tab key, which should be set at five to seven spaces, or ½ in. The default settings in most word-processing programs are acceptable. Type the remaining lines of the manuscript to a uniform left-hand margin. The only exceptions to these requirements are (a) the abstract, (b) block quotations, (c) titles and headings, (d) table titles and notes, and (e) figure captions.

Order of manuscript pages. Arrange the pages of the manuscript as follows:

- title page

The title page includes five elements: title, running head, author byline, institutional affiliation, and author note. Identify the title page with the page number 1. The remaining pages should be numbered consecutively, using Arabic numerals (except for artwork and figures).

The running head is an abbreviated title that is printed at the top of the pages of a manuscript or published article to identify the article for readers. The running head should be a maximum of 50 characters, counting letters, punctuation, and spaces between words. It should appear flush left in all uppercase letters at the top of the title page and all subsequent pages.

- abstract (start on separate page, numbered page 2)
- text (start on a separate page, numbered page 3)

- references (start on a separate page)
- tables (start each on a separate page)
- figures (start each on a separate page; include caption on page with figure)
- appendices (start each on a separate page)

Page numbers and running heads. After the manuscript pages are arranged in the correct order, number them consecutively, beginning with the title page. Pages occasionally are separated during the editorial process, so identify each manuscript page with the running head along with the page number. (Do not use your name to identify each page, because the name will have to be removed if the manuscript receives masked review.)

Use the automatic functions of your word-processing program to generate headers and page numbers for your file. (Do not type these manuscript page headers repeatedly in your word-processing file.)

Spelling check. Most word-processing programs have a function that checks spelling. Use it. Although an electronic spelling check cannot take the place of proofreading the article, because words spelled correctly may be used incorrectly, it will lessen the chance that typographical errors in the manuscript will make their way into print when your electronic file is used to publish the article.

Supplemental materials. If you are submitting supplemental materials with your manuscript (see section 2.13), check the journal's website to determine the preferred format. If you are submitting your manuscript to an APA journal, you will need to

- submit a separate file for each supplemental document and specify the format, naming your files consistently and including the file format in the naming convention;
- provide a title for each document, bearing in mind that the file will be viewed separately from the article and will need to be sufficiently identified to be useful for the reader;
- include a context statement for each file that specifies precisely what the document or file is intended to communicate (readers should be able to ascertain what they will find in the file from the statement, whether it contains several sentences or just a few); and
- prepare each document so it is complete—that is, tables and figures intended for supplemental material should include captions in the document just as if they were appearing in the published article.

Obtain and submit necessary permission to reproduce images (in addition to copyrighted material, keep in mind that images of human subjects require the subjects' permission; see http://www.apa.org/journals for more guidance on supplemental material).

Cover letter. Check the journal's website for the current editor's name and for specific instructions on submission. When submitting a manuscript for consideration, enclose a letter that includes the following elements:

- specific details about the manuscript (title, length, number of tables and figures);
- a request for masked review, if that is an option for the journal and you choose to use it;
- recommendations for potential reviewers or reviewers to avoid (optional);
- information about any previous presentation of the data (e.g., at a scientific meeting);

- information about the existence of any closely related manuscripts that have been submitted for simultaneous consideration to the same or to another journal;
- notice of any interests or activities that might be seen as influencing the research (e.g., financial interests in a test or procedure, funding by pharmaceutical companies for drug research);
- verification that the treatment of subjects (human or animal) was in accordance with established ethical standards; and
- a copy of the permission granted to reproduce or adapt any copyrighted material from another source or a notice that permissions are pending. (The publisher will need copies of all granted permissions on receipt of your accepted manuscript.)

The corresponding author is responsible for ensuring that all authors are in agreement with the content of the manuscript and with the order of authorship before submitting an original or revised submission (see section 1.13). The cover letter should assure the editor that such agreements have been reached and that the corresponding author will take responsibility for informing coauthors in a timely manner of editorial decisions, reviews received, changes made in response to editorial review, and the content of revisions. If the manuscript is accepted, all the authors will need to certify authorship.

Finally, include your telephone number, fax number, e-mail address, and mailing address for future correspondence. (See Figure 8.1 for a sample cover letter.)

Interim correspondence. While a manuscript is under consideration, be sure to inform the editor of any substantive corrections needed, any change in address, and so forth. In all correspondence, include the complete manuscript title, the authors' names, and the manuscript number (which is assigned by the editor when the manuscript is first received).

8.04 Complying With Ethical, Legal, and Policy Requirements

In Chapter 1, we noted that authors are responsible for demonstrating that they have complied with the ethical standards that govern scholarly publishing. When you submit a manuscript to a journal editor for consideration, you may be asked to provide proof of compliance with these standards. You are also expected to comply with legal standards of fair use when reprinting or adapting the work of others and to comply with the publication policies established by the journal publisher.

Ethical conduct of research and conflicts of interest. When you submit your manuscript, you may be asked to verify that you have complied with ethical standards in the conduct of your research. You may also be asked to disclose potential conflicts of interest and to indicate financial agreements or affiliations with any product or services used or discussed in your papers as well as any potential bias against another product or service. The forms used by APA for this purpose are provided in Figures 8.2 and 8.3.

Permission to reprint or adapt the work of others. If your paper includes material borrowed from another source, you must cite the original source in your paper (for more on including your own previously published work in a paper, see section 1.10 on self-plagiarism). It is the author's responsibility to (a) obtain letters of permission from copyright holders to reproduce copyrighted material and (b) enclose copies of these letters with the accepted manuscript.

Figure 8.1. Sample Cover Letter

April 2, 2008

Meredith S. Simpson, PhD
Editor, *Journal of Poetry and Psychology*
Department of Psychology
University of Xanadu
9 Prentice Hall
Xanadu, NY 10003-1212

Dear Dr. Simpson:

I am enclosing a submission to the *Journal of Poetry and Psychology* entitled, "Poetry and the Cognitive Psychology of Metrical Constructs." The manuscript is 40 pages long and includes 4 tables and 1 figure. I wish for the manuscript to be given a masked review and request that it not be sent to my ex-husband [name blocked out] for review. Although he is an expert in the area, I do not believe that he would be able to provide an unbiased review at this time.

Some of the data from this paper were previously presented at the annual meeting of the Poetry and Psychology Society in San Diego (May 2006). This is one of a series of papers examining cognition and creative writing (see references for a listing of those published and in press). There is some overlap in the content of the introduction sections, which we have noted in the text. We would be happy to provide copies of the other manuscripts if there should be any concern about duplicate or fragmented publication. My coauthors and I do not have any interests that might be interpreted as influencing the research, and APA ethical standards were followed in the conduct of the study.

I have enclosed a copy of the permission granted us for the adaptation we made to the figure; permission is pending from the publisher for the poetry that is reproduced.

I will be serving as the corresponding author for this manuscript. All of the authors listed in the byline have agreed to the byline order and to submission of the manuscript in this form. I have assumed responsibility for keeping my coauthors informed of our progress through the editorial review process, the content of the reviews, and any revisions made. I understand that, if accepted for publication, a certification of authorship form will be required that all coauthors will sign.

Sincerely,

Janet Sestina, PhD, Associate Professor
University of Melville
112 Oceanside Drive
Quequeeg, ME 20031-2221
218-555-1212 (voice)
218-555-1213 (fax)
jsestina@melville.edu

The following are some examples of material that require permission:

- **Figures and tables:** Along with directly reprinted figures and tables, this also includes figures and tables that have been adapted from or are very similar to previously published figures and tables.
- **Data:** This applies only to data that are directly reproduced from another source; data that have been reconfigured or reanalyzed to produce different numbers do not require permission.

Figure 8.2. APA Compliance With Ethical Principles Form

CERTIFICATION OF COMPLIANCE WITH APA ETHICAL PRINCIPLES

The APA Publications and Communications Board has added to the Instructions to Authors for each APA journal the following statement: "Authors will be required to state in writing that they have complied with APA ethical standards in the treatment of their sample, human or animal, or to describe the details of treatment." (A copy of the APA Ethical Principles may be obtained at http://www.apa.org/ethics/ or by writing the APA Ethics Office, 750 First Street, NE, Washington, DC 20002-4242.)

For your information, the APA Ethical Principles concerning research and publication are reprinted below. Please review the Principles and sign the form provided on the back of this sheet to indicate that you are in compliance.

From Ethical Principles of Psychologists and Code of Conduct. (2002). *American Psychologist, 57,* 1060–1073.

8.01 Institutional Approval

When institutional approval is required, psychologists provide accurate information about their research proposals and obtain approval prior to conducting the research. They conduct the research in accordance with the approved research protocol.

8.02 Informed Consent to Research

(a) When obtaining informed consent as required in Standard 3.10, Informed Consent, psychologists inform participants about (1) the purpose of the research, expected duration, and procedures; (2) their right to decline to participate and to withdraw from the research once participation has begun; (3) the foreseeable consequences of declining or withdrawing; (4) reasonably foreseeable factors that may be expected to influence their willingness to participate such as potential risks, discomfort, or adverse effects; (5) any prospective research benefits; (6) limits of confidentiality; (7) incentives for participation; and (8) whom to contact for questions about the research and research participants' rights. They provide opportunity for the prospective participants to ask questions and receive answers. (See also Standards 8.03, Informed Consent for Recording Voices and Images in Research; 8.05, Dispensing With Informed Consent for Research; and 8.07, Deception in Research.)

(b) Psychologists conducting intervention research involving the use of experimental treatments clarify to participants at the outset of the research (1) the experimental nature of the treatment; (2) the services that will or will not be available to the control group(s) if appropriate; (3) the means by which assignment to treatment and control groups will be made; (4) available treatment alternatives if an individual does not wish to participate in the research or wishes to withdraw once a study has begun; and (5) compensation for or monetary costs of participating including, if appropriate, whether reimbursement from the participant or a third-party payor will be sought. (See also Standard 8.02a, Informed Consent to Research.)

8.03 Informed Consent for Recording Voices and Images in Research

Psychologists obtain informed consent from research participants prior to recording their voices or images for data collection unless (1) the research consists solely of naturalistic observations in public places, and it is not anticipated that the recording will be used in a manner that could cause personal identification or harm, or (2) the research design includes deception, and consent for the use of the recording is obtained during debriefing. (See also Standard 8.07, Deception in Research.)

8.04 Client/Patient, Student, and Subordinate Research Participants

(a) When psychologists conduct research with clients/patients, students, or subordinates as participants, psychologists take steps to protect the prospective participants from adverse consequences of declining or withdrawing from participation.

(b) When research participation is a course requirement or an opportunity for extra credit, the prospective participant is given the choice of equitable alternative activities.

8.05 Dispensing With Informed Consent for Research

Psychologists may dispense with informed consent only (1) where research would not reasonably be assumed to create distress or harm and involves (a) the study of normal educational practices, curricula, or classroom management methods conducted in educational settings; (b) only anonymous questionnaires, naturalistic observations, or archival research for which disclosure of responses would not place participants at risk of criminal or civil liability or damage their financial standing, employability, or reputation, and confidentiality is protected; or (c) the study of factors related to job or organization effectiveness conducted in organizational settings for which there is no risk to participants' employability, and confidentiality is protected or (2) where otherwise permitted by law or federal or institutional regulations.

8.06 Offering Inducements for Research Participation

(a) Psychologists make reasonable efforts to avoid offering excessive or inappropriate financial or other inducements for research participation when such inducements are likely to coerce participation.

(b) When offering professional services as an inducement for research participation, psychologists clarify the nature of the services, as well as the risks, obligations, and limitations. (See also Standard 6.05, Barter With Clients/Patients.)

8.07 Deception in Research

(a) Psychologists do not conduct a study involving deception unless they have determined that the use of deceptive techniques is justified by the study's significant prospective scientific, educational, or applied value and that effective nondeceptive alternative procedures are not feasible.

(b) Psychologists do not deceive prospective participants about re-search that is reasonably expected to cause physical pain or severe emo-tional distress.

(c) Psychologists explain any deception that is an integral feature of the design and conduct of an experiment to participants as early as is feasible, preferably at the conclusion of their participation, but no later than at the conclusion of the data collection, and permit participants to withdraw their data. (See also Standard 8.08, Debriefing.)

8.08 Debriefing

(a) Psychologists provide a prompt opportunity for participants to obtain appropriate information about the nature, results, and conclusions of the research, and they take reasonable steps to correct any misconceptions that participants may have of which the psychologists are aware.

This form can be found on the APA Journals web page (http://www.apa.org/journals).

- **Test and scale items, questionnaires, vignettes, and so forth:** This applies mainly to items that are from copyrighted and commercially available tests (e.g., the Minnesota Multiphasic Personality Inventory, the Wechsler Adult Intelligence Scale, and the Stanford–Binet Intelligence Scales).
- **Long quotations:** Each copyright holder has a definition of what is considered fair use. It is your responsibility to determine whether the copyright holder requires permission for long quotations.

Figure 8.2. APA Compliance With Ethical Principles Form (continued)

(b) If scientific or humane values justify delaying or withholding this information, psychologists take reasonable measures to reduce the risk of harm.

(c) When psychologists become aware that research procedures have harmed a participant, they take reasonable steps to minimize the harm.

8.09 Humane Care and Use of Animals in Research

(a) Psychologists acquire, care for, use, and dispose of animals in compliance with current federal, state, and local laws and regulations, and with professional standards.

(b) Psychologists trained in research methods and experienced in the care of laboratory animals supervise all procedures involving animals and are responsible for ensuring appropriate consideration of their comfort, health, and humane treatment.

(c) Psychologists ensure that all individuals under their supervision who are using animals have received instruction in research methods and in the care, maintenance, and handling of the species being used, to the extent appropriate to their role. (See also Standard 2.05, Delegation of Work to Others.)

(d) Psychologists make reasonable efforts to minimize the discomfort, infection, illness, and pain of animal subjects.

(e) Psychologists use a procedure subjecting animals to pain, stress, or privation only when an alternative procedure is unavailable and the goal is justified by its prospective scientific, educational, or applied value.

(f) Psychologists perform surgical procedures under appropriate anesthesia and follow techniques to avoid infection and minimize pain during and after surgery.

(g) When it is appropriate that an animal's life be terminated, psychologists proceed rapidly, with an effort to minimize pain and in accordance with accepted procedures.

8.10 Reporting Research Results

(a) Psychologists do not fabricate data. (See also Standard 5.01a, Avoidance of False or Deceptive Statements.)

(b) If psychologists discover significant errors in their published data, they take reasonable steps to correct such errors in a correction, retraction, erratum, or other appropriate publication means.

8.11 Plagiarism

Psychologists do not present portions of another's work or data as their own, even if the other work or data source is cited occasionally.

8.12 Publication Credit

(a) Psychologists take responsibility and credit, including authorship credit, only for work they have actually performed or to which they have substantially contributed. (See also Standard 8.12b, Publication Credit.)

(b) Principal authorship and other publication credits accurately reflect the relative scientific or professional contributions of the individuals involved, regardless of their relative status. Mere possession of an institutional position, such as department chair, does not justify authorship credit. Minor contributions to the research or to the writing for publications are acknowledged appropriately, such as in footnotes or in an introductory statement.

(c) Except under exceptional circumstances, a student is listed as principal author on any multiple-authored article that is substantially based on the student's doctoral dissertation. Faculty advisors discuss publication credit with students as early as feasible and throughout the research and publication process as appropriate. (See also Standard 8.12b, Publication Credit.)

8.13 Duplicate Publication of Data

Psychologists do not publish, as original data, data that have been previously published. This does not preclude republishing data when they are accompanied by proper acknowledgment.

8.14 Sharing Research Data for Verification

(a) After research results are published, psychologists do not withhold the data on which their conclusions are based from other competent professionals who seek to verify the substantive claims through reanalysis and who intend to use such data only for that purpose, provided that the confidentiality of the participants can be protected and unless legal rights concerning proprietary data preclude their release. This does not preclude psychologists from requiring that such individuals or groups be responsible for costs associated with the provision of such information.

(b) Psychologists who request data from other psychologists to verify the substantive claims through reanalysis may use shared data only for the declared purpose. Requesting psychologists obtain prior written agreement for all other uses of the data.

8.15 Reviewers

Psychologists who review material submitted for presentation, publication, grant, or research proposal review respect the confidential-

JOURNAL ____________________

TITLE OF MANUSCRIPT ____________________

AUTHOR(S) ____________________

I certify that I (we) have complied with the APA ethical principles regarding research with human participants and/or care and use of animals in the conduct of the research presented in this manuscript.

____

(Signature of corresponding author) (date)

1-13-03

The journal publisher typically owns the copyright on material published in its journals. Provided that the purpose of the use is scholarly comment, noncommercial research, or educational use and full credit is given to the author and the publisher as copyright holder through a complete and accurate citation, many scientific, technical, and medical publishers require no written permission or fees for

Figure 8.3. APA Disclosure of Interests Form

AMERICAN PSYCHOLOGICAL ASSOCIATION

Full Disclosure of Interests

This section to be completed by author(s):

Journal: ______________________ Issue: ______________________
Article title: ______________________

Authors: ______________________

In psychology, as in other scientific disciplines, professional communications are presumed to be based on objective interpretations of evidence and unbiased interpretations of fact. An author's economic and commercial interests in products or services used or discussed in their papers may color such objectivity. Although such relationships do not necessarily constitute a conflict of interest, the integrity of the field requires disclosure of the possibilities of such potentially distorting influences where they may exist. The reader may then judge and, if necessary, make allowance for the impact of the bias on the information being reported.

In general, the safest and most open course of action is to disclose activities and relationships that, if known to others, might be viewed as a conflict of interest, even if you do not believe that any conflict or bias exists.

Whether an interest is "significant" will depend on individual circumstances and cannot be defined by a dollar amount. Holdings in a company through a mutual fund are not ordinarily sufficient to warrant disclosure, whereas salaries, research grants, consulting fees, and personal stock holdings would be. Being the copyright holder of and/or recipient of royalties from a psychological test might be another example. Participation on a board of directors or any other relationship with an entity or person that is in some way part of the paper should also be carefully considered for possible disclosure.

In addition to disclosure of possible sources of positive bias, authors should also carefully consider disclosure where circumstances could suggest bias **against** a product, service, facility, or person. For example, having a copyright or royalty interest in a competing psychological test or assessment protocol might be seen as a possible source of negative bias against another test instrument.

Please check one line only:

I have read the above APA policy on full disclosure, and I declare that

_____ Neither I nor any member of my immediate family have a significant financial arrangement or affiliation with any product or services used or discussed in my paper, nor any potential bias against another product or service.

_____ I (or an immediate family member) have a significant financial interest or affiliation with the following products or services used or discussed in my paper:

Name of product or service and nature of relationship with each (e.g., stock or bond holdings, research grants, employment, ownership or partnership, consultant fees or other remuneration).

Name of Product or Service	Relationship/Interest

If an author note should be added to your manuscript in reference to any disclosure(s) noted above, please check the line below and attach to this form the text of the author note.

_____ Author Note Attached

Author signature *(All contributing authors must sign this form or duplication of thereof)* Date

This form can be found on the APA Journals web page (http://www.apa.org/journals).

- a maximum of three figures (including tables) from a journal article or book chapter and a maximum of five figures (including tables) from a whole book or
- single text extracts of fewer than 400 words or series of text extracts totaling fewer than 800 words.

In addition, permission granted for print formats extends in most cases to electronic formats, to all second and subsequent editions, and to foreign language editions.

Permissions policies differ from publisher to publisher. Consult your publisher directly to determine the policies that apply. Requests for permission to reproduce material should be directed to the publisher's permissions office (see, e.g., http://www.apa.org/about/copyright.html).

When permissions are required, you must request permission to reproduce the material in all formats. Some publishers may also require that you obtain permission from the author of the original work. Publishers normally grant permission contingent on the inclusion of a copyright notice on the first page of reproduced material and payment of a fee per table, figure, or page.

Allow ample time (several weeks) to secure permission. At the time of submission, identify the copyright holder and request permission to reprint or adapt the material in both print and electronic form. Determining who holds the copyright can be a challenge, particularly for older works, because publishers may merge and copyrights may change hands. The permissions request should specify the source material (title of work, year of publication, page number, etc.) and the nature of the reuse (e.g., reusing in a journal). (See Figure 8.4 for the APA form used to request permission.)

Permission can be secured via fax, mail, or e-mail. Many publishers have online submission forms for requesting permission that can be accessed from their websites (e.g., see http://www.apa.org/journals and click on Copyright and Permission Information to request permission to reproduce material published by APA). Most publishers will not allow your article to enter into production until all print and electronic permissions are secured for reproduced items and forwarded with your manuscript.

Once permission is granted, the author needs to include a permissions notice in the manuscript, following the wording and format shown in section 2.12 or the specific wording at the copyright holder's request.

8.05 Publisher Policy Requirements

Transfer of copyright. When a manuscript is accepted for publication, the journal editor sends to the author a legal form regarding copyright and authorship. By transferring copyright, authors permit publishers to (a) more widely distribute the work, (b) control reuse by others, and (c) handle the paperwork involved in copyright registration and administration. The publisher in turn represents the author's interests and permits authors to reuse their work in several ways.

The corresponding author (a) transfers the copyright on the article to the publisher or (b) certifies that the majority of the authors or the primary authors are employees of the U.S. government and that the work was performed as part of their employment and is not protected by U.S. copyright law (therefore, it is in the public domain). In the case of work performed under U.S. government contract, the publisher may retain the copyright but grant the U.S. government royalty-free permission to reproduce all or portions of the article and authorize others to do so for U.S. government purposes. By law, publishers own the copyright on their journal articles for 95 years from the time of publication. The copyright transfer includes both print and electronic rights to the article to allow the publisher to disseminate the work as broadly as possible.

Posting articles on the Internet. Certain rights are linked to copyright ownership, including the exclusive right to reproduce and distribute the copyrighted work. Journals are committed to publishing original scholarship and distributing peer-

Figure 8.4. APA Copyright Permission Request Form

American Psychological Association

Copyright Permission Request Form

If you want to reuse APA journal or book material, please use our new Online Permission Rightslink® service for fast, convenient permission approval. For instructions, please visit http://www.apa.org/about/copyright/process.html

Please make sure the material you want to use is copyrighted by American Psychological Association (APA).

After filling out the information below, email this form to permissions@apa.org.

Additional contact information:
APA Permissions Office, 750 First Street, NE, Washington, DC 20002-4242
Phone: 1-800-374-2722 or 202-336-5650
Fax: 202-336-5633
www.apa.org/about/copyright.html

For Use of APA Material

Date:

Your contact information:
Name:
Organization name:
Department:
Complete postal address:
Country:
Office phone:
Fax number:
Email:
Your reference code number (if required):

1. **The APA material you want to use:**
   Complete citation (Ex: URL, Title, Source, Author, Publication year, Pagination, etc.)

2. **Do you want to use:**
   ☐ The entire material, unedited?
   ☐ Portions of the material?
   ☐ Please give APA page number(s) ___
   ☐ A specific section? Please give APA page number(s) ___
   ☐ Scale or test material? Please give APA page number ___
   ☐ A photo? Please give APA page number ___
   ☐ Appendix material? Please give APA page number ___
   ☐ Other / Please specify:

This form can be found on the APA Journals web page (http://www.apa.org/journals).

reviewed articles, in both print and electronic formats, that serve as the version of record. Thus, many publishers have policies delineating the terms under which an article may be posted on the Internet by the author.

If a paper is unpublished, the author may distribute it on the Internet or post it on a website but should label the paper with the date and a statement that the paper has not (yet) been published.

Figure 8.4. APA Copyright Permission Request Form (continued)

3. **What media do you want to use the APA material in?**
   ☐ Print only
   ☐ Electronic / Please give details:
   ☐ Both print and electronic / Please give details:
   ☐ Other / Please give details:

4. **The material will be used in:**
   ☐ Journal ☐ Book ☐ Newsletter ☐ Magazine
   ☐ Directory ☐ Newspaper ☐ Other / Please specify:
   Publication name:
   Publisher:
   Estimated publication date:
   Estimated print run:

   ☐ Presentation or Seminar
   Title:
   Date:
   Number of copies needed:
   Is the presenter the author of the APA material? YES NO
   Is the presentation or seminar continuing education? YES NO
   Is there a fee for attendees? YES NO

   ☐ Dissertation or Thesis

   ☐ Email distribution ☐ Listserv
   Please give details:

   ☐ Secure Intranet site ☐ Public Internet site ☐ Restricted Internet site
   Please give URL and other details:

   ☐ Classroom use (Print)
   Institution name:
   Course name:
   Course start date:

   ☐ 1 semester (6 months)
   ☐ 2 semesters (12 months)
   Instructor's name:
   Number of students enrolled:

   ☐ Classroom use (Electronic reserve)
   Institution name:
   Course name:
   Course start date:

   ☐ Other / Please specify:

   ☐ Online CE course
   Organization:
   Course name:
   Course start date:

   ☐ 6 months ☐ 12 months ☐ Other / Please specify:

   If your school has a PsycARTICLES or PsycBOOKS license, your site license policy grants permission to put the content into password protected electronic (not print) course packs or electronic reserve for your users. Please see the license policy at www.apa.org/librarians/policies/course-packs.html for more information, and discuss this use with your librarian.

   ☐ Other / Please give details:

5. **Any additional information to tell us:**

Example:

> Draft version 1.3, 1/5/99. This paper has not been peer reviewed. Please do not copy or cite without author's permission.

Upon submitting the paper for publication, you are obligated to inform the editor if the paper has been or is posted on a website. Some editors may consider such a web posting to be prior publication and may not review the paper. Authors of articles published in APA journals may post a copy of their final manuscript (e.g., as a word-processing file) on a personal website or on the author's employer's server after it is accepted for publication. The following conditions prevail:

- The posted manuscript must carry an APA copyright notice and include a link to the APA journal home page (http://www.apa.org/journals).
- The posted manuscript must include the following statement: "This manuscript may not exactly replicate the final version published in the APA journal. It is not the copy of record."
- APA does not permit archiving with any other non-APA repositories.
- APA does not provide electronic copies of the APA published version for this purpose, and authors are not permitted to scan in the APA published version.

Complying with the National Institutes of Health (NIH) public access policy. The "Revised Policy on Enhancing Public Access to Archived Publications Resulting from NIH-Funded Research," notice number NOT-OD-08-033, took effect April 7, 2008.

Under this policy, NIH-funded investigators (or their publishers) are required to deposit to PubMed Central an electronic version of their final, peer-reviewed and accepted manuscript at acceptance to be made publicly available within 12 months of publishers' final publication date.

For detailed guidance about this policy, check with your publisher. If you are publishing in an APA journal, consult the APA Journals website (http://www.apa.org/journals).

8.06 Working With the Publisher When the Manuscript Has Been Accepted

After your manuscript has been accepted for publication, your publisher will contact you with detailed instructions on working with copyeditors, proofreading the typeset manuscript, and monitoring the production process.

Preparing the word-processing file for copyediting and typesetting. Most publishers request that authors provide the electronic word-processing files containing their manuscript, figures, and other materials to the production office for copyediting and production. You may be asked to provide the electronic manuscript files by e-mail or through a submission portal. Consult the instructions to authors for the journal to which you are submitting your paper for the latest guidance on manuscript file preparation.

Reviewing the proofs. Both journal editors and copyeditors introduce changes in manuscripts to correct errors of form, to achieve consistency of style, or to clarify expression. The corresponding author needs to review the edited manuscript carefully, being alert for changes in meaning and being attentive to levels of heading and to markup of statistics, equations, and tables. It is important to check the proofs word for word against the manuscript to catch typographical errors.

Limit changes on these proofs to corrections of production errors and to updates of reference citations or addresses. This is not the time to rewrite the text. Be sure to check the following:

- Are all queries fully answered?
- Is the hierarchy of headings and subheadings correct?

- Are all numbers and symbols in text, tables, and mathematical and statistical copy correct?
- Are tables correct? Are table alignment notes, superscripts, and footnotes correct?
- Are figures correct? Are captions and numbers correct? Are all labels properly spelled? Do symbols in the legends match those in the figure? Are your photographs reproduced successfully?

If coauthors participate in the review of the copyedited manuscript, the corresponding author is responsible for consolidating necessary changes and forwarding them to the publisher. It is important to submit your requested changes to the publisher within the established deadline so publication of your article will not be delayed.

Retaining raw data. The tradition in scientific publishing is to retain data, instructions, coding systems, details of procedure, and analyses so that copies may be made available in response to inquiries from interested readers (see section 1.08). APA, for example, expects you to retain these materials for a minimum of five years after your article has been published.

Initial observations may take many forms, including, for example, participant responses to individual test or survey items, videotapes of participant performances, interviewer or observer notes, and physiological recordings. They need to be retained in a form that to the extent possible ensures that the information available to the original researcher is also available to the researcher seeking to confirm the original findings. For example, retaining only an electronic data file containing scale scores derived from a questionnaire is insufficient. A scoring or coding system for the logging or transformation of data should also be retained. Choose an archival form for retaining data that ensures that no information is lost; do not simply opt for the most expedient means of archiving (e.g., using optical scanners to record response sheets may cause future problems; Sackett, 2000).

Correction notices. From time to time, errors occur in published journal articles. If you detect an error in your published article and think that a correction notice is warranted, submit a proposed correction notice to the journal editor. The notice should contain the following elements: (a) full journal title and year, volume number, issue number (when appropriate), and inclusive page numbers of the article being corrected; (b) complete article title and names of all authors, exactly as they appear in the published article; (c) precise location of the error (e.g., page, column, line); (d) exact quotation of the error or, in the case of lengthy errors or an error in a table or figure, an accurate paraphrasing of the error; and (e) concise, unambiguous wording of the correction. Because it is not the purpose of corrections to place blame for mistakes, correction notices do not identify the source of the error.

8.07 Checklist for Manuscript Submission

Numbers following entries refer to relevant section numbers in the *Publication Manual* (this checklist can also be found online at http://www.apa.org/journals).

Checklist for Manuscript Submission

Format

- ☐ Have you checked the journal's website for instructions to authors regarding specific formatting requirements for submission (8.03)?
- ☐ Is the entire manuscript—including quotations, references, author note, content footnotes, and figure captions—double-spaced (8.03)? Is the manuscript neatly prepared (8.03)?
- ☐ Are the margins at least 1 in. (2.54 cm; 8.03)?
- ☐ Are the title page, abstract, references, appendices, author note, content footnotes, tables, and figures on separate pages (with only one table or figure per page)? Are the figure captions on the same page as the figures? Are manuscript elements ordered in sequence, with the text pages between the abstract and the references (8.03)?
- ☐ Are all pages numbered in sequence, starting with the title page (8.03)?

Title Page and Abstract

- ☐ Is the title no more than 12 words (2.01)?
- ☐ Does the byline reflect the institution or institutions where the work was conducted (2.02)?
- ☐ Does the title page include the running head, article title, byline, and date, and author note (8.03)? (Note, however, that some publishers prefer that you include author identification information only in the cover letter. Check with your publisher and follow the recommended format.)
- ☐ Does the abstract range between 150 and 250 words (2.04)? (Note, however, that the abstract word limit changes periodically. Check http://www.apa.org/journals for updates to the APA abstract word limit.)

Paragraphs and Headings

- ☐ Is each paragraph longer than a single sentence but not longer than one manuscript page (3.08)?
- ☐ Do the levels of headings accurately reflect the organization of the paper (3.02–3.03)?
- ☐ Do all headings of the same level appear in the same format (3.02–3.03)?

Abbreviations

- ☐ Are unnecessary abbreviations eliminated and necessary ones explained (4.22–4.23)?
- ☐ Are abbreviations in tables and figures explained in the table notes and figure captions or legends (4.23)?

Mathematics and Statistics

- ☐ Are Greek letters and all but the most common mathematical symbols identified in the manuscript (4.45–4.49)?
- ☐ Are all non-Greek letters that are used as statistical symbols for algebraic variables in italics (4.45)?

Units of Measurement

- ☐ Are metric equivalents for all nonmetric units provided (except measurements of time, which have no metric equivalents; see 4.39)?
- ☐ Are all metric and nonmetric units with numeric values (except some measurements of time) abbreviated (4.27, 4.40)?

References

- ☐ Are references cited both in text and in the reference list (6.11–6.21)?
- ☐ Do the text citations and reference list entries agree both in spelling and in date (6.11–6.21)?
- ☐ Are journal titles in the reference list spelled out fully (6.29)?
- ☐ Are the references (both in the parenthetical text citations and in the reference list) ordered alphabetically by the authors' surnames (6.16, 6.25)?
- ☐ Are inclusive page numbers for all articles or chapters in books provided in the reference list (7.01, 7.02)?
- ☐ Are references to studies included in your meta-analysis preceded by an asterisk (6.26)?

Notes and Footnotes

- ☐ Is the departmental affiliation given for each author in the author note (2.03)?
- ☐ Does the author note include both the author's current affiliation if it is different from the byline affiliation and a current address for correspondence (2.03)?
- ☐ Does the author note disclose special circumstances about the article (portions presented at a meeting, student paper as basis for the article, report of a longitudinal study, relationship that may be perceived as a conflict of interest; 2.03)?
- ☐ In the text, are all footnotes indicated, and are footnote numbers correctly located (2.12)?

Tables and Figures

- ☐ Does every table column, including the stub column, have a heading (5.13, 5.19)?
- ☐ Have all vertical table rules been omitted (5.19)?

- ☐ Are all tables referred to in text (5.19)?
- ☐ Are the elements in the figures large enough to remain legible after the figure has been reduced to the width of a journal column or page (5.22, 5.25)?
- ☐ Is lettering in a figure no smaller than 8 points and no larger than 14 points (5.25)?
- ☐ Are the figures being submitted in a file format acceptable to the publisher (5.30)?
- ☐ Has the figure been prepared at a resolution sufficient to produce a high-quality image (5.25)?
- ☐ Are all figures numbered consecutively with Arabic numerals (5.30)?
- ☐ Are all figures and tables mentioned in the text and numbered in the order in which they are mentioned (5.05)?

Copyright and Quotations

- ☐ Is written permission to use previously published text, tests or portions of tests, tables, or figures enclosed with the manuscript (6.10)?
- ☐ Are page or paragraph numbers provided in text for all quotations (6.03, 6.05)?

Submitting the Manuscript

- ☐ Is the journal editor's contact information current (8.03)?
- ☐ Is a cover letter included with the manuscript? Does the letter
  - ☐ include the author's postal address, e-mail address, telephone number, and fax number for future correspondence?
  - ☐ state that the manuscript is original, not previously published, and not under concurrent consideration elsewhere?
  - ☐ inform the journal editor of the existence of any similar published manuscripts written by the author (8.03, Figure 8.1)?
  - ☐ mention any supplemental material you are submitting for the online version of your article?

APPENDIX

Journal Article Reporting Standards (JARS), Meta-Analysis Reporting Standards (MARS), and Flow of Participants Through Each Stage of an Experiment or Quasi-Experiment

Journal Article Reporting Standards (JARS)

Information Recommended for Inclusion in Manuscripts That Report New Data Collections Regardless of Research Design

Table 1
Journal Article Reporting Standards (JARS): Information Recommended for Inclusion in Manuscripts That Report New Data Collections Regardless of Research Design

Paper section and topic	Description

Title and title page	Identify variables and theoretical issues under investigation and the relationship between them
	Author note contains acknowledgment of special circumstances:
	  Use of data also appearing in previous publications, dissertations, or conference papers
	  Sources of funding or other support
	  Relationships that may be perceived as conflicts of interest

Abstract	Problem under investigation
	Participants or subjects; specifying pertinent characteristics; in animal research, include genus and species
	Study method, including:
	  Sample size
	  Any apparatus used
	  Outcome measures
	  Data-gathering procedures
	  Research design (e.g., experiment, observational study)
	Findings, including effect sizes and confidence intervals and/or statistical significance levels
	Conclusions and the implications or applications

Introduction	The importance of the problem:
	  Theoretical or practical implications
	Review of relevant scholarship:
	  Relation to previous work
	  If other aspects of this study have been reported on previously, how the current report differs from these earlier reports
	Specific hypotheses and objectives:
	  Theories or other means used to derive hypotheses
	  Primary and secondary hypotheses, other planned analyses
	How hypotheses and research design relate to one another

Method	
Participant characteristics	Eligibility and exclusion criteria, including any restrictions based on demographic characteristics Major demographic characteristics as well as important topic-specific characteristics (e.g., achievement level in studies of educational interventions), or in the case of animal research, genus and species

Sampling procedures	Procedures for selecting participants, including:
	  The sampling method if a systematic sampling plan was implemented
	  Percentage of sample approached that participated
	  Self-selection (either by individuals or units, such as schools or clinics)
	Settings and locations where data were collected
	Agreements and payments made to participants
	Institutional review board agreements, ethical standards met, safety monitoring

Table 1 (*continued*)

Paper section and topic	Description
Method (*continued*)	
Sample size, power, and precision	Intended sample size
	Actual sample size, if different from intended sample size
	How sample size was determined:
	Power analysis, or methods used to determine precision of parameter estimates
	Explanation of any interim analyses and stopping rules
Measures and covariates	Definitions of all primary and secondary measures and covariates:
	Include measures collected but not included in this report
	Methods used to collect data
	Methods used to enhance the quality of measurements:
	Training and reliability of data collectors
	Use of multiple observations
	Information on validated or ad hoc instruments created for individual studies, for example, psychometric and biometric properties
Research design	Whether conditions were manipulated or naturally observed
	Type of research design; provided in Table 3 are modules for:
	Randomized experiments (Module A1)
	Quasi-experiments (Module A2)
	Other designs would have different reporting needs associated with them
Results	
Participant flow	Total number of participants
	Flow of participants through each stage of the study
Recruitment	Dates defining the periods of recruitment and repeated measurements or follow-up
Statistics and data analysis	Information concerning problems with statistical assumptions and/or data distributions that could affect the validity of findings
	Missing data:
	Frequency or percentages of missing data
	Empirical evidence and/or theoretical arguments for the causes of data that are missing, for example, missing completely at random (MCAR), missing at random (MAR), or missing not at random (MNAR)
	Methods for addressing missing data, if used
	For each primary and secondary outcome and for each subgroup, a summary of:
	Cases deleted from each analysis
	Subgroup or cell sample sizes, cell means, standard deviations, or other estimates of precision, and other descriptive statistics
	Effect sizes and confidence intervals
	For inferential statistics (null hypothesis significance testing), information about:
	The a priori Type I error rate adopted
	Direction, magnitude, degrees of freedom, and exact *p* level, even if no significant effect is reported
	For multivariable analytic systems (e.g., multivariate analyses of variance, regression analyses, structural equation modeling analyses, and hierarchical linear modeling) also include the associated variance–covariance (or correlation) matrix or matrices
	Estimation problems (e.g., failure to converge, bad solution spaces), anomalous data points
	Statistical software program, if specialized procedures were used
	Report any other analyses performed, including adjusted analyses, indicating those that were prespecified and those that were exploratory (though not necessarily in level of detail of primary analyses)
Ancillary analyses	Discussion of implications of ancillary analyses for statistical error rates
Discussion	Statement of support or nonsupport for all original hypotheses:
	Distinguished by primary and secondary hypotheses
	Post hoc explanations
	Similarities and differences between results and work of others
	Interpretation of the results, taking into account:
	Sources of potential bias and other threats to internal validity
	Imprecision of measures
	The overall number of tests or overlap among tests, and
	Other limitations or weaknesses of the study
	Generalizability (external validity) of the findings, taking into account:
	The target population
	Other contextual issues
	Discussion of implications for future research, program, or policy

Table 2
Module A: Reporting Standards for Studies With an Experimental Manipulation or Intervention (in Addition to Material Presented in Table 1)

Paper section and topic	Description
Method	
Experimental manipulations or interventions	Details of the interventions or experimental manipulations intended for each study condition, including control groups, and how and when manipulations or interventions were actually administered, specifically including:
	Content of the interventions or specific experimental manipulations
	Summary or paraphrasing of instructions, unless they are unusual or compose the experimental manipulation, in which case they may be presented verbatim
	Method of intervention or manipulation delivery
	Description of apparatus and materials used and their function in the experiment
	Specialized equipment by model and supplier
	Deliverer: who delivered the manipulations or interventions
	Level of professional training
	Level of training in specific interventions or manipulations
	Number of deliverers and, in the case of interventions, the *M*, *SD*, and range of number of individuals/units treated by each
	Setting: where the manipulations or interventions occurred
	Exposure quantity and duration: how many sessions, episodes, or events were intended to be delivered, how long they were intended to last
	Time span: how long it took to deliver the intervention or manipulation to each unit
	Activities to increase compliance or adherence (e.g., incentives)
	Use of language other than English and the translation method
Units of delivery and analysis	Unit of delivery: How participants were grouped during delivery
	Description of the smallest unit that was analyzed (and in the case of experiments, that was randomly assigned to conditions) to assess manipulation or intervention effects (e.g., individuals, work groups, classes)
	If the unit of analysis differed from the unit of delivery, description of the analytical method used to account for this (e.g., adjusting the standard error estimates by the design effect or using multilevel analysis)
Results	
Participant flow	Total number of groups (if intervention was administered at the group level) and the number of participants assigned to each group:
	Number of participants who did not complete the experiment or crossed over to other conditions, explain why
	Number of participants used in primary analyses
	Flow of participants through each stage of the study (see Figure 1)
Treatment fidelity	Evidence on whether the treatment was delivered as intended
Baseline data	Baseline demographic and clinical characteristics of each group
Statistics and data analysis	Whether the analysis was by intent-to-treat, complier average causal effect, other or multiple ways
Adverse events and side effects	All important adverse events or side effects in each intervention group
Discussion	Discussion of results taking into account the mechanism by which the manipulation or intervention was intended to work (causal pathways) or alternative mechanisms
	If an intervention is involved, discussion of the success of and barriers to implementing the intervention, fidelity of implementation
	Generalizability (external validity) of the findings, taking into account:
	The characteristics of the intervention
	How, what outcomes were measured
	Length of follow-up
	Incentives
	Compliance rates
	The "clinical or practical significance" of outcomes and the basis for these interpretations

Table 3
Reporting Standards for Studies Using Random and Nonrandom Assignment of Participants to Experimental Groups

Paper section and topic	Description
	Module A1: Studies using random assignment
Method	
Random assignment method	Procedure used to generate the random assignment sequence, including details of any restriction (e.g., blocking, stratification)
Random assignment concealment	Whether sequence was concealed until interventions were assigned
Random assignment implementation	Who generated the assignment sequence
	Who enrolled participants
	Who assigned participants to groups
Masking	Whether participants, those administering the interventions, and those assessing the outcomes were unaware of condition assignments
	If masking took place, statement regarding how it was accomplished and how the success of masking was evaluated
Statistical methods	Statistical methods used to compare groups on primary outcome(s)
	Statistical methods used for additional analyses, such as subgroup analyses and adjusted analysis
	Statistical methods used for mediation analyses
	Module A2: Studies using nonrandom assignment
Method	
Assignment method	Unit of assignment (the unit being assigned to study conditions, e.g., individual, group, community)
	Method used to assign units to study conditions, including details of any restriction (e.g., blocking, stratification, minimization)
	Procedures employed to help minimize potential bias due to nonrandomization (e.g., matching, propensity score matching)
Masking	Whether participants, those administering the interventions, and those assessing the outcomes were unaware of condition assignments
	If masking took place, statement regarding how it was accomplished and how the success of masking was evaluated
Statistical methods	Statistical methods used to compare study groups on primary outcome(s), including complex methods for correlated data
	Statistical methods used for additional analyses, such as subgroup analyses and adjusted analysis (e.g., methods for modeling pretest differences and adjusting for them)
	Statistical methods used for mediation analyses

From "Reporting Standards for Research in Psychology: Why Do We Need Them? What Might They Be?" by APA Publications and Communications Board Working Group on Journal Article Reporting Standards, 2008, *American Psychologist, 63,* pp. 842–845.

Meta-Analysis Reporting Standards (MARS)

Information Recommended for Inclusion in Manuscripts Reporting Meta-Analyses

Table 4
Meta-Analysis Reporting Standards (MARS): Information Recommended for Inclusion in Manuscripts Reporting Meta-Analyses

Paper section and topic	Description
Title	Make it clear that the report describes a research synthesis and include "meta-analysis," if applicable Footnote funding source(s)
Abstract	The problem or relation(s) under investigation Study eligibility criteria Type(s) of participants included in primary studies Meta-analysis methods (indicating whether a fixed or random model was used) Main results (including the more important effect sizes and any important moderators of these effect sizes) Conclusions (including limitations) Implications for theory, policy, and/or practice
Introduction	Clear statement of the question or relation(s) under investigation: Historical background Theoretical, policy, and/or practical issues related to the question or relation(s) of interest Rationale for the selection and coding of potential moderators and mediators of results Types of study designs used in the primary research, their strengths and weaknesses Types of predictor and outcome measures used, their psychometric characteristics Populations to which the question or relation is relevant Hypotheses, if any
Method	
Inclusion and exclusion criteria	Operational characteristics of independent (predictor) and dependent (outcome) variable(s) Eligible participant populations Eligible research design features (e.g., random assignment only, minimal sample size) Time period in which studies needed to be conducted Geographical and/or cultural restrictions
Moderator and mediator analyses	Definition of all coding categories used to test moderators or mediators of the relation(s) of interest
Search strategies	Reference and citation databases searched Registries (including prospective registries) searched: Keywords used to enter databases and registries Search software used and version Time period in which studies needed to be conducted, if applicable Other efforts to retrieve all available studies: Listservs queried Contacts made with authors (and how authors were chosen) Reference lists of reports examined Method of addressing reports in languages other than English

Table 4 (*continued*)

Paper section and topic	Description
Search strategies (*continued*)	Process for determining study eligibility: Aspects of reports were examined (i.e, title, abstract, and/or full text) Number and qualifications of relevance judges Indication of agreement How disagreements were resolved Treatment of unpublished studies
Coding procedures	Number and qualifications of coders (e.g., level of expertise in the area, training) Intercoder reliability or agreement Whether each report was coded by more than one coder and if so, how disagreements were resolved Assessment of study quality: If a quality scale was employed, a description of criteria and the procedures for application If study design features were coded, what these were How missing data were handled
Statistical methods	Effectsizemetric(s): Effect sizes calculating formulas (e.g., *M*s and *SD*s, use of univariate *F* to *r* transform) Corrections made to effect sizes (e.g., small sample bias, correction for unequal *n*s) Effect size averaging and/or weighting method(s) How effect size confidence intervals (or standard errors) were calculated How effect size credibility intervals were calculated, if used How studies with more than one effect size were handled Whether fixed and/or random effects models were used and the model choice justification How heterogeneity in effect sizes was assessed or estimated *M*s and *SD*s for measurement artifacts, if construct-level relationships were the focus Tests and any adjustments for data censoring (e.g., publication bias, selective reporting) Tests for statistical outliers Statistical power of the meta-analysis Statistical programs or software packages used to conduct statistical analyses
Results	Number of citations examined for relevance List of citations included in the synthesis Number of citations relevant on many but not all inclusion criteria excluded from the meta-analysis Number of exclusions for each exclusion criterion (e.g., effect size could not be calculated), with examples Table giving descriptive information for each included study, including effect size and sample size Assessment of study quality, if any Tables and/or graphic summaries: Overall characteristics of the database (e.g., number of studies with different research designs) Overall effect size estimates, including measures of uncertainty (e.g., confidence and/or credibility intervals) Results of moderator and mediator analyses (analyses of subsets of studies): Number of studies and total sample sizes for each moderator analysis Assessment of interrelations among variables used for moderator and mediator analyses Assessment of bias including possible data censoring
Discussion	Statement of major findings Consideration of alternative explanations for observed results: Impact of data censoring Generalizability of conclusions: Relevant populations Treatment variations Dependent (outcome) variables Research designs General limitations (including assessment of the quality of studies included) Implications and interpretation for theory, policy, or practice Guidelines for future research

Flow of Participants Through Each Stage of an Experiment or Quasi-Experiment

Figure 1
Flow of Participants Through Each Stage of an Experiment or Quasi-Experiment

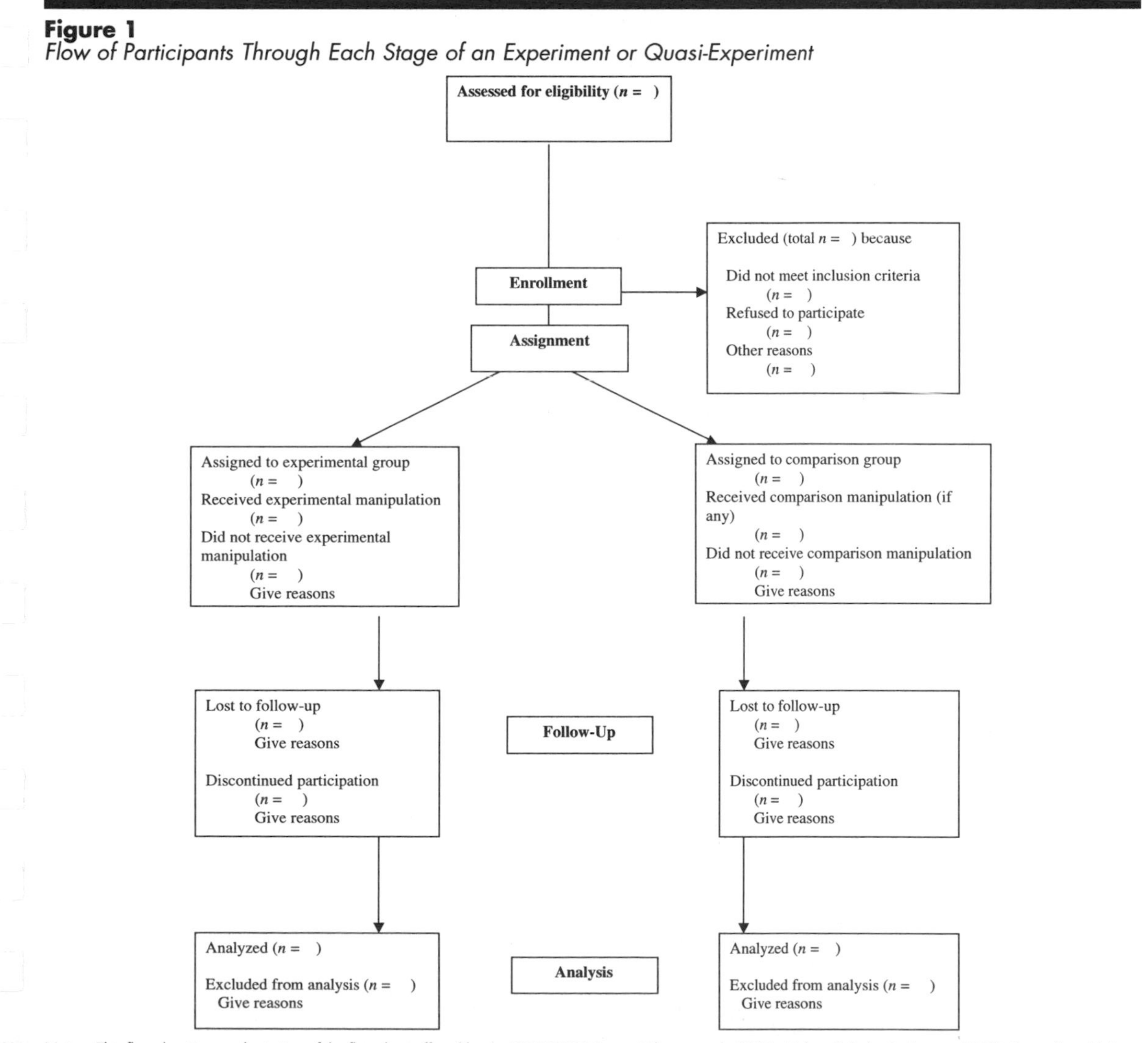

Note. This flowchart is an adaptation of the flowchart offered by the CONSORT Group (Altman et al., 2001; Moher, Schulz, & Altman, 2001). Journals publishing the original CONSORT flowchart have waived copyright protection.

From "Reporting Standards for Research in Psychology: Why Do We Need Them? What Might They Be?" by APA Publications and Communications Board Working Group on Journal Article Reporting Standards, 2008, *American Psychologist, 63,* p. 846.

References

American Psychiatric Association. (2000). *Diagnostic and statistical manual of mental disorders* (4th ed., text rev.). Washington, DC: Author.

American Psychological Association. (1994). *Publication manual of the American Psychological Association* (4th ed.). Washington, DC: Author.

American Psychological Association. (2002). Ethical principles of psychologists and code of conduct. *American Psychologist, 57*, 1060–1073. doi:10.1037/0003-066X.57.12.1060

American Psychological Association. (2004). Guidelines for psychological practice with older adults. *American Psychologist, 59*, 236–260. doi:10.1037/0003-066X.59.4.236

American Psychological Association, Committee on Lesbian, Gay, and Bisexual Concerns Joint Task Force on Guidelines for Psychotherapy With Lesbian, Gay, and Bisexual Clients. (2000). *Guidelines for psychotherapy with lesbian, gay, and bisexual clients*. Washington, DC: Author. Retrieved from http://www.apa.org/pi/lgbc/guidelines.html

American Psychological Association, Presidential Task Force on the Assessment of Age-Consistent Memory Decline and Dementia. (1998). *Guidelines for the evaluation of dementia and age-related cognitive decline*. Washington, DC: Author. Retrieved from http://www.apa.org/practice/dementia.html

APA Publications and Communications Board Working Group on Journal Article Reporting Standards. (2008). Reporting standards for research in psychology: Why do we need them? What might they be? *American Psychologist, 63*, 839–851. doi:10.1037/0003-066X.63.9.839

Bentley, M., Peerenboom, C. A., Hodge, F. W., Passano, E. B., Warren, H. C., & Washburn, M. F. (1929). Instructions in regard to preparation of manuscript. *Psychological Bulletin, 26*, 57–63. doi:10.1037/h0071487

The bluebook: A uniform system of citation (18th ed.). (2005). Cambridge, MA: Harvard Law Review Association.

Consolidated Standards of Reporting Trials. (2007). *CONSORT: Strength in science, sound ethics*. Retrieved from http://www.consort-statement.org/

Copyright Act of 1976 (title 17 of the *United States Code*).

Devlin, J. T., & Poldrack, R. A. (2007). In praise of tedious anatomy. *NeuroImage, 37*, 1033–1041. doi:10.1016/j.neuroimage.2006.09.055

Fisher, C. (2003). *Decoding the ethics code: A practical guide for psychologists*. Thousand Oaks, CA: Sage.

Gay & Lesbian Alliance Against Defamation. (2007). *GLAAD media reference guide* (7th ed.). Retrieved from http://www.glaad.org/media/guide/

Gray literature. (2006). In *Crossref glossary* (Version 1.0). Retrieved from http://www.crossref.org/02publishers/glossary.html

Grissom, R. J., & Kim, J. J. (2005). *Effect sizes for research: A broad practical approach*. Mahwah, NJ: Erlbaum.

Harlow, L. L., Mulaik, S. A., & Steiger, J. H. (Eds). (1997). *What if there were no significance tests?* Mahwah, NJ: Erlbaum.

Hegarty, P., & Buechel, C. (2006). Androcentric reporting of gender differences in APA articles, 1965–2004. *Review of General Psychology, 10*, 377–389. doi:10.1037/1089-2680.10.4.377

Hyde, J. S. (2005). The gender similarities hypothesis. *American Psychologist, 60*, 581–592. doi:10.1037/0003-066X.60.6.581

Jones, L. V., & Tukey, J. W. (2000). A sensible formulation of the significance test. *Psychological Methods, 5*, 411–414. doi:10.1037/1082-989X.5.4.411

Kasdorf, W. E. (Ed.). (2003). *The Columbia guide to digital publishing*. New York, NY: Columbia University Press.

Kline, R. B. (2004). *Beyond significance testing: Reforming data analysis methods in behavioral research*. Washington, DC: American Psychological Association. doi:10.1176/appi.ajp.162.3.643-a

Knatterud, M. E. (1991, February). Writing with the patient in mind: Don't add insult to injury. *American Medical Writers Association Journal, 6*, 10–17.

Merriam-Webster's collegiate dictionary (11th ed.). (2005). Springfield, MA: Merriam-Webster.

Meyer, W., Bockting, W. O., Cohen-Kettenis, P., Coleman, E., DiCeglie, D., Devor, H., . . . Wheeler, C. C. (2001). The Harry Benjamin International Gender Dysphoria Association's standards of care for gender identity disorders, sixth version. *Journal of Psychology & Human Sexuality, 13*(1), 1–30. doi:10.1300/J056v13n01_01

Mildenberger, P., Eichenberg, M., & Martin, E. (2002). Introduction to the DICOM standard. *European Radiology, 12*, 920–927. doi:10.1007/s003300101100

National Lesbian & Gay Journalists Association. (2005). *Stylebook supplement on lesbian, gay, bisexual & transgender terminology*. Retrieved from http://www.nlgja.org/resources/stylebook.html

Picton, T. W., Benton, S., Berg, P., Donchin, E., Hillyard, S. A., Johnson, R. J., . . . Taylor, M. J. (2000). Guidelines for using human event-related potentials to study cognition: Recording standards and publication criteria. *Psychophysiology, 37*, 127–152. doi:10.1111/1469-8986.3720127

Rappaport, J. (1977). *Community psychology: Values, research and action*. New York, NY: Holt, Rinehart, & Winston.

Sackett, P. (2000, March 24–26). Some thoughts on data retention. In *American Psychological Association Board of Scientific Affairs Agenda* (Item 8, Exhibit 1). (Unpublished letter, available from the American Psychological Association, Publications Office, 750 First Street, NE, Washington, DC 20002-4242)

Schaie, K. W. (1993). Ageist language in psychological research. *American Psychologist, 48*, 49–51. doi:10.1037/0003-066X.48.1.49

Sick, L. (Ed.). (2009). *Record structure for APA databases*. Retrieved from http://www.apa.org/databases/training/record-structure.pdf

Tuckett, D. (2000). Reporting clinical events in the journal: Towards the construction of a special case. *International Journal of Psychoanalysis, 81*, 1065–1069.

University of Chicago Press. (2003). *The Chicago manual of style* (15th ed.). Chicago, IL: Author.

University of Kansas, Research and Training Center on Independent Living. (2008). *Guidelines for reporting and writing about people with disabilities*. Lawrence, KS: Author.

U.S. Copyright Office. (1981). *Circular R1: Copyright basics* (Publication No. 341-279/106). Washington, DC: Government Printing Office.

VandenBos, G. R. (2001). *Disguising case material for publication*. Unpublished manuscript, Publications Office, American Psychological Association, Washington, DC.

VandenBos, G. R. (Ed.). (2007). *APA dictionary of psychology*. Washington, DC: American Psychological Association.

Wainer, H. (1997). Improving tabular displays: With NAEP tables as examples and inspirations. *Journal of Educational and Behavioral Statistics, 22*, 1–30.

Webster's third new international dictionary, unabridged. (2002). Springfield, MA: Merriam-Webster.

Wilkinson, L., and the Task Force on Statistical Inference. (1999). Statistical methods in psychology journals: Guidelines and explanations. *American Psychologist, 54*, 594–604. doi:10.1037/0003-066X.54.8.594

Index

Numbers in bold refer to section numbers.

A

B

D

E

F

G

H

I

J

K

L

M

N

O

P

S

T

U

V

W

Y

Z